Nation and Migration

SOUTH ASIA SEMINAR SERIES

A listing of the books in this series appears at the back of this volume

Nation and Migration

The Politics of Space in the South Asian Diaspora

Edited by Peter van der Veer

University of Pennsylvania Press

Philadelphia

Library of Congress Cataloging-in-Publication Data
Nation and migration: the politics of space in the South Asian
diaspora / edited by Peter van der Veer.
    p.   cm. — (South Asia seminar series)
  Papers presented at the 47th Annual South Asia Seminar held at the
University of Pennsylvania, 1991/1992.
  Includes bibliographical references and index.
  ISBN 0-8122-3259-3 (cloth). — ISBN 0-8122-1537-0 (paper)
  1. South Asians—Foreign countries.   2. South Asia—Emigration and
immigration.   3. South Asia—Politics and government.   I. Veer,
Peter van der.   II. South Asia Seminar (47th: 1991: University of
Pennsylvania).   III. Series.
DS339.4.N37   1995
909'.04914—dc20

94-28888
CIP

Contents

Acknowledgments   vii

Introduction: The Diasporic Imagination
Peter van der Veer   I

1. A Sikh Diaspora? Contested Identities and Constructed
Realities
Verne A. Dusenbery   17

2. *Bhakti* and Postcolonial Politics: Hindu Missions to Fiji
John D. Kelly   43

3. Projecting Identities: Empire and Indentured Labor
Migration from India to Trinidad and British Guiana,
1836–1885
Madhavi Kale   73

4. Homeland, Motherland: Authenticity, Legitimacy, and
Ideologies of Place among Muslims in Trinidad
Aisha Khan   93

5. Hindus in Trinidad and Britain: Ethnic Religion,
Reification, and the Politics of Public Space
Steven Vertovec   132

6. New York City's Muslim World Day Parade
Susan Slyomovics   157

7. Indian Immigrants in Queens, New York City: Patterns of
Spatial Concentration and Distribution, 1965–1990
Madhulika S. Khandelwal   178

8. Gendering Diaspora: Space, Politics, and South Asian
Masculinities in Britain
Sallie Westwood   197

9. New Cultural Forms and Transnational South Asian
Women: Culture, Class, and Consumption among British
Asian Women in the Diaspora
Parminder Bhachu   222

Contributors   245

Index   249

Acknowledgments

This book is the outcome of the 47th Annual South Asia Seminar, held at the University of Pennsylvania during the academic year 1991–92. All the essays in this volume were originally presented at that seminar. I want to thank Karen Vorkapich for her management of the lecturers' travel arrangements and Richard Cohen and the successive chairmen of the South Asia Regional Studies Center, Arjun Appadurai and David Ludden, for their steady support. Editing a volume of essays is never an easy task, but my departure from Penn in the summer of 1992 definitely made it more complicated. Without Victoria Farmer's superb handling of diasporic communications the manuscript would never have been prepared for publication. I am very grateful for her efficiency and thoroughness. Finally, I would like to thank Patricia Smith of the University of Pennsylvania Press for her calm support of the project.

Peter van der Veer

Introduction: The Diasporic Imagination

In a recent study of the South Asian diaspora, Colin Clarke, Ceri Peach, and Steven Vertovec (1990: 1) observe that the number and proportion of people of South Asian descent living outside South Asia—some 8 million worldwide (compared to the 1 billion residents of South Asia) — is small in relation to other migrant populations, such as the Chinese (22 million worldwide; 1 billion in China), the Jews (11 million worldwide; 3.5 million in Israel), the Africans (300 million worldwide; 540 million in Africa), and the Europeans (350 million worldwide; 700 million in Europe). Nevertheless, the complexity and diversity of the South Asian diaspora offer important insights for the understanding of international migration processes. Overseas South Asian communities have different historical trajectories because they have developed in widely divergent historical contexts in many parts of the world. It is the fragmented nature of these contexts and experiences that complicates the use of "the South Asian diaspora" as a transparent category.

The complexities and contradictions of the South Asian diasporic experience enable us to approach a politics of space which evolves in shifting historical contexts. International migration is clearly one of the most important political issues in today's world. The European Community's attempt to remove its internal borders has made its external borders with the rest of the world even more significant. Processes of globalization create new bounded entities which entertain complex relations with older constructions of territoriality. Some nations are seen to be closer—both spatially and racially—than others, so that, for example, German immigrants in Britain, despite the history of warfare between Britain and Germany, can be regarded as part of a relatively unproblematic "internal" migration within the European Community, whereas immigrants from India—though coming from a country once part of the British empire — are regarded as a threat to the political stability of Britain. The English language is in this context not enough to signify the unity of the British, since the immigrants from the former colonies usually speak perfect English. Race and culture or religion appear to have displaced language as markers of unity in the politics of space in the European Community.

Immigration is a major political theme in the United States as well, despite a global ideology stressing that this is a settler's society. Everyone is either a migrant or a self-conscious descendant of a migrant; even White Anglo-Saxon Protestants who belong to a firmly established elite have their story of the *Mayflower.* To be an immigrant in the United States seems, therefore, a typical situation. In addition, spatial and social mobility are seen as connected and positively valued in the United States. Nevertheless, some ambiguities exist. First is the patent hostility toward recent immigrants—and most of the South Asians are recent arrivals. Despite the fact that the United States is an "immigrant country," there is a strong sense of the nation and of national boundaries which have to be protected against diseases (such as communism and AIDS) brought in by immigrants, a sense best expressed by that huge, impenetrable bureaucracy, the Immigration and Naturalization Service. Second, while a strong sense of a single American nation and its historic mission exists, one finds also the preservation of firm ethnic boundaries and a continuing interest of ethnic groups in their roots. The search for "Africa" among African Americans is one of the most fascinating examples of this interest in origins elsewhere. In the South Asian case, especially given the construction of "Asian" as a category (including Chinese, Koreans, Japanese, Indians, Pakistanis, Bangladeshis, and so on), there is a fascination with a similarly elusive "Asia" in ethnic politics. Third is a continuing involvement of these immigrant groups in the affairs of the countries of origin. This is most obvious in the Jewish and Irish lobbies in the United States, but it is also present among South Asian immigrants.

These ambiguities can, of course, be found in other regions besides the United States and Western Europe. They derive from the contradictions between the notion of discrete territoriality in the discourse of nationalism and the transgressive fact of migration. Inter*national* migration and trans*national* flows of information and goods are, as these terms themselves indicate, intimately connected to the discourse of nationalism. Let us look, initially, more closely at the first term in the title of this volume: *nation.*

Nationalism is neither a very old nor a very recent phenomenon in world history. By and large, its ideological roots were in the American and French revolutions of the eighteenth century, after which it spread over the world in the nineteenth century. Contrary to what is often thought, nationalism is perhaps less an isolated European invention than the product of

European colonial expansion. Influential analyses of nationalism by Ernest Gellner (1983) and Eric Hobsbawm (1991) present it squarely in terms of the modernization of Europe. Although Benedict Anderson (1991) shares this general perspective, he points out how important the desire for independence from the mother country in the American settler societies was for the development of the idea of the nation. One should not forget that the American Revolution preceded the French Revolution. More important, however, would be to realize that colonialism and nationalism go hand in hand in both the colonizing and the colonized countries of the world. The colonial project produced reified national cultures both in the colonies and "at home" (cf. Breckenridge and van der Veer 1993). The scholarly discourses that informed the colonial and later the national project were developed not only in the Western metropolis, but also in the colonies. It was in colonized Bengal at the end of the eighteenth century that Sir William Jones brought Johann Gottfried Herder's notion that everyone belonged to a nation and that the nation was a linguistic community a significant step further by developing a comparative philology. Again, the idea of a territorially bounded national community arises in the same period that witnesses the growing interdependence of societies in the world-system. It is fruitful therefore to see that connections between colonialism and nationalism are important not only in the colonized societies but also in the colonizing societies.

The nation is a modern construction that became salient in South Asia in the second part of the nineteenth century, or more or less the same period as in many parts of Europe. Migration, however, is definitely an old phenomenon. There is often a tendency to see displacement, disjuncture, and diaspora as something new in human experience, or, at least, to see its speed and scale adding up to something that is not even modern, but postmodern (see, e.g., Gupta and Ferguson 1992). I have some hesitations about emphasizing a Great Transformation from modernity to postmodernity, because it resembles so much the rhetoric of the earlier one from tradition to modernity. The discourse of modernity emphasizes the "boundedness" of the traditional community and compares it to the individual freedom of movement in modern society. To a point the discourse of postmodernity does the same by celebrating marginality, hybridity, and syncretism and by rejecting notions of pure origins and identities (see, e.g., Bhabha 1990).

This discursive opposition of traditional restrictions and modern individual freedom is expressed well in V. S. Naipaul's great novel *A House for Mr. Biswas,* describing the struggle of an individual to escape from the stranglehold of his "traditional" Indo-Trinidadian community. Parenthetically, it should be observed that one of the ironies of the story is that this so-called traditional community is in fact a product of the colonial migration process. The radical opposition between modernity and tradition is an Enlightenment illusion which has afflicted other realms besides modern literature. The idea that Indians lived their lives with restricted notions of time and space in autarkic villages until colonialism came to wake them up, as Karl Marx (1972 [1853]) thought, is still very much among us. Even in modern ethnographies that deal with situations in which there is evidence of considerable migration, the village community has often continued to be the research unit and migration is not taken into account. One sometimes wonders whether the anthropologist is perhaps the only one who is not involved in this constant movement from and to the village.

Precolonial society was not static at all. Migration within South Asia was, in fact, pervasive in the precolonial period (see Kolff 1990). Moreover, there is a long and fascinating history connecting Gujarat with the Persian Gulf and East Africa and connecting South India with the so-called Indic civilizations of South East Asia. The pervasiveness of precolonial migration inside and outside of India may at least lead us to question the radical modernity of the experience of displacement, disjuncture, and diaspora. Migration has ambiguities of its own, based on what I would call the dialectics of "belonging" and "longing." The theme of belonging opposes rootedness to uprootedness, establishment to marginality. The theme of longing harps on the desire for change and movement, but relates this to the enigma of arrival, which brings a similar desire to return to what one has left. These themes are often regarded as typically modern predicaments, but I am not so sure.

My reservation should not be taken, however, as synonymous with the ahistorical view that everything has remained essentially the same over a long stretch of time. Obviously, there are huge differences between, say, the relations Indian trading communities had with the Persian Gulf in the precolonial period and the post-1960 mass migration of South Asian laborers to that region. I believe that the notion of national territory provides modern possibilities to interpret facts and experiences of migration that have been around much longer. To understand the modern articulation of nation and migration we have to look first at colonialism, since colonialism has transformed older notions of community and movement (see van der Veer 1994).

The scale and nature of migration changed with colonialism. Before bringing South Asians to other parts of the empire, colonialism brought British traders, soldiers, and missionaries to South Asia. It also created its own flows of migration within South Asia: Anglo-Indian railway communities, Sikh and Gurkha soldiers, Bengali officials. Natives played an important role in British India, but, as members of the bureaucracy, moved to places where they were not native. Moreover, at a certain point, they went to the colonial metropolis for further education. Benedict Anderson (1991: 114–15) has shown the significance of this bureaucratic migration for the transformation of the colonial state into the nation-state.

> In each constricted journey he [the official] found bilingual travelling companions with whom he came to feel a growing commonality. In his journey he understood rather quickly that his point of origin—conceived either ethnically, linguistically, or geographically—was of small significance . . . it did not fundamentally determine his destination or his companions. Out of this pattern came that subtle, half-concealed transformation, step by step, of the colonial-state into the national-state, a transformation made possible not only by a solid continuity of personnel, but by the established skein of journeys through which each state was experienced by its functionaries.

Although the connection between the emergence of a Bengali class of officials, the Bengal renaissance, and Bengali nationalism probably provides the best illustration of Anderson's argument, it may also be worthwhile to look at the migrant experience of Mahatma Gandhi. Arguably, Gandhi's stay in England and South Africa opened his eyes to the nationalist cause. He not only acquainted himself firsthand with the discriminatory treatment of Indians as "British subjects" under South African racial laws, but also learned to see Indians as an ethnic group, a "nation." The marginal position of the migrant, and the special qualities of group formation among exiles, seem in general to play a significant role in the formulation of nationalist discourse. Although this may already be the case with the "Westernized" intellectual who becomes marginal to both his or her own culture and the colonial culture, it is even stronger when such a Western-educated person has a vivid migrant experience. To see one's society from the outside with the eyes of "the other," yet still experience a marginality and strangeness that is enhanced by colonial discrimination, leads to bold personal transformations which may have paradigmatic significance for the society at large.

Gandhi's experience of migration also helped him launch his first successful political campaign in India. In 1919 the Indian National Congress, under Gandhi's leadership, forced the British to stop recruiting Indian laborers for indentured labor in other colonies. The indenture system was the new colonial organization of labor migration after the abolishment of slavery throughout the British empire with the Act of Abolition of 1833. Under the system, 1.5 million people migrated to colonies as far apart as Mauritius, Fiji, and Guyana, a large part of them from Hindustan. Only about a third of them chose to return after expiry of the five- or ten-year contract (see Tinker 1974). In this volume Madhavi Kale shows the extent to which the British debate about this system as the successor of slavery has from the start been based on stereotypical reifications of Indian culture. The sexual morality of Indian women under the indenture system was a particularly crucial issue. Because much of this debate was already framed in terms of Indian culture and Indian national character, it should not surprise us that the nationalist attack on the system was focused precisely on its alleged failure to protect the virtue of Indian women (see Kelly 1991). The treatment of female laborers was constructed by the nationalists as an insult to the nation's honor. This is one case among many in which the plight of Indian migrants provided symbolic capital for the nationalist cause. Another example is the discrimination of Punjabis in California and Canada in the beginning of the twentieth century. News of this reached India and caused great nationalist agitation.

One would perhaps not expect connections between nation and migration to exist, since nationalist ideology seems so opposed to the fact of migration. Nationalism stresses *Blut und Boden,* "the sons of the soil" (*bhumiputra*), and as such the soil, or territory. It appears to deny the idea of migration and the mixing and mingling of populations by its metaphor of "roots" and its emphasis on the boundedness of populations in time and space. Nationalism is a discourse that depends on notions of space, of territory. Outsiders do not belong, are not rooted in the soil, and indeed have immigrated from outside. Sometimes this boundary is enforced by denying "immigrants," such as Jews in Europe and Indians in Fiji, despite their long presence on the soil, the right to own land and become rooted. I would suggest that this opposition of nation and migrant has an ideological function. Nationalism needs this story of migration, the diaspora of others, to establish the rootedness of the nation.

On a general level, what we see in the negative valuation of migration is the function of outsiders for creating social cohesion among the established. It does not matter how long these groups in fact have been present on the soil; they continue to be migrants and thus fulfill the need for outsiders in the formation of a national identity. This can be called the myth of migrants' "transience," both in time and in space — a quality that makes them simultaneously marginal and threatening. It is a negative valuation by the "established" of the unsettling movement of "strangers."

Whereas the diaspora of others fortifies the sense of belonging among the established, one's own diaspora tends to strengthen the longing to be elsewhere. In an interesting manner the presence of the migrant "other" is used not only in the nationalist discourse of the established; this discourse, which marginalizes and demonizes the migrant, also breeds nationalism among those who are marginalized.

Eric Hobsbawm (1987) emphasizes the importance of mass emigration in the emergence of the later phase of European nationalism (which he calls "right-wing," replacing the liberating legacy of the French Revolution). The half-century before 1914 witnessed the greatest international migration in history. It produced nationalism in two ways. It created xenophobia among the people already well-established, both the middle and working classes, in the countries of immigration. This led to forms of nationalism, highly focused on the "defense of the nation" against the threatening immigrant. We see similar behavior today in Europe. The negative identity imposed by xenophobia certainly also encouraged a nationalist sentiment among migrants. In general, the migratory experience can lead to more embracing identifications on the margin of the host society: Those who do not think of themselves as Indians before migration become Indians in the diaspora. The element of romanticization which is present in every nationalism is even stronger among nostalgic migrants, who often form a rosy picture of the country they have left and are able to imagine the nation where it did not exist before. The example Hobsbawm gives is that of Thomas Masaryk (1850–1937), founder and first president of Czechoslovakia, who had to come to Pittsburgh to sign an agreement to form a state uniting Czechs and Slovaks, since Slovak nationalism was more alive in Pennsylvania than in Slovakia.

The present volume is concerned with the ways in which the South Asian diaspora produces a politics of space that has diverse forms and dynamics in different historical contexts. The contributors certainly do not want to unify and homogenize these differences into "Indian culture overseas," as in the following amusing anecdote narrated by V. S. Naipaul: "At an official reception of a former governor of a state someone called across to me, as we sat silently in deep chairs set against the walls of the room, 'How is Indian culture getting on in your part of the world?'" (1965: 223). The differences are real and important and should be taken seriously; on the other hand, we do not want to deconstruct the South Asian diaspora to the point of dissolution. Within the politics of space produced by the South Asian diaspora, the articulation of nation and migration forms an important, structural feature.

The Ethnicization of Religion

This volume explores also another articulation, that of nation and religion, which is of great importance in the South Asian case. Major forms of nationalism in South Asia articulate discourse on the religious community and discourse on the nation. Hindu, Muslim, Sikh, and Buddhist nationalisms are salient not only in South Asia, but also in the diaspora. It is important to realize that these religious nationalisms of the colonized had their counterpart in an allegedly "secular" nationalism of the colonizer. At the end of the nineteenth century when religious nationalisms emerged in South Asia, the experience of empire fostered among the colonizers the notion of the distinctiveness of "being British," member of a ruling race. The characteristics of that national identity were defined in terms of difference from the identity of the "ruled" colonized peoples.

Being British was and is very much the province of a liberal English elite. One of the core elements of this identity seems to be a secular rationality which deems (Christian) religious faith a private matter and which allows for religious tolerance in the public sphere. This identity enabled the British to rule those who could not distinguish the public and the private in religious matters, such as Hindus and Muslims in India, and guide them to enlightened progress, making them British as it were. It is fascinating to see how this problematic has returned with a vengeance after the dissolution of the empire. From the end of the 1950s to the end of the 1960s, Britain imported workers from the ex-colonial countries — mostly the Caribbean, India, Pakistan, and Bangladesh. As Talal Asad (1990) has convincingly shown, the Salman Rushdie affair and the debate on multiculturalism in Britain focus on the clash between the transformative ideals of "being British," fostered by the state, and the transformative ideals of "being Muslim," fostered by the religious institutions of, mainly, South Asian Muslim immigrants.

Probably the best example of the articulation of nation, migration, and religion is the emergence of Zionism in the Jewish diaspora. Here we have an ethnic community, living in diaspora, without what comes to be called a homeland, suddenly discovering the need of such a national territory and a national language, Hebrew (not spoken since the days of the Babylonian captivity), to go with it. Again, this is a nationalism that is directly related to — and can only be understood in relation to — the emerging German and French nationalisms of the "established" majorities among whom Jews happened to live. The Jewish diaspora raises the same question of the relation between religious and nationalist forms of identity that is of importance in the South Asian diaspora.

Three chapters in this volume — those by John Kelly, Steven Vertovec, and Aisha Khan — deal explicitly with the articulation of religious and nationalist discourse in the construction of the communities of the indentured laborers' descendants. Together with Madhavi Kale's chapter, they form a cluster of essays that engage the specificities of the diaspora of (ex-)indentured peoples in Fiji and Trinidad. Kelly argues that religious organization and identity have become central both to the construction of the indigenous people of Fiji as a "Fijian nation" and to the construction of the ex-indentured laborers as an "Indian nation" in Fiji. Christian missions have played a major role in identity formation among the indigenous Fijians, while missions of the Arya Samaj and the Sanatan Dharm have played a similar role among the Indo-Fijians. Christianity and Hinduism thus have become the signs of the bipolar ethnic opposition between Fijians and Indians. Since the 1987 military coups in Fiji, which ensured "traditional" Fijian dominance, Indians have experienced a growing political marginalization. Temples and mosques are the sacred spaces with which the Indo-Fijians are identified. In 1989 a group of young Fijian men and women set fire to four of these structures, saying that it was their Christian duty to do so. The message was clear: Indians should convert to the Fijian way of life, which is increasingly defined as Christian.

As Kelly argues, the articulation of nation and religion takes place not within one community, but in the interaction between a so-called indigenous group and a so-called immigrant group, between the nation and the nonnation. The opposition between the two groups, which is played out in terms of religious space, has obviously as much to do with secular space, that is landownership: Indo-Fijians (about half of the population) are not allowed to own land in Fiji. As in the case of the African Sikhs in the 1960s and 1970s (see Bhachu 1985), they have reacted to that by voting with their feet, a second migration. Not a return to India, though, but a move to the West. In this situation the Sai Baba and Hare Krishna missions of modern Hinduism cater to feelings of political impotence by making politics irrelevant and to diasporic imaginations by offering a transnational Hinduism, not bound to any particular soil. These new missions appear to have a renunciatory and apolitical rhetoric.

Vertovec compares the situation of an ex-indentured Indian population in Trinidad with the much more recently immigrated Indians in Britain. In Trinidad Vertovec sees a political Hinduism, an ethnicized religion which was, as in Fiji, conditioned by bipolar ethnic competition. He argues that, since the 1950s, there has been a depoliticization of Hinduism in Trinidad, though less dramatic than the one Kelly observed in Fiji.

In Britain, no unified, ethnic Hindu identity appears to have arisen. The main reason seems to be that there is no bipolar competition between two colonized peoples of almost the same size, as in the case of Fiji and Trinidad. The main issue for Hindus in Britain is not so much the competition with one other ethnic group, but the construction of their own multiple identities in the face of the unifying projects of a British nation-state, such as assimilation and multiculturalism. It is clear from Vertovec's contribution, as well as earlier work by David Pocock (1976) on Britain and Raymond Williams (1988) on the United States, that the constraints of the immigrant situation force Hindus to make new distinctions between the essential and the nonessential in their religious doctrines and practices. This self-conscious reflection on religious tradition and identity in itself already contributes to an ethnicization of religion, in which religion becomes a marker of ethnic identity. Such a process is inherently political, since it prevents Hinduism from becoming a mere exotic contribution to the multicultural British school curriculum. The multiple origins and migration histories of the Indo-British Hindus will, however, also remain an important obstacle to the formation of a unified, ethnic Hinduism in Britain.

With a universalist religion like Islam, attempts at unification of the community of believers, whatever their origin, seem easier than with Hinduism. As Aisha Khan shows in her chapter, however, there are a great number of myths of origin and purity to which Muslims in Trinidad can refer. Again, as for Hindus in Trinidad, it is the bipolar competition with the "others," the Afro-Trinidadians, which defines discourse on identity. The fact that some Afro-Trinidadians do belong to the universal Muslim community (*'umma*) poses interesting conceptual difficulties for Indian Muslims. Khan shows the extent to which Afro-Trinidadian Muslims are the subject of discussion among Indian Muslims, although they avoid direct interaction with them. The universalism of religious ideas does not extend to religious space and Islamic practice does not transcend the bi-polar ethnic boundaries between Afro-Trinidadians and Indo-Trinidadians.

Khan's contribution also draws attention to the importance of authenticity among diasporic peoples. Muslims in Trinidad form a small minority far from the centers of Islamic authentication. Muslim identity is a highly insecure one, and the debates about authentic beliefs and practices gain an extra dimension in what Khan calls a "frontier" situation. This uncertainty about tradition is especially strong among Afro-Trinidadians, for whom "Africa" itself is a highly contested trope in the narrative construction of relations among pasts, presents, and futures (see Scott 1991).

No doubt, the question of cultural continuity also exists in the Indo-Trinidadian community. It is important to note here that it is not an uncertainty that arises in the postcolony among V. S. Naipaul's "mimic men," but that it is deeply embedded in colonial discourse, as Madhavi Kale shows in her contribution. Kale looks at the debates that accompanied the introduction of Indian laborers to the Caribbean in the nineteenth century. She argues that the various positions in this debate about the conditions of indenture tended to result in static and reified notions of Indian culture which had their "truth-effects" in colonial policies. These notions did indeed constrain the attempts of Indian workers to define themselves, but they were forcefully challenged in festivals, such as Hosay, a Trinidadian elaboration of the Indo-Muslim festival of Muharram. As in nineteenth-century India, it is in the arena of public festivals that the colonial state and its definitions of "Indian culture" came to be challenged (see Freitag 1989). The question of authenticity and continuity can be interpreted, to an important extent, as a question of discursive and performative power.

Territory

A major feature of nationalism is the politics of space. Bordered territory symbolizes the fixity, stability, and sovereignty of the nation-state, so that borders have become the contested sites for international warfare, refugees, and immigration policies. Those who see themselves as a nation often seek a spatial, territorial expression of their nationhood. The Indian Muslim League spoke of a "homeland" for Muslims when it demanded Pakistan in the 1940s. This expression was imitated by Sikh leaders when the Punjab region was cut in two by the Partition of 1947. As Harjot Oberoi (1987) has shown, for most of Sikh history territory has not played a key role in defining Sikh identity, but the politics of space in nationalism has led to the demand of Khalistan. Since Punjabis and especially the Sikhs among them are almost the proverbial migrants in India, it is interesting to see how in the Sikh case religion, territory, and nationhood have become articulated with the facts of migration, as is brought out in Verne Dusenbery's chapter on the Sikhs of Vancouver. His starting point is that a regional identity, such as "Punjabi," was as imagined as a religious identity, such as "Sikh," at the beginning of this century. Dusenbery makes an interesting distinction between *bhum bhai* (brother of the land) and *guru bhai* (coreligionist), which highlights his main theme: the relation between territoriality and identity. The notion of *bhum bhai* seems very localized and limited to the physical space of the village, but it may have been extended to the larger *bhumi* of the Punjab. To an important extent, this notion remained disconnected from the transterritorial notions of the guru and the holy book, the *Granth Sahib,* until it came to be articulated with the discourse of modern territorial nationalism.

Dusenbery argues convincingly that an interest in Khalistan among diasporic Sikhs may have an almost opposite meaning from what one would expect. Their interest is connected not so much with a wish to leave for such a "homeland," but with a desire to belong in the countries of immigration. Multiculturalist discourse in the West tends to recognize only national cultures, each connected to an independent nation-state. Sikhs are thus lumped in the general category of Indians or South Asians and they are not always happy with that categorization. For Sikh migrants the Punjab has become a spiritual homeland on which they depend to gain respect in Canada, the real homeland, but to which they do not want to return.

Territory plays a different role in the identity formation of the black men who are the subject of Sallie Westwood's contribution. These men understand that as citizens they are legally British, but not culturally English. Their masculine identity is worked out in a number of public spaces, such as inner-city streets and soccer fields. These spaces are defined as "ours" in what Westwood calls a "nationalism of the neighborhood." The men of the neighborhood are tied together by shared territory as *bhum bhai,* as Dusenbery describes it in discussing Punjabi identity. They are South Asians and Afro-Caribbeans, interestingly transcending the bipolar competition that exists between these groups in the Caribbean. It is fascinating to read in Westwood's account how black men have responded to the racism of the professional soccer league by recreating their own tournaments, one of which is organized around the Sikh festival of Vaisakhi. Soccer is clearly a space that allows not only for the display of individual skills, but also for the creation of an important level of self-organization in a rather dismal situation of discrimination and unemployment.

Madhulika Khandelwal discusses other aspects of the relation between identity and the politics of space in the immigrant neighborhood of Flushing in New York City. She describes the emergence of concentration areas for Indian immigrants in the 1970s. This has not led, however, to a mobilization of these immigrants for shared interests. There is hardly a community center in Flushing, while religious and cultural activities, in general, continue to be held at private residences. On the other hand, despite the fragmented nature of the "Indian community," there is a clear business concentration that has created an "Indian Bazaar" atmosphere, which is perceived from the outside by other Americans as a form of ethnic separatism and a rejection of American civic culture.

Seemingly straightforward participation in American civic culture appears to be enacted by Muslims who participate in the annual Muslim World Day Parade in New York City. City parades are performances of ethnic diversity in America's multicultural society. Here, however, religious identity replaces ethnicity. Nevertheless, as in Trinidad, the parade has a distinct South Asian imprint with Pakistani leadership, because African American Muslims do not participate. Susan Slyomovics shows in her chapter the interesting negotiations of Muslim notions of space and movement in a pattern provided by the oldest of the parades, the more than two-hundred-year-old Irish Saint Patrick's Day Parade. Muslims claim a respectable place in American society through this public performance, but, as Slyomovics argues, they are keenly aware that they have to restrain Sufi ecstatic dances and the noise of the call for prayer in order not to disturb the image of secular respectability.

Marginality

In her contribution Khandelwal emphasizes the greater importance of transnational links over spatial identities. These networks ensure a continuous multiplicity of identities and a political marginality of the community as a whole in the American context. However, it is not a marginality in an economic sense. The general economic profile of Indians in the United States in 1985 showed an average household income of $58,200 (Helweg

and Helweg 1990: 262). We should not conclude from this statistic, however, that every Indian in the United States is wealthy. Clearly, the pattern is
changing and, as Khandelwal shows, especially in a "receiving" area of
immigration such as New York City. Obviously, the income and life-style of
an Indian taxi driver in New York City are totally different from those of an
Indian doctor or an engineer in a New Jersey suburb.

The stereotypical image of the poor, marginal immigrant is also
convincingly refuted by Parminder Bhachu, who discusses middle-class,
British-born, and British-educated Sikh women. The Asian woman has
long been the sign of the backwardness of Asian cultures in the orientalist
imagination. The narrative of her subjection and lack of freedom has in the
Indian case especially focused on arranged marriages with bridewealth, or
dowry. In British media images they are often portrayed as passive working-
class victims forced to struggle with their "oppressive cultural systems."
Bhachu counters this essentializing narrative by focusing on the current
labor market and education profile of Asian women as well as on regional
and class differences in their consumption patterns. She shows that South
Asian women actively engage with the British economy and education and
that the different niches they occupy within it exert a strong influence on
their cultural patterns and consumption styles, examined here through an
analysis of their marriage and dowry patterns. As she argues, the vast
majority of South Asian women in Britain in the 1990s are either locally
born or raised and are thus British women, but at the same time they are
active cultural entrepreneurs within their ethnic communities.

In some respects Bhachu's cultural analysis is similar to a recent argument made by Pnina Werbner (1990) about the position of women in a
Pakistani community in Manchester. Like the Sikh women in Bhachu's
analysis, the Pakistani women have gained considerable command over
economic resources and mainstream cultural capital. Werbner discusses at
length the importance of ritual gift giving in the construction of community
and the crucial role women play in this. She describes convincingly the way
balanced gifting defines friendship networks which are basically maintained
by women. Although this taking and giving is based on the role of the
daughter receiving from her patrikin, Werbner demonstrates that this system extends to much larger interhousehold networks.

Although the image of the "marginality" of South Asian women can be
understood as a media product, the larger forces of racism and discrimination also inflict "marginality" on South Asian men. This is particularly clear
from Westwood's account of how Asian men are constantly subject to the

"empire of the gaze." They are subjected to routine harassment by the police and, occasionally, to racial attacks. This contributes forcefully to their sense of separateness and their feeling of safety only "in their own space."

I would submit that "marginality" as a construct has to be understood in the same interpretive framework as "centrality." The "established" and the "outsiders" need each other and should be understood as structurally interdependent. Moreover, in a number of cases we can see that those who are outsiders in one context are established in another and that the images used to portray the outsiders can be used by them in reverse. There is a whole gamut of possible relations between marginality and centrality here that we seek to explore in this volume.

References

Anderson, Benedict
  1991 *Imagined Communities*. London: Verso.
Asad, Talal
  1990 "Multiculturalism and British Identity in the Wake of the Rushdie Affair." *Politics and Society* 18: 455–80.
Bhabha, Homi
  1990 *Nation and Narration*. London: Routledge.
Bhachu, Parminder
  1985 *Twice Migrants: East African Sikh Settlers in Britain*. London: Tavistock.
Breckenridge, Carol A., and Peter van der Veer, eds.
  1993 *Orientalism and the Postcolonial Predicament: Perspectives on South Asia*. Philadelphia: University of Pennsylvania Press.
Clarke, C., C. Peach, and S. Vertovec, eds.
  1990 *South Asians Overseas: Migration and Ethnicity*. Cambridge: Cambridge University Press.
Freitag, Sandria
  1989 *Collective Action and Community*. Berkeley: University of California Press.
Gellner, Ernest
  1983 *Nations and Nationalism*. Ithaca: Cornell University Press.
Gupta, Akhil, and James Ferguson
  1992 "Beyond 'Culture': Space, Identity and the Politics of Difference." *Cultural Anthropology* 7, 1: 6–24.
Helweg, Arthur, and Usha Helweg
  1990 *An Immigrant's Success Story*. Philadelphia: University of Pennsylvania Press.
Hobsbawm, E. J.
  1987 *The Age of Empire, 1875–1914*. New York: Pantheon.

1990   *Nations and Nationalism since 1780*. Cambridge: Cambridge University Press.

Kelly, John

1991   *A Politics of Virtue*. Chicago: University of Chicago Press.

Kolff, D. H. A.

1990   *Naukar, Rajput and Sepoy*. Cambridge: Cambridge University Press.

Marx, Karl

1972   *On Colonialism* [1853]. New York: International Publishers.

Naipaul, V. S.

1961   *A House for Mr. Biswas*. London: André Deutsch.

1965   *An Area of Darkness*. London: André Deutsch.

Oberoi, Harjot

1987   "From Punjab to 'Khalistan': Territoriality and Metacommentary." *Pacific Affairs* 60, 1: 26–41.

Pocock, David

1976   "Preservation of the Religious Life: Hindu Immigrants in England." *Contributions to Indian Sociology* (n.s.) 10: 341–65.

Scott, David

1991   "That Event, This Memory: Notes on the Anthropology of African Diasporas in the New World." *Diaspora* 1, 3: 261–84.

Tinker, Hugh

1974   *A New System of Slavery*. New York: Oxford University Press.

van der Veer, Peter

1994   *Religious Nationalism*. Berkeley: University of California Press.

Werbner, Pnina

1990   *The Migration Process*. Oxford: Berg.

Williams, Raymond

1988   *Religions of Immigrants from India and Pakistan: New Threads in the American Tapestry*. Cambridge: Cambridge University Press.

Verne A. Dusenbery

1. A Sikh Diaspora? Contested Identities and Constructed Realities

When does a diaspora come into existence? Does the use of the term necessarily imply a geographically dispersed but unitary "people" with a common "culture" and an ancestral "homeland" (imagined or otherwise) from which they have been "uprooted," either temporarily or indefinitely (Malkki 1992; Safran 1991)? If, as Peter van der Veer suggests (in the Introduction to this volume), diaspora and the nation have become inextricably intertwined, is territoriality crucial to the identity of the diasporan person? If so, is there a *Sikh* diaspora unless and until there is the concept of a "Sikh homeland"? And does the concept of a *Sikh* homeland "naturalize" efforts to realize a separate Sikh nation-state? What, in short, is the conceptual relationship, if any, between the idea of a Sikh diaspora, the assertion that Sikhs are a "nation," and the call for a territorially separate Sikh nation-state of Khalistan? And how, if at all, has modernist discourse — as reflected, for instance, in colonial administrative directives, Western academic writings, and state policies concerning race, ethnicity, and religion — been implicated in naturalizing connections between people, place, and culture?

My starting point for considering these questions is the recent conference volume, *The Sikh Diaspora: Migration and the Experience Beyond Punjab*, which I edited with N. Gerald Barrier (1989). In conceptualizing the topic for the conference and volume, we had taken the existence of a "Sikh diaspora" to be a relatively unproblematic social fact; but two of the contributing historians, W. H. McLeod (1989a) and Karen Leonard (1989), raised the issue of whether it was in fact appropriate to speak of a *Sikh* diaspora at the time (late nineteenth and early twentieth century) and among the peoples (Punjabi immigrants in New Zealand and rural California, respectively) with whom they had conducted their research. As McLeod noted (1989a: 32), a volume he had preliminarily entitled "Sikhs in New Zealand" he chose ultimately to publish as *Punjabis in New Zealand* (1986), because "when we talk about *Sikh* migration we are choosing to use an imprecise adjective" (1989a: 32) since "the Punjabi village of the early twentieth century was no place to go looking for clear-cut normative identities" (ibid.: 42). Leonard was even more blunt. She argued:

> It has become common to talk of the Sikh diaspora, but there is some question whether or not "Sikh" is the most appropriate category for analysis of these emigrants from South Asia. While the overwhelming majority of the Punjabi pioneers in early twentieth century California were indeed Sikhs, my research indicates that religion was less salient than other characteristics of these men. It was in fact a Punjabi diaspora, and to go back and emphasize Sikhs and Sikhism does violence to the historical experiences of the immigrants and their descendants. (1989: 120)

According to these historians, then, early international migrants from colonial Punjab, whatever their religious practices before or after migration, were not conscious of themselves as forming a "Sikh diaspora." For McLeod and Leonard, it was their *Punjabi* identity—their common "culture," "place of origin," and "mother tongue"—that was most meaningful to these early twentieth-century migrants.

The question, then, is when and where and for whom can one legitimately speak of a Sikh diaspora? Both McLeod and Leonard allow that the Sikh aspect of the migrants' identity became increasingly salient as time went by. And it is surely salient in the contemporary context of the political crisis in Punjab and the movement for the Khalistan, a separate Sikh state. Was there then a historical moment when the Sikh diaspora came to know itself as a unitary collectivity of people dispersed in geographic space but sharing a common "culture" and "homeland," a "community" structurally distinct from and opposed to equivalent sociological units? If so, what were the terms by which this collective "identity" was made known and expressed? Was it as a "nation," defined as a conjunction of people, culture, and place? And has this Sikh diasporan identity become so thoroughly naturalized as to subordinate alternative collective identities?

McLeod and Leonard make an important point in alerting us to analytic anachronisms that may not reflect the subjective experiences of historical subjects but may well reflect an interested retrospective inscription of some putatively collective history. However, in phrasing the issue in the terms of whether this was a Punjabi diaspora or a Sikh diaspora, McLeod and Leonard themselves appear to be overly constrained by high modernist sensibilities that anticipate "clear-cut normative identities"— including radical distinctions of religious and secular identities (see Dusenbery 1981) and unambiguous mappings of peoples and their cultures on places (see Gupta and Ferguson 1992: 8). My argument, by contrast, is: (1) that there are good reasons why the Punjabi village of the early twentieth century was no place to go looking for clear-cut normative identities; (2) that these reasons have had to do with the prevailing understanding of persons and groups that has allowed Punjabis to strategically emphasize different aspects of their partially shared personhood (e.g., caste, region, language, religion) in different historical contexts; (3) that the colonial and diasporan experience has confronted South Asians with an alternative modernist discourse of identity that would have them possess — in the possessive individualist sense (see Handler 1988: 50–51) — a fixed, superordinant "cultural"/"ethnic"/"national" identity, such that Sikhs have increasingly come to represent themselves as an "ethnoterritorial community" (Oberoi 1987: 40); but, finally, (4) that there exist alternative deterritorialized and supraterritorial terms by which Sikhs can, and in fact do, construct their collective identity.

*   *   *

McLeod's point about the lack of "clear-cut normative identities" in Punjabi villages at the turn of the century is an appropriate place from which to begin consideration of a Punjabi ethnosociology. The forty years from 1880 to 1920 were a period of extensive international migration from the hard-pressed villages of central Punjab (see Dusenbery 1989; McLeod 1989a; Fox 1985). It was also a time during which a new cultural elite of neo-orthodox Sikhs, responding to the British colonial and Christian missionary presence in Punjab, successfully sought to "subsume a variety of Sikh sub-traditions . . . under a monolithic, codified and reified religion" (Oberoi 1988: 149). As Harjot Oberoi, writing of the late nineteenth century, notes: "Far from there being a single 'Sikh' identity, most Sikhs moved in and out of multiple identities" (ibid.: 137; see also Oberoi 1994). And, as historical work on the British census in Punjab shows (see Barrier 1970), how to categorize and enumerate the population in Punjab was a challenge to the British, who were confused and frustrated by what they perceived to be the lack of clear-cut normative identities among Punjabis.

In Punjab, different kinds of people or different human "genera" (Panjabi, *zat;* Hindi, *jati*) were locally distinguished by, among other criteria, "worship," "territorial," "occupational," "linguistic" substances incorporated as a result of their different ritual practices, places of residence, productive modes, and languages used (see Dusenbery 1988, 1990b). Of the indigenous distinctions that Punjabis were making among local people, the British were most cognizant of — and concerned with enumerating and rationalizing for administrative purposes — two identities: occupational genera (which for British purposes becomes reified as "caste") and worship genera (which for the British becomes "religion"). By fixing on these identities and then trying to affix said identities to a bounded subpopulation within the province, the British did two things. First, they imposed conceptual boundaries and structural rigidity on a fluid interpersonal and intrapersonal transactive space. This was especially so in the case of caste and religion, where "cultivating" and "noncultivating" castes and "martial" and "nonmartial" castes were now legally and administratively distinguished, and one was pushed to declare oneself to be unequivocally "Sikh," "Hindu," or "Muslim." Second, the British made caste and religion increasingly salient political categories around which the local population might organize and be organized, while at the same time making territorial genera (the localized "regional" identities) less salient and, ultimately, making territory itself a free-floating sign — which, at partition, became aligned with "communal" distinctions.

One result of modernist discourse among Sikhs (emanating from the Singh Sabha/Tat Khalsa movement) was to help establish this newly emergent canonical Sikh identity, such that it became possible for the Sikh public in the early twentieth century "to think, imagine and speak in terms of a universal community of believers united by uniform rites, symbols and scripture" (Oberoi 1988: 154). If this made sharper and more categorical the distinctions between Sikhs, Hindus, and other "communities of believers," it still did not make all members of the Sikh worship genus or *panth* (lit., path or way), identical in their personal natures, since they also continued to belong to other, different human genera — territorial, occupational, and even linguistic (given the existence of Sikhs speaking Sindhi and other South Asian languages). A Sikh Jat (agriculturalist) from Doaba (the region of central Punjab between the Beas and Sutlej rivers) and a Sikh Mazhbi (sweeper) from Majha (the region of central Punjab between the Beas and Ravi rivers) might partake of similar worship substances, making them coequal members of the Sikh Panth, but they would otherwise be distinguished by occupational genus and territorial genus — as is clear from the continued evidence of what becomes reified, in Western sociological terms, as "caste endogamy" and "regional endogamy" within the Sikh Panth.

In South Asian ethnosociological terms, the Punjabi person was thus a "dividual," a confluence of different biomoral substances, partially shared with other persons.[1] Political mobilization and social solidarity in Punjab and among Punjabis abroad have been at different times effected through appeals to these partially shared ties made in the name of caste, religious, linguistic, or territorial "brotherhood" (the Panjabi terms *biradari* and *bhaichara* being potentially applicable to persons thought to share natural substances and codes for conduct). In imposing their own ethnosociology, the British colonial policy of "divide and rule" made certain fault lines (especially caste and communal [i.e., religious]) that much more rigid and impermeable than might otherwise have been the case. Nevertheless, the historical experience of Punjabis has been of shifting personal and political alliances based on appeals to partially shared personal natures. Many Khatris, for instance, judging their caste similarities (as urban merchants) to outweigh their religious differences, continued to blend and unite Khatri Sikh and Khatri Hindu families long after Jat Sikhs, Jat Hindus, and Jat Muslims had come to marry almost exclusively with coreligionists. The successful Sikh-led, postindependence agitation for Punjabi Suba, a linguistically based state in secular India, could be couched in linguistic terms precisely because Punjabi Hindus, in declaring Hindi rather than Panjabi as their mother tongue, renounced what they could have constituted as their brotherhood with Punjabi Sikhs through a shared language. At the same time, Sikhs themselves have been unable to establish political hegemony in India's reorganized Sikh majority state of Punjab because Mazhbi Sikhs (former "untouchables") usually have been unwilling to commit their votes to the Jat-dominated Sikh party, the Akali Dal. In the aftermath of the attack on the Golden Temple and the Delhi riots of 1984, however, a sense of shared suffering and dishonor *as Sikhs* was sufficient to override caste differences, sweeping the Akali Dal into power in the Punjab elections of 1985. In Punjab, social, political, and economic interests commonly run along channels laid down in terms of local understandings of persons and their particular natures.

Given these indigenous distinctions of persons, for the early twentieth century at least, one might well talk of a Jat diaspora in North America (since the overwhelming majority of migrants across the Pacific were Jats) or a Ramgarhia diaspora in East Africa (since the vast majority of Punjabi migrants there were of this artisan caste) or even a Bhatra diaspora in England (since the first wave of Punjabi immigrants were from this small peddler caste). Or one could conceivably talk of Malwai, Majhai, or Doabi diasporas, recognizing the indigenous Punjabi territorial distinctions of persons that played a part and continue to play a part in the lives of Sikhs in the diaspora — where marriage networks and even local gurdwaras (Sikh temples) have been organized by Punjabi regions, as well as by caste and sect (see, e.g., Ballard 1989).

McLeod and Leonard are right to suggest that Sikh identities were not the only salient identities that early migrants brought with them from Punjab. Not only were the lines between Sikh, Hindu, and Muslim Punjabis not yet drawn as absolutely as they would be by later migrants, but also those who followed different religious practices often shared and were bound together by caste, regional, and linguistic ties. At the same time, however, the notion of a "Punjabi diaspora" is itself problematic if it implies some clearly delineated, internally undifferentiated cultural-cum-geographic group. Here McLeod and Leonard come close to imposing their modernist sensibilities about the correspondence of culture, language, and place on their informants' subjective understandings of their fluid and relatively unbounded social world. Punjab (lit., [land of] five rivers) might have broad territorial and linguistic referents, but the administrative boundaries that the British drew did not mark off some "natural" sociocultural or political unit. And turn-of-the-century migrants are likely to have interacted and mobilized on the basis of shared worship, occupational, regional, and/or linguistic ties, but not on the basis of some superordinant "Punjabi" cultural identity.[2]

Insofar as these indigenous distinctions of persons by worship, occupational, territorial, and linguistic genera have remained salient among Punjabi Sikhs, "religion" and "place" would appear to be analytically separate sources of social identity and solidarity. How, then, has a sense of territoriality — of a rootedness to Punjab or Khalistan — come to be tied to an understanding of the Sikh Panth as a distinct worship genus (*zat*) or brotherhood (*biradari*)? In the ethnosociology sketched earlier, one's territory marked one with the natural substances of the place (i.e., the land and its products), making people of the same place into *bhum bhai* (brothers of the earth), whereas one's ritual practices involved incorporating the worship substances — *darshan* (glances), *bani* (speech), *prashad* (leavings), *amrit* (nectar) — of the guru, making those who worship alike into *guru bhai* (brothers of the [same] guru). Members of a Punjabi village might expect to share qualities with their local *bhum bhai* without expecting all fellow villagers to be *guru bhai*. At the same time, Sikhs of different regions within and even outside Punjab might recognize one another as *guru bhai,* without expecting their personal natures to be identical. Worship and territoriality would apparently generate different aspects of a person's nature.

In fact, the collective actions of Sikhs in the diaspora, as reported in the historical and ethnographic literature, suggest that Sikhs have attempted to nourish and sustain the various ancestral genera — worship, territorial, linguistic, occupational — of which the migrants conceive themselves to be a part. Where possible, Sikh migrants have constructed gurdwaras, maintained facility in Panjabi, remitted to and visited the natal village, and avoided inappropriate occupations (see Dusenbery 1990a, 1990b). Although it is beyond the scope of this chapter to detail how such actions have been sustained, through stereotyping, gossip, and exclusionary practices (see Helweg 1986: 12–21; Dusenbery 1990a), a Sikh's *izzat* (honor), even in the diaspora, has usually entailed following actions considered appropriate to one's nature as a specific kind of person. And these different aspects of the person continue to be indexed in marriage practices, such that a Panjabi-speaking, Doabi, Jat Sikh living in Vancouver, Yuba City, or Southall will usually seek a spouse of similar personal character. But since this is a dynamic and fluid ethnosociology that can logically incorporate new coded substances, it is also not surprising that for the generation born and raised in the English-speaking diaspora, England, Canada, the United States, Singapore, and Malaysia have over time come to complement Majha, Malwa, and Doaba in imparting their "territorial" natures — complete with corresponding regional stereotypes and presumed marital compatibilities — to persons.[3]

*   *   *

Yet if, as I have been arguing, worship and territorial genera have long been conceptually distinct for Punjabis, how are we to account for the territorial claims in contemporary Sikh political discourse? And how does an inclusive, unbounded Sikh sacred space, defined by the presence of the Guru, articulate with the demand for an exclusive Sikh nation-state defined by territorial boundaries?

The *janam-sakhi* literature, the popular accounts of the life of the first Sikh Guru, recounts Guru Nanak's travels in the late fifteenth and early sixteenth centuries to the extremities of the known world to spread his divinely inspired message. The first Guru is credited with journeys north to

Nepal and Tibet, east to Assam and Bengal, south to Ceylon, west to Mecca and Baghdad. The message is of the Guru's expansiveness, of a royal assertion of a Sikh presence throughout the world, of conquest of the world in all four directions along familiar *digvajaya* lines (see McLeod 1989b: 20). Like an Indian ruler surveying his domain, the founder of Sikhism in effect circumambulates — and thus metonymically and metaphorically incorporates — the known world. The effect is intentionally outward looking and inclusionary. Far from delimiting a territorial boundary to the Sikh world, the Guru's travels suggest a boundless and boundaryless world of Sikh sacred space which carries itself into the very heart of Hindu, Buddhist, and Muslim lands.

Nor does the distribution of historical Sikh shrines and relics suggest any attempt to define the Sikh realm as coterminous with the boundaries of Punjab. Like their followers in later centuries, the Gurus traveled widely. Shrines and relics said to be associated with the lives of the Gurus can be found throughout India and beyond. The five most important historical shrines associated with the lives of the Gurus, those that have been recognized as the five *takhat*s (lit., thrones) of the Sikhs, include two — Patna Sahib in Bihar and Nander in Maharashtra — that are located well outside any of the variable historical boundaries of Punjab.[4] It would appear that the presence of the Guru bestows sanctity on a place, not the reverse.

If Amritsar, the home of Darbar Sahib (the "Golden Temple") and the Akal Takhat (lit., immortal throne; the highest seat of Sikh religiotemporal authority), has over time become a pilgrimage center of the Sikh world, it is a symbolic center for a world without boundaries. Unlike caste Hindus, Sikhs suffered no loss of rank or merit from travel overseas. Indeed, Sikhs journeying beyond Punjab, far from Amritsar and the sacred shrines, could take comfort from the pronouncement attributed to the tenth and last human Guru, Gobind Singh, that wherever five Sikhs gather together in the presence of their sacred scripture, the Adi Granth or Guru Granth Sahib, there too is the eternal Guru. Sikhs of the diaspora may be dispersed from ancestral homes in Punjab and far from most of the historical Sikh shrines; but insofar as the Guru is believed to coreside in the Guru Granth, the divine Word inscribed in the sacred scripture, and the Guru Panth, the corporate community created by the congregation of any five worthy Sikhs, Sikhs are never at a distance from the Guru, whose presence defines the sacred center. The local gurdwaras (lit., door of the Guru), to be found wherever Sikhs have settled, are sacred spaces in which the Guru's divine substances are made available to any Sikh wherever resident.

Clearly the rhetoric of a territorially delimited Sikh nation-state is not grounded in this vein of Sikh discourse.

*   *   *

In one of his many important articles tracing the subjective and symbolic dimensions of Sikh historical experience, Harjot Oberoi has recently explored "how the expression of Punjab as a homeland was woven into the self-definitions of the Sikh Panth" (1987: 27). It is Oberoi's contention that "the affective attachment with the Punjab is fairly recent, and it does not date back to the early annals of the Sikh community, as some ideologues of 'Khalistan' would like to assert today" (ibid.). Indeed, he presents a convincing argument that it was only with the impending partition of Punjab at the close of the colonial era that Sikhs began to suggest that "Sikhs belonged to the Punjab; the Punjab belongs to the Sikhs" (ibid.: 37). Oberoi shows that throughout what he calls the Guru Phase (1600 to 1707), the Heroic Phase (1708 to 1849), and through much of the Colonial Phase (1849 to 1947), including the neo-orthodox Singh Sabha/Tat Khalsa period at the turn of the century, Sikh discourse showed no concern with tying Sikhs and Sikhism to the territory of Punjab. It was the person of the Guru — the human Gurus in their lifetimes and then the scriptural Guru (Guru Granth) and corporate Guru (Guru Panth) — that bound together the Sikhs (lit., disciples).

Only when the British were on the verge of splitting Punjab between Muslims and Hindus — in effect, making territorial groups out of religious communities — did Sikhs demand a "Sikhistan" based on Sikh "intimate bonds" to Punjab and, failing to achieve it, bemoan: "The Hindus got Hindustan, the Muslims got Pakistan, what did the Sikhs get?" Oberoi goes on to show how Sikh commentary over the past four decades has since spread the idea of a special Sikh tie to the "land of five rivers" (Punjab), with what he calls "an undeniable nexus between the Punjab and Sikh consciousness" (ibid.: 39) having been firmly established during the protracted struggle for Punjabi Suba, reinforced by the Green Revolution miracle in Punjab, and given full voice by proponents of Khalistan. And he concludes by suggesting that the equation of the Sikhs with Punjab — now transformed into Khalistan (the so-called land of the pure) — has become thoroughly "naturalized."

Oberoi provides us with the historical time frame in which to place this transformation of Sikhs into an "ethnoterritorial community." But how was the symbol of territory added to what Oberoi calls the "evolving inventory of Sikh ethnicity" (ibid.: 40)? And what was the impetus for this conceptual or rhetorical shift?

One of the subtle ways in which this reconceptualization has taken place is through increasing substitution in Sikh discourse of the Persian loan word *qaum* (lit., people who stand together) or the English word "nation" in reference to the Sikh collectivity. The term *panth* seems particularly appropriate to a self-definition that focuses on ritual practice as the source of shared worship substances that unite Sikhs as a brotherhood of *gursikhs* (followers of the Guru). As McLeod has noted, *qaum*, by contrast, "possesses an ethnic dimension . . . and retains the kind of overtones which have done so much to debase the English words 'community' and 'communal' in their distinctively Indian usage" (1978: 294). But precisely for these reasons, *qaum* might serve as an appealing alternative when one is advancing political and territorial claims. All the more would this be the case with "nation," which even more clearly has come in contemporary political discourse to imply rights to the possession of a sovereign homeland or territory.

This creative tension over how to conceptualize the Sikh collectivity is telling. As McLeod points out, Sir John Malcolm, writing from Punjab early in the nineteenth century, referred to the Sikhs as both a "sect" and a "nation"; and "the two terms have since recurred in the ongoing attempt to find an English word which will accurately describe, in the corporate sense, those . . . who call themselves Sikhs" (ibid.: 287). It has apparently not been easy for Western observers to categorize Sikhs neatly as either a religious community or an ethnic group. I see this and similar conceptual problems for Western would-be interpreters of the Sikhs (see, e.g., Juergensmeyer and Barrier 1979; McLeod 1989b; Dusenbery 1990b) as reflecting deep-seated and recurrent Western ontological and sociological dualisms (e.g., spirit and matter, sacred and secular, religion and ethnicity). To the extent that the dominant Punjabi ethnosociology has not been premised on the same dualisms, the issue of Sikh corporate identity presumably has not posed the same problem for Sikhs as it has for Western-trained observers. But, and this is the important point, to the extent that Sikhs do not neatly fall into familiar Western social categories, they may find it useful in given fields of power to manipulate the rhetoric of their personhood so as to represent themselves more or less as a religious community (as may be suggested by the term *panth*) or as an ethnic group or nation (as may be suggested by the term *qaum*). Certainly, as territorially based nationalism became a prevailing discourse of the world in the nineteenth century (see Anderson 1991), it affected discourses of identity and belonging on the Indian subcontinent. Thus, when at partition the British moved to provide Indian Muslims with their own nation-state of Pakistan, it served Sikh purposes as another "communal" group to emphasize their "intimate bonds" to the Punjab and the "rights of the Sikh nation" to "the creation of a Sikh state," as in the oft-cited Akali Dal resolution of March 1946 which called on the British to create a "Sikhistan" to be located between India and West Pakistan (quoted in Oberoi 1987: 37; see also Madan 1991: 620).

*   *   *

What Robin Jeffrey (1987) has called modern Sikh "rhetorical history" is replete with claims that have proven useful to recent proponents of a Sikh nation-state. Foremost among these rhetorical claims is that of past and future Sikh sovereignty. The case for Sikh political as well as religious sovereignty is advanced on many fronts. According to Sikh hagiography, the sixth Guru, Hargobind, was invested with two swords at his installation as Guru, one representing spiritual authority (*piri;* from the Persian, *pir,* a religious teacher) and the other representing temporal authority (*miri;* from *amir,* commander). The Akal Takhat, the preeminent "throne" of the Sikhs (destroyed by the Indian Army in its 1984 raid on the Golden Temple complex), is commonly referred to as "the seat of Sikh sacred and secular authority" and was intentionally built higher than the palaces or thrones of local potentates. The line, *Raj karega Khalsa* (The Khalsa shall rule), from Ardas, the communal Sikh prayer sung at the conclusion of Sikh worship, is seen by many Sikhs as a prophetic pronouncement of Sikh sovereignty made by the tenth Guru, Gobind Singh.[5] And the reign of Maharaj Ranjit Singh over greater Punjab in the early nineteenth century is taken by some as a Golden Age in which Guru Gobind Singh's prophecy of Sikh rule was fulfilled. The past century and a half, including both colonial and postindependence Indian history, is then presented as a long series of plots by various parties intent on depriving Sikhs of their rightful sovereignty.[6]

But contemporary Sikh nationalist rhetoric goes beyond reasserting Singh Sabha/Tat Khalsa claims to Sikh distinctiveness—encapsulated in the phrase, *Ham Hindu Nahin* (We are not Hindus) — or reiterating the rhetorical history of Sikh sovereignty—encapsulated in the phrase, *Raj karega Khalsa*. Instead, proponents of a Sikh nation-state attempt to represent Sikh realities as in full conformity with the tenets of modern nationalism, including the correspondence of people, culture, and place. Thus, Mehar Singh Chaddah, in *Are Sikhs a Nation?* starts with a general (modern, Western) definition and proceeds to argue that Sikhs are a separate "nation" because "the Sikhs are bound by common race, common language and literature, common land, common history, common religion, common joys and sorrows, and common political aims and aspirations" (1982: 79; see also Surjan Singh 1982: 113–18). It is then but a short step from claiming nationhood to demanding statehood, especially in the contemporary world climate of crumbling empires and political devolution. Thus, in a recent joint appeal to the United Nations, the two most powerful mainstream Sikh institutions — the Sikh political party, the Shiromani Akali Dal, and the committee charged with control of Sikh shrines in Punjab, the Shiromani Gurdwara Parbandhak Committee — argue for "decolonisation of Punjab" on the basis that "Sikhs are a religious community and a political nation simultaneously. . . . Sikhism and its apotheosis, the Khalsa[,] is a unique political society with a distinct religion, language, culture, ethos, a historic territory and political thought" (Shiromani Akali Dal 1992: 6).

In short, the logic of Sikh nationalist rhetoric leads inexorably to the notion that the Sikhs belong to Punjab and Punjab belongs to the Sikhs. Internal homogeneity and historical continuity within fixed spatial boundaries is the dominant imagery, and a unique Punjabi Sikh patrimony is the dominant claim. To make their case, however, Sikh nationalist rhetoricians are perforce required to ignore or explain away such uncomfortable facts as coresidence and intermarriage with Punjabi Hindus, the existence of Sindhi-speaking Sikhs and Euro-American Sikh converts, and long-standing caste, regional, and sectarian differences among Sikhs.[7] The entire thrust of such nationalist rhetoric, with its neatly bounded and differentiated social units, flies in the face of much that we know about the social history of Punjab over the past five centuries. Nevertheless, given that nationalist discourse has become a dominant political discourse of the contemporary world, it is hardly surprising that Sikhs might represent themselves in its terms to advance their claims.

It would be naive to act as though such discourse has had a life entirely unrelated to the changing political economy in which Sikhs have lived their lives. Whatever the sources of these concepts, they find resonance among human agents when conditions are favorable to their propagation. Oberoi's analysis suggests that Sikh claims of constituting a distinct "ethnoterritorial community" gained general currency on the eve of partition, when Sikhs felt that they, as a "communal" group, would be net political and economic losers. In the postindependence era, the Government of India acquiesced to the creation of Punjabi Suba only at a time when Punjab was a frontline state and Sikh troops were needed in the 1965 war with Pakistan. Although the demand for a Sikh-majority state within the Indian union had to be cloaked in linguistic rather than religious terms to satisfy the requirements of secular India's constitution, the ultimate acceptance of this demand seemed to confirm in principle the right of the Sikh "nation" (defined, as earlier in Chaddah's formulation, to include both linguistic and religious referents) to "self-determination" within a territorial "homeland" (as the contemporary nationalist slogan would have it). Thus it only temporarily dampened the overt nationalist and separatist rhetoric. After the initial productive success of the Green Revolution, the world and national political economy turned against certain classes in the reorganized state of Punjab, creating a crisis of honor for marginal Sikh farmers and for educated but unemployed Sikh youth. It was in this context that Sant Jarnail Singh Bhindranwale, himself of a small farmer family, and Amrik Singh, head of the All India Sikh Student Federation, found a receptive audience (particularly among youth from less well-off Jat Sikh families) for visions of a better, more honorable life that might be realized in a fully sovereign Punjab or an imagined Khalistan.[8] And after the cataclysmic events of 1984 (the assault on the Golden Temple complex and the Delhi riots following Indira Gandhi's assassination), other Sikhs, feeling their own interests and the collective honor of the community to be threatened by the Indian state, found sufficient cause to seriously entertain separatist visions.[9]

*   *   *

But why should Sikhs of the diaspora be moved by such imagery, given the presumably very different political and economic situations they are experiencing? The Government of India, particularly under the Congress party rule of Indira Gandhi and Rajiv Gandhi, has made much of the supposed intellectual leadership and material support that the Khalistan movement and "Sikh terrorists" have received from Sikhs of the diaspora. Clearly, as Arthur Helweg has detailed (1989), specific Sikh individuals and organizations in the United Kingdom, the United States, Canada, and elsewhere have been major proponents of Khalistan, although it is hardly surprising that Sikhs supporting a separatist agenda might find it easier to voice their claims from outside India. As for the charge of widespread material support of and active complicity in "terrorism" on the part of Sikhs in North America and the United Kingdom, the evidence is less convincing. Indeed, it has even been suggested by credible third parties that Indian agents themselves may have been responsible for some of the violence popularly attributed to diasporan Sikhs (see Kashmeri and McAndrew 1989). Nevertheless, it is true that Sikh nationalists pushing a separatist agenda (which should not be confused with terrorism) after 1984 established apparent political hegemony, through a combination of moral suasion and intimidation of their critics, among diasporan Sikhs in England, Canada, and the United States, as in Punjab. The question is, given their remove from the immediate political and economic problems troubling the state of Punjab, why has it served some Sikhs of the diaspora to emphasize Sikh nationhood, to proclaim Sikh territorial ties to Punjab, and to promote a new state of Khalistan?

Various explanations have been advanced for diasporan Sikh support for Khalistan. Helweg emphasizes alienation, anomie, and opportunity. That is, he attributes Khalistani sympathies to what he calls a supportive "psychological and cultural framework" among diasporan Sikhs (1989: 331), consisting of a perceived threat of extinction, a migrant's loneliness, and a desire for honor in the eyes of others combined with the organizational capacities of the gurdwaras and the absence of sanctions on nationalist activities. Harry Gouldbourne (1991: 126–69), focusing on the British case, emphasizes the cohesion of the migrant community and its disenchantment with British society, claiming that "any sense of insecurity in this country tends to encourage articulate Sikhs to support the demand for an independent and secure homeland in the sub-continent" (ibid.: 152). Mark Juergensmeyer, on the other hand, argues that Sikhs of the diaspora have actively promoted Khalistan mainly because as emigrants they were "socially marginal to the [home] community [in Punjab]" and "were looking for a centre to Sikhism and wanted to be associated with it" so as to gain "a sense of belonging" (1988: 79, 80). Although there is something to be said for these varied explanations, each on its own terms seems unduly general and overly mechanistic. Are diasporan Sikhs in fact demonstrably lonelier, more insecure (in their new abode), or more marginal (to their old) than other nonseparatist migrant groups? And, more to the point, are Sikhs of the diaspora who actively support Khalistan lonelier, more insecure, and more marginal than those who do not support Khalistan? My own analysis, therefore, is focused less on the psychological profile of the diasporan Khalistani than on dialectical linkages between (1) Sikh notions of collective identity and personal honor, and (2) the sociology and politics of ethnic representation in those countries with significant Sikh populations. I emphasize this dialectical relationship since, as the discussion here suggests, Sikh identities — including the notion of Sikhs as an "ethnoterritorial community" — have been constructed in fields of power, where ideologies and policies of the state can significantly affect Sikh self-identity.

Along these lines, Peter van der Veer (in the Introduction to this volume) has written of the imposition by xenophobia of a negative identity, enhancing among migrants a nationalist sentiment characterized by a "longing" to be elsewhere. Certainly, the discrimination and hostility that the first generation of South Asian immigrants (overwhelmingly Sikh) experienced in Canada and the United States contributed to the widespread support that they gave the North American–based Ghadar (Revolution) party in the early part of this century. A major ideological motivation for the Ghadar effort to oust the British from India was the perceived failure of the British Indian authorities to protect the interests of South Asian immigrants in North America from hostile, exclusionary actions of Canadian and American authorities. If Indians only controlled their own state, it was argued, they would be able to deal effectively on a state-to-state basis with Canadian and American authorities on behalf of the interests of Indian subjects residing in North America. In his definitive account, Harish Puri (1993) shows how an "autointoxication of disgrace" over their own treatment in North America, as well as that of their "brothers" in British India, led a significant number of Sikh immigrants to commit their money and lives to this heroic but premature effort to drive the British from India. What is notable about the Ghadar episode is the way in which, as van der Veer suggests, the xenophobia of Canadians and Americans generates a "nationalist" consciousness among the South Asians. Juergensmeyer labels this the "Ghadar syndrome," what he defines as "a militant nationalist movement . . . created abroad by expatriates, for whom the movement is also an outlet for economic and social frustrations, and a vehicle for their ethnic identities" (1979: 14; see also Juergensmeyer 1982). But Ghadar was still a pan-Indian nationalist movement, uniting Sikhs, Hindus, and Muslims from various parts of the subcontinent. And accounts focused on Indian nationalism of the Ghadarites have often ignored or underplayed alternative, non-nationalist ideologies present at the same time among North American Sikhs (Dusenbery 1985; Puri 1985). How do we then shift from Indian nationalism to *Sikh* nationalism among Sikhs in North America?

Ghadar sought primarily to address the political situation in India, with the hope that this would positively affect the situation of South Asians in North America. From the beginning, in Canada, political mobilization to address Canadian authorities on the migrants' concerns as Canadian residents of South Asian origins was consistently channeled through the Sikh gurdwara societies — most notably through the Khalsa Diwan Society in British Columbia. It was not until the 1950s that a nominally pan–"East Indian" organization was founded (again, in British Columbia). And only in the 1970s was a national organization for Canada's "East Indians" formed. I have advanced situational and cultural factors to explain the failure of South Asians to develop separate religious and ethnic-political organizations in Canada — that is, the demographic predominance of Sikhs among the immigrants and the long-standing tradition among Sikhs of conjoined religious and political authority (see Dusenbery 1981). But the success of the Ghadar party in attracting diasporan Sikh support for an Indian "nationalist" agenda (as would later be the case with support given the Indian National Army and Indian Congress) suggests that Sikh political action could be mobilized along nonreligious lines.

Let me now implicate the ethnosociology and local politics of the state (what used to be called "the host country") in this analysis. State ideologies and public policies of race, ethnicity, and multiculturalism pursued in such pluralistic countries as Canada, Malaysia, Singapore, and, increasingly, the United States and United Kingdom over the past several decades seem predicated on a common modernist assumption that one's ancestral "place of origin" — and, in particular, one's "national origins" or "country of origin" — in some sense provides the natural building blocks out of which social units — the various ethnic, racial, or cultural communities — are constructed in pluralist nation-states. (At the same time, religion is often differentiated from these other identities as private, voluntaristic, and achieved rather than public, essentialistic, and ascribed.)

Given this ethnosociology, it is not surprising that Sikhs in Canada were being encouraged in the 1970s to funnel their public activities through what were at least in theory pan–"East Indian" ethnic-political organizations. While conducting fieldwork in Vancouver, British Columbia, in the late 1970s, I was struck by two contending models and discourses of political mobilization being pursued by local Sikhs. The modernist Sikh elite in Vancouver, including many second-generation and even third-generation Canadians, was active in organizing and providing leadership for a newly established ethnic-political organization, the National Association of Canadians of Origins in India (NACOI). This group accepted the conventional fiction of the Canadian government's new multiculturalism policy (Canada 1971) — to wit, that Canadians of origins in India not only shared a common ancestral place of origin but also a common "culture" and, it was assumed, similar political interests. The logic of Canadian multiculturalism was of a world of discrete cultures mapped unproblematically onto people who had definitive places of origin. India, as a nation-state, was a recognized place of origin. According to this line of thinking, Sikhs — at least those Sikhs of Punjabi ancestry — like other Canadians whose ancestral roots led back to present-day India, ought to address the government and society-at-large through pan-Indian ethnic-political organization such as NACOI (leaving the gurdwaras and other "places of worship" to deal with distinctly "religious" matters). Indeed, the government would actively nurture NACOI to be this umbrella ethnic-political organization.[10]

Struggling to be heard against this logic of Canadian multiculturalism was a popular Sikh alternative, supported especially by the more recent immigrants and enunciated most vociferously at the time by the local Shiromani Akali Dal of Canada — to wit, that Sikhs are "a separate people" who should be known neither as East Indians nor as Canadians of Origins in India but simply as Canadian Sikhs. Moreover, according to the Shiromani Akali Dal line, political representation of Sikh interests in Canada should come from local gurdwara societies or other representatives "of the Sikh people," and not channeled through pan–"East Indian" ethnic-political organizations like NACOI — however strong Sikh representation might be in such organizations. When it became clear in the late 1970s and early 1980s that the Canadian government preferred Sikhs to petition the government through ethnic-political organizations, it gave these anti-NACOI Sikhs all the more incentive to promote the message that Sikhs constitute a distinct "ethnoterritorial community" and, even before the traumatic events of 1984, to join the call for Khalistan.[11]

One of the appeals of Khalistan to diasporan Sikhs may be the creation of a publicly recognized "country of origin," from which Sikhs may legitimately make claim to their own political voice and to the perquisites of public support for cultural diversity (e.g., funding made available under multiculturalism programs or protection under local human rights codes) in their countries of residence. If the local logic of multiculturalism in these pluralist polities requires a distinctive source "culture" derived from a recognized homeland or country of origin, then Sikhs who believe their religion, culture, and politics to be indivisible will endeavor to supply the territorial basis for their "separate identity as Sikhs."

Since 1984, it has in fact been increasingly difficult to sustain a plausible fiction that Canada's "East Indians" or Britain's "Asians" or Singapore's "Singaporean Indians" share not only a collective identity but also common political interests. And Sikhs seem to realize that in pressing the claims of Sikh nationhood, especially if realized territorially through the achievement of Khalistan, the right of diasporan Sikhs to a separate identity and political voice can be established in local ethnosociological and policy terms. Thus I would argue that much as Ghadar party members sought to end the disgrace following from their treatment in North America by changing the colonial map of India, so too Khalistan supporters in the diaspora can be seen to be attempting to gain a measure of respect and power in countries of the diaspora by changing the contemporary political map of South Asia. In van der Veer's terms, the "longing" for Khalistan is for some Sikhs a means of and to "belonging" in their current country of residence.

*   *   *

However successfully links between the Sikhs and Punjab or Khalistan may have been naturalized in recent Sikh discourse, there is nothing in fact "natural" (i.e., intrinsic and inevitable and thus beyond human agency) about these links, nor does such discourse exhaust the ways that Sikhs envision their collective identity. And as Richard Handler has forcefully reminded us, anthropologists might do well to distance themselves from a discourse of nationalism and ethnicity that naturalizes such links between people, culture, and place, especially since it is based on a theory of social difference that implicates both "mainstream anthropology" and "Western common sense" (1985: 171).[12] Thus, it is useful to remind ourselves that understandings of the Sikh collectivity as a "nation" having a "homeland" and a "diaspora" are emergent, contested, and contestable social facts. If in entitling our volume *The Sikh Diaspora* Barrier and I seemed thereby to be committing ourselves to a view of the world or to a political position naturalizing Sikh demands for Khalistan, we were unwitting collaborators. My position is that "the Sikhs of the diaspora are an integral part of a worldwide Sikh society" (1989: 9). How such social ties — including those with Punjab — are to be conceptualized and represented is an open subject, one of considerable concern to various interested Sikh and non-Sikh parties. Obviously, the stakes are high. As Oberoi notes:

Having derived sustenance from the stories of territoriality, the Sikhs are now trapped in the depths of a classic dilemma: if they pursue its resolution, they are faced with a situation similar to that of the Basques, the Kurds, and the Palestinians (which are fellow ethnoterritorial communities), but if they abandon this newly constituted emblem they undermine an element of their own identity. One possible way out of the labyrinth would be gradually to invent new myths. (1987: 40)

One such possible new myth is not really a new myth at all. By creatively playing within the field of possibilities implicit in the Punjabi notion of a *panth,* Sikhs can plausibly reemphasize the deterritorialized notion of the Sikh Panth as a "worship genus" composed of any and all persons who share the Guru's substances, acquired through their "physiological engagement" with the scriptural Guru and corporate Guru, not with the land of Punjab.[13] Or, if they must represent their collective identity in more familiar Western terms, they can build logically on the supraterritorial notion of Sikhism as a "world religion" uniting Sikhs of whatever ethnicity or nationality as fellow believers.[14] If such discourse is temporarily submerged by talk of the Sikh nation and of Khalistan, it is by no means dead (see, e.g., Sidhu 1989).

Indeed, there are many diasporan Sikhs for whom the "natural" underpinnings of the Sikh-Punjab nexus are less than compelling. These would include such groups as the recent non-Punjabi North American Sikh converts who, as I have noted elsewhere (Dusenbery 1988), commonly despair of parochial "Indian politics" contaminating what they take to be a "universal religion"; many diasporan non-Jat Sikhs, such as Parminder Bhachu's "twice migrant" Ramgarhias (1985, 1989), who in their move to East Africa and then to Britain have cut their social links to Punjab; members of Sikh sects, like the Namdharis (Tatla 1991), who have reason to fear a fundamentalist Khalistan; and even a good many second, third-, and now fourth-generation descendants of earlier Jat Sikh migrants, whose own affective ties to Punjab are attenuated. If these Sikhs look to Punjab as a "spiritual homeland," the birthplace of their Gurus, and the site of historical shrines, and if they remain concerned about the treatment of historic Sikh sites and their fellow Sikhs at the hands of the state, they nevertheless do not necessarily accept the notion that only a Punjabi can be a Sikh, or that only Sikhs should inhabit Punjab, or that Sikhs should inhabit only Punjab. Not coincidentally, these are among the Sikhs whose very existence is particularly problematic for the nationalist rhetoricians, who wish to emphasize the Punjabi patrimony (via common language, history, culture, religion, territory, and blood) of the Sikhs. It is hardly surprising, therefore, that these Sikhs have been among the least ardent Khalistan supporters or that, in pursuing Sikh collective interests in their countries of residence, they have (at least in North America) commonly used the rhetoric of "religious rights" rather than those of "race," "ethnicity," or "national origins" in pressing claims of Sikh social distinctiveness.[15]

In their recent postmodernist celebration of deterritorialization and reterritorialization, Akhil Gupta and James Ferguson note that "remembered places have often served as symbolic anchors of community for dispersed peoples" (1992: 11), but that the "naturalizations" of people, place, and culture underlying such images are often analytically problematic, even if politically potent (ibid.: 12). As we have seen, for Sikhs in Punjab and dispersed beyond, the notion of Sikhs as an "ethnoterritorial community" bound by natural ties to Punjab/Khalistan has recently served as one powerful way to conceptualize their place in the world. And representations, in academic or popular discourse, of Sikhs outside Punjab as constituting a "diaspora" may well serve to further strengthen the Sikh-Punjab nexus. Yet this territorialization has never been "the *only* grid on which cultural difference could be mapped" (ibid.: 20). Sikh collective identity has been and can be envisioned and bespoken in other, nonterritorialized terms — as, for example, in Sikhs understanding themselves to be a particular "worship genus" or an inclusive "world religion." The terms by which Sikhs know and represent themselves ultimately must be determined by Sikhs as human agents operating within multiple fields of power. At the moment, Sikh identity remains contested; and it would therefore be premature to represent the issue and the terms of debate as closed.

Notes

1. On South Asian ethnosociology, see Marriott 1990. On the ethnosociology of the Sikh person, see Dusenbery 1988, 1990b.

2. In any case, "Punjabi" was rarely a term by which the early migrants were known in the diaspora. North Indians in Southeast Asia were known as "Bangalees"; South Asians in North America were known indiscriminantly as "Hindoos" or "East Indians."

3. I do not mean to be seen as making an essentialist argument. Not only is this Punjabi ethnosociology flexible enough to incorporate new languages, territories, and occupations, but also it is and long has been challenged by alternative ethnosociologies through which Sikhs can understand their social world. What seems

notable to me has been the persistence among many diasporan Sikhs, even after long residence abroad, of what I take to be the dominant Punjabi socio-logic.

4. The other three *takhats* are the Akal Takhat in Amristar, Keshgarh at Anandapur Sahib, and Damdama Sahib near Batinda. Nominally, the *jathedars* (lit., commanders) of the five *takhats* constitute an exalted *panj piare* (lit., five beloved) who can, in consultation with the Guru Granth (the scriptural Guru), make pronouncements in the name of the Guru Panth (the corporate Guru). In practice, since they are appointed by different administrative bodies, they rarely function as a cohesive consultative board.

5. See Dhanoa 1990 and Singh and Dhillon 1992 for conflicting views on whether the phrase *Raj karega Khalsa* necessarily implies the establishment of a territorial state under Sikh rule.

6. Dilgeer and Sekhon (1992) present the most sustained argument on how Sikh sovereignty has been thwarted by various parties over the past two centuries.

7. In advancing his claim that Sikhs are a distinct "race," Chaddah (1982: 75) goes to heroic lengths to minimize the significance of non-Punjabi Sikh converts, whose emergence on an unprecedented scale in the early 1970s had been heralded by Sikh leaders in Punjab as a sign that Sikhism is a modern world religion of mass appeal and not simply a parochial faith (see Dusenbery 1988). Furthermore, as Andrew J. Major has pointed out, it is not easy to sustain the nationalist's claim for "commonality of blood" when "everyone is aware of the commonplaceness of marriages between Sikhs and non-Sikhs, especially Punjabi Hindus" (1985: 178).

8. For analyses of some of Bhindranwale's imagery, see Pettigrew 1987, Juergensmeyer 1988, and Madan 1991.

9. It might only be fair to note that the territorial association of Sikhs with Punjab has probably been most compelling for Jat Sikhs, the traditional landholding class/caste of central Punjab, whose honor as Jats has been significantly tied to their independence gained from maintaining the family homestead. Those Sikhs from castes less tied to the land may in general be less moved by naturalizing the links to Punjab. This seems to be one lesson to be derived from the work of Parminder Bhachu (1985, 1989) on the "twice migrant" Sikh Ramgarhias who, having resettled in England after their expulsion from East Africa, have cut their marital and property ties to Punjab. But since Jats predominate within the Panth, their moral and political visions tend to dominate Sikh discourse.

10. The Canadian folk category "East Indian" has been used to refer to all people of South Asian ancestry. But under the logic of Canadian multiculturalism, each nation-state in South Asia could serve as a separate "country of origin" for purposes of self-identification and political organization. This meant, for example, that the numerically smaller Pakistani Canadian community was able to get official recognition and support for their separate ethnic-political organization, while Canadian Sikhs were being urged to use NACOI to advance their political agenda.

11. On the rise and eclipse of NACOI, see Dusenbery 1981 and Paranjpe 1986 (especially pp. 76–77). It should be noted that despite its lack of popular support among Sikhs, NACOI continues to represent all "Canadians of Origins in India" on the Canadian Ethnocultural Council (CEC), a representative body that advises the government on multicultural issues. A recent attempt by the World Sikh Orga-

nization (Canada) to gain a seat on the CEC was turned down largely on the basis of NACOI's argument that it already represents Canadian Sikh interests (personal communication, Anna Chiappa, Executive Director, Canadian Ethnocultural Council).

12. Handler's argument is that essentialistic anthropological and popular Western concepts of culture, which commonly align an ahistoric "culture" with a "people" and a "place," have proven useful to nationalist ideologues. Handler argues for a "destructive analysis of our shared presuppositions" as "the anthropologist's contribution to a dialogue that respects natives by challenging rather than romanticizing them" (1985: 181).

13. The term "physiological engagement" is taken from Babb 1983. I explicate its logic as it applies in the Sikh case in Dusenbery 1992.

14. On the significance of world religions as "the longest lasting of civilization's primary institutions" and as a source of "self-identification," see Hefner 1993. Part of the ongoing project of religious rationalization begun by Singh Sabha/Tat Khalsa reformers at the turn of the last century was to make Sikhism into a world religion on par with Hinduism, Islam, and Christianity (see Oberoi 1994).

15. As I have noted elsewhere, in the Canadian human rights codes and in Canadian multiculturalism funding, a radical distinction is made between discrimination, whether negative or positive, on the basis of "religion" or on the basis of "race, ethnicity, and national origins" (see Dusenbery 1981). A similar distinction is operative in the United States. In North America, Sikhs have commonly sought protections and exemptions (e.g., from dress codes that would require giving up turbans) as a matter of fundamental "religious rights." In the United Kingdom, by contrast, Sikhs have apparently used laws against "racial" discrimination (see Wallman 1982) to pursue similar ends. As McLeod suggests (1989b: 106), the effect of British law and public policy might be to further strengthen among British Sikhs the Punjab-Sikh nexus and thus "ethnoterritorial community" over "world religion" rhetoric and social identities.

References

Anderson, Benedict
 1991 *Imagined Communities: Reflections on the Origin and Spread of Nationalism.* Revised edition; original 1983. New York and London: Verso.
Babb, Lawrence A.
 1983 "The Physiology of Redemption." *History of Religions* 22, 4 (May): 293–312.
Ballard, Roger
 1989 "Differentiation and Disjunction amongst the Sikhs in Britain." In Barrier and Dusenbery, *The Sikh Diaspora,* 200–234.
Barrier, N. Gerald
 1970 *The Sikhs and Their Literature.* Delhi: Manohar.

Barrier, N. Gerald, and Verne A. Dusenbery, eds.
  1989 *The Sikh Diaspora: Migration and the Experience Beyond Punjab.* Columbia, Mo.: South Asia Publications; Delhi: Chanakya Publications.
Bhachu, Parminder
  1985 *Twice Migrants: East African Sikh Settlers in Britain.* London: Tavistock.
  1989 "The East African Sikh Diaspora: The British Case." In Barrier and Dusenbery, *The Sikh Diaspora,* 235–60.
Canada
  1971 "Canadian Culture: Announcement of Implementation of Policy of Multiculturalism within a Bilingual Framework." *House of Commons Debates* (October 8, 1971).
Chaddah, Mehar Singh
  1982 *Are Sikhs a Nation?* Delhi: Delhi Sikh Gurdwara Management Committee.
Dhanoa, S. S.
  1990 "The Meaning of Raj Karega Khalsa." *The Sikh Review* 38, 12 (December):24–26.
Dilgeer, H. S. and A. S. Sekhon
  1992 *The Sikhs' Struggle for Sovereignty: An Historical Perspective.* A. T. Kerr, ed. Oslo: Guru Nanak Institute of Sikh Studies.
Dusenbery, Verne A.
  1981 "Canadian Ideology and Public Policy: The Impact on Vancouver Sikh Ethnic and Religious Adaptation." *Canadian Ethnic Studies* 13, 3 (Winter): 101–19.
  1985 "Review of Harish K. Puri's *Ghadar Movement.*" *South Asia in Review* 9, 3 (March): 5.
  1988 "Punjabi Sikhs and Gora Sikhs: Conflicting Assertions of Sikh Identity in North America." In Joseph T. O'Connell et al., eds., *Sikh History and Religion in the Twentieth Century.* Toronto: Centre for South Asian Studies, University of Toronto, 334–55.
  1989 "Introduction: A Century of Sikhs beyond Punjab." In Barrier and Dusenbery, *The Sikh Diaspora,* 1–28.
  1990a "On the Moral Sensitivities of Sikhs in North America." In Owen M. Lynch, ed., *Divine Passions: The Social Construction of Emotion in India.* Berkeley: University of California Press; Delhi: Oxford University Press, 239–61.
  1990b "The Sikh Person, the Khalsa Panth, and Western Sikh Converts." In Bardwell L. Smith, ed., *Religious Movements and Social Identity.* Vol. 4 of "Boeings and Bullock-Carts," festschrift for K. Ishwaran. Delhi: Chanakya Publications, 117–35.
  1992 "The Word as Guru: Sikh Scripture and the Translation Controversy." *History of Religions* 31, 4 (May): 379–96.
Fox, Richard G.
  1985 *Lions of the Punjab: Culture in the Making.* Berkeley: University of California Press.

Goulbourne, Harry
    1991   *Ethnicity and Nationalism in Post-Imperial Britain*. Cambridge: Cambridge University Press.
Gupta, Akhil, and James Ferguson
    1992   "Beyond 'Culture': Space, Identity, and the Politics of Difference." *Cultural Anthropology* 7, 1 (February): 6–23.
Handler, Richard
    1985   "On Dialogue and Destructive Analysis: Problems in Narrating Nationalism and Ethnicity." *Journal of Anthropological Research* 41, 2 (Summer): 171–82.
    1988   *Nationalism and the Politics of Culture in Quebec*. Madison: University of Wisconsin Press.
Hefner, Robert W.
    1993   "Introduction: World Building and the Rationality of Conversion." In Robert W. Hefner, ed., *Conversion to Christianity: Historical and Anthropological Perspectives on a Great Transformation*. Berkeley: University of California Press, 3–44.
Helweg, Arthur W.
    1986   *Sikhs in England*. 2d ed. Delhi: Oxford University Press.
    1989   "Sikh Politics in India: The Emigrant Factor." In Barrier and Dusenbery, *The Sikh Diaspora*, 305–36.
Jeffrey, Robin
    1987   "Grappling with History: Sikh Politicians and the Past." *Pacific Affairs* 60, 1 (Spring): 59–72.
Juergensmeyer, Mark
    1979   "The Ghadar Syndrome: Nationalism in an Immigrant Community." *Punjab Journal of Politics* 1, 1 (October): 1–22.
    1982   "The Ghadar Syndrome: Ethnic Anger and Nationalist Pride." *Population Review* 25, 1 and 2: 48–58.
    1988   "The Logic of Religious Violence: The Case of the Punjab." *Contributions to Indian Sociology* (n.s.) 22, 1: 65–88.
Juergensmeyer, Mark, and N. Gerald Barrier
    1979   "Introduction: The Sikhs and the Scholars." In Mark Juergensmeyer and N. Gerald Barrier, eds., *Sikh Studies: Comparative Perspectives on a Changing Tradition*. Berkeley, Calif.: Graduate Theological Union, 1–9.
Kashmeri, Zuhair, and Brian McAndrew
    1989   *Soft Target: How the Indian Intelligence Service Penetrated Canada*. Toronto: James Lorimer.
Leonard, Karen
    1989   "Pioneer Voices from California: Reflections on Race, Religion and Ethnicity." In Barrier and Dusenbery, *The Sikh Diaspora*, 120–40.
Madan, T. N.
    1991   "The Double-Edged Sword: Fundamentalism and the Sikh Religious Tradition." In Martin E. Marty and R. Scott Appleby, eds., *Fundamentalisms Observed*. Chicago: University of Chicago Press, 594–627.

Major, Andrew J.
    1985   "Sikh Ethno-Nationalism, 1967–1984: Implications for the Congress." *South Asia: Journal of South Asian Studies* (n.s.) 8, 1 and 2 (June and December): 168–81.

Malkki, Liisa
    1992   "National Geographic: The Rooting of Peoples and the Territorialization of National Identity among Scholars and Refugees." *Cultural Anthropology* 7, 1 (February): 24–44.

Marriott, McKim
    1990   "Constructing an Indian Ethnosociology." In McKim Marriott, ed., *India Through Hindu Categories.* Newbury Park, Calif.: Sage, 1–39.

McLeod, W. H.
    1978   "On the Word *Panth:* A Problem of Terminology and Definition." *Contributions to Indian Sociology* (n.s.) 12, 2: 287–95.
    1986   *Punjabis in New Zealand.* Amritsar: Guru Nanak Dev University Press.
    1989a "The First Forty Years of Sikh Migration: Problems and Possible Solutions." In Barrier and Dusenbery, *The Sikh Diaspora,* 29–48.
    1989b *Who Is a Sikh? The Problem of Sikh Identity.* Oxford: Clarendon Press.

Oberoi, Harjot S.
    1987   "From Punjab to 'Khalistan': Territoriality and Metacommentary." *Pacific Affairs* 60, 1 (Spring): 26–41.
    1988   "From Ritual to Counter-Ritual: Rethinking the Hindu-Sikh Question, 1884–1915." In Joseph T. O'Connell et al., eds., *Sikh History and Religion in the Twentieth Century.* Toronto: Centre for South Asian Studies, University of Toronto, 136–58.
    1994   *The Construction of Religious Boundaries: Culture, Identity and Diversity in the Sikh Tradition.* Delhi: Oxford University Press.

Paranjpe, A. C.
    1986   "Identity Issues among Immigrants: Reflections on the Experience of Indo-Canadians in British Columbia." In Richard Harvey Brown and George V. Coelho, eds., *Tradition and Transformation: Asian Indians in America.* Williamsburg, Va.: College of William and Mary (Studies in Third World Societies, no. 38), 71–94.

Pettigrew, Joyce
    1987   "In Search of a New Kingdom of Lahore." *Pacific Affairs* 60, 1 (Spring): 1–25.

Puri, Harish K.
    1985   "Singh Sabhas and Ghadar Movement: Contending Political Orientations." *Punjab Journal of Politics* 7, 2 (July–December): 12–26.
    1993   *Ghadar Movement: Ideology, Organisation and Strategy.* 2d ed. Amritsar: Guru Nanak Dev University Press.

Safran, William
    1991   "Diasporas in Modern Societies: Myths of Homeland and Return." *Diaspora* 1, 1 (Spring): 83–99.

Shiromani Akali Dal
    1992   "Appeal by Shiromani Akali Dal and Shiromani Gurdwara Parbandhak
            Committee to the United Nations." *World Sikh News* (June 26): 6–7.
Sidhu, M. S.
    1989   "The Punjabi-Sikh Nexus." *Sikh Courier* 29, 67 (Spring–Summer): 22–
            24.
Singh, Kharak, and Gurdarshan Singh Dhillon
    1992   "Raj Karega Khalsa." In Kharak Singh, Gobind Singh Mansukhani,
            and Jasbir Singh Mann, eds., *Fundamental Issues in Sikh Studies*. Chan-
            digarh: Institute of Sikh Studies, 187–95.
Singh, Surjan
    1982   *Case for Republic of Khalistan*. Vancouver: Babbar Khalsa.
Tatla, Darshan Singh
    1991   "A Note on Namdhari Sikhs in Britain." *Khera* 10, 1 (January–March):
            50–57.
Wallman, Sandra
    1982   "Turbans, Identities and Racial Categories." *RAIN* (*Royal Anthropolog-
            ical Institute News*) 52: 4.

John D. Kelly

2. *Bhakti* and Postcolonial Politics: Hindu Missions to Fiji

Pacific island groups are isolated, and small. The islands of the Fiji group are surrounded by thousands of kilometers of ocean. Fiji's current population, about three-quarters of a million people, is found mainly on Fiji's two largest islands, neither of which is more than 200 kilometers wide. In the late nineteenth century one of the early British colonial governors described Fiji as "the most outer or remote British colony in the world" (quoted in Young 1984: 25).

Social relations and identities in the Pacific have been discussed many ways. Early in the twentieth century, European colonists' generalizations about native "races," "chiefdoms," and "kingdoms," missionary tales of Christian conversion and travelers' romances about swaying palm trees were joined by ethnographic investigations into islander societies and cultures. But it was only quite recently that the idea of "nations" has become important in the Pacific. In a place like Fiji, where "race" and "religion" have been salient markers of social place and powers for more than a century, where indigenous "custom" and "culture" have been discussed for almost as long, the idea of *nation* is very new. National independence was forced on the indigenous Fijians, despite the misgivings of their chiefs, who knew that British power had backed their local privileges. Small wonder then, that race, religion, and culture have become lines of disabling fracture as Fiji now tries to work politically as a nation-state.

Fiji's population is currently 48 percent "Indo-Fijian," of South Asian descent, and 48 percent of indigenous Fijian descent. The Indo-Fijians are 80 percent Hindu, 15 percent Muslim; the indigenous Fijians are more than 99 percent Christian. This chapter is about religion and politics, nation and identity in postcolonial Fiji. It is about political and religious violence in Fiji, about the currently active Hindu missions, especially the Sai Baba and the ISKCON (Hare Krishna) missions, and about their predicament and response in the face of the violence. What is the social and political content of the new Hinduisms that have been so successful across the South Asian diaspora, the missions that owe so much of their shape and style to the conditions of the diaspora? In my view these Hindu missions are more than virtually commercial suppliers of an ersatz version of an eroding Hindu "tradition." They address the present as well as the past. And, as I think this story about the violence in Fiji will show, they are religious movements engaging with forms of experience and self-consciousness that lie outside the settled world of stable national identities, addressing the present from an angle different from that of comfortably national people.

The Missions to Fiji

Fiji has active Christian, Hindu, and Muslim religious missions. The Hare Krishna and Sai Baba organizations in Fiji are comparable to several of the Christian (and Muslim) missions there, especially the Assembly of God, the Seventh-Day Adventists, and the Mormons, in that they attend to people who are already Hindus, just as the radical Christian groups seek converts among people already Christian (and Muslims among Muslims). The second-conversion Christian groups differ significantly from each other in tactics and style. Members of the Assembly of God are known for their emotion-laden evangelicalism, for their personal prayers to Jesus, for the guitars they allow in church, and generally for their relaxed style. The Mormons and the Seventh-Days (as they are locally called) are known for their severity and for restrictions on drinking alcohol and kava, the former group also for encouraging an entrepreneurial work ethic, the latter for their rejection of indigenous Fijian kinship duties. In different ways each of the three offers indigenous Fijian Christians social and moral alternatives to the Methodist orthodoxy that has become the Fiji equivalent of High Church, and each has more or less deliberately snarled its theological specifics into the dilemmas of indigenous Fijian custom in the late twentieth century (the Mormons less than the others, with fewer converts). How similarly can we read the situation of the recent Hindu missions, Sai Baba and Hare Krishna?

I had planned long ago to write a paper about the Hare Krishna and Sai Baba missions, before recent political events significantly changed my sense of what should be said. I had intended to contrast these two transnational Hinduisms.[1] Members of ISKCON, the Hare Krishna group, are deliberately arrogant, dismissive of other Hindu leadership, strict and dictatorial in their religious instruction, hierarchical and exclusive in their interior order. The ISKCON leaders, especially the Americans and Australians who come through Fiji on periodic tours, adopt an aggressive and patronizing tone toward their audiences, who are told that they are doomed to interminable ugly and degraded rebirths if they do not quickly and fundamentally change their habits. The same leaders, especially Srila Tamal Krishna Goswami Gurudeva, the Initiating Spiritual Master for Fiji and one of the leaders of ISKCON as a whole, try to promote a cult of personality centered on themselves as superior beings. In short, the whole enterprise has a colonizing tone and feel.

In contrast, the Sai Baba efforts in Fiji are ambiguous where ISKCON is dogmatic and structured, proliferating where ISKCON is planned and controlled, self-contradictory where ISKCON is clear, gentle where ISKCON is stern, and to put it most broadly, open where ISKCON is closed. Unlike ISKCON, the Sai organization does not ask its members to undergo special initiations or to commit themselves to obey particular leaders. There are sixteen official Sai centers in Fiji. In addition, several other Sai miracle sites exist but are not accepted as official centers because they include types of miracles that Sathya Sai Baba disavows, especially possession episodes, manifestations of him in the bodies of devotees. All these centers, official and unofficial, are under local management and are highly individualized in style. The principal vehicle of dissemination of Sai Baba around Fiji, in contrast to the ISKCON lecture and sermon tours, is through images of Sathya Sai Baba himself, which I think can be found in the prayer places (*bhagwan sthan*) of at least half of the Hindus in Fiji.

The points of greatest local success for ISKCON in Fiji correlate with their strengths in organization and discipline: they run successful restaurants and other businesses, including the best local incense factory. Almost every Hindu in Fiji, whatever he or she thinks of the Hare Krishna, uses their incense, and for many Hindu women theirs are the only public restaurants that are trusted. Sai Baba is clearly much more popular in Fiji, if one were to survey the presence of his image in public and private places, but beyond this generality are some interesting ambiguities. The Sai centers and temples are not always well attended, and knowledge about Sai Baba varies greatly, even among people who pray to him on a daily basis. Theologically the Sai message is multitiered; the Sai that is truly well known is the man of miracles, the powerful avatar who grants whatever you ask for, and is friendly enough to be asked for anything. Money, for example. Despite the clear suggestions in the Sai videos and texts, it is a much smaller audience of Sai Baba devotees who understand that it is foolish to ask God for jobs, health, or money, when one could ask God for superior forms of self-discipline and self-understanding. These more subtle, sober bourgeois forms of Sai devotion exist in urban Fiji. In fact, these pockets of earnest, middle-class devotees run the national Sai organization, manage the importation of Sai images, videos, and literature, and represent Fiji at the international Sai conferences. They instruct their children to fill out methodically the prayer, school, and chore daily schedules that rival the ones devised by Benjamin Franklin, the ones that so impressed Max Weber. But this middle-class Sai group struggles to teach its version of Baba worship to a much larger audience that is more interested in health and money miracles.[2]

Bhakti is the devotional branch of Hinduism, which privileges love for God in various forms as the way to live both morally and effectively. It has a long, complex history in South Asia, including many centuries of important saint-poets, and exists in many new elaborations in this century. Both the Sai Baba and the Hare Krishna forms of *bhakti* devotionalism came to Fiji after Fiji had become an independent member of the British Commonwealth in 1970. A bit of comparative chronology might be helpful here: Sathya Sai Baba was born in Andhra Pradesh, India, in 1926; disclosed in 1940 that he was the reincarnation of Sai Baba of Shirdi and began to gather a national following in India; disclosed in 1963 that he was an incarnation of Shiva and Shakti; and by the 1970s was one of the most popular, and possibly the most popular, Hindu religious leader among urban, middle-class Hindus in India (see Babb 1986: 162–67). Meanwhile, a twentieth-century devotee of the sixteenth-century Bengali Vaishnava saint-poet Caitanya, a man named Prabhupada (or as he is now officially titled, His Divine Grace A. C. Bhaktivedanta Swami Prabhupada), decided that the only hope for Vaishnava *bhakti* was to have it return to India from the West. He went to New York to begin gathering Western disciples in 1965. Fiji's ISKCON spiritual master, Gurudeva, met Prabhupada in 1966 and became one of his American initiates. Gurudeva took up his role as Fiji's spiritual master in 1977. By this time the most important ISKCON initiation in Fiji had already been accomplished. Businessman Deoji Punja became Vasudeva Dasa, but was still one of the Sons of "Hari Punja and Sons," one of Fiji's two or three biggest locally founded multinational corporations. Vasudeva Dasa, initiated by Prabhupada himself, underwrote and oversaw the construction in Lautoka of the massive ISKCON Krishna-Kaliya Temple, one of Fiji's biggest temples, completed in 1977. Meanwhile, the first Sai Baba devotees were also Gujarati businesspeople, but based mainly in Suva. Their Sai Baba circle began in the 1970s, and shortly thereafter they built their impressive Shri Shirdi Sai Baba Mandir. This temple still stands more or less as it was when built, but the Krishna-Kaliya Temple in Lautoka was rebuilt in 1990, after major damage from firebombs thrown by members of a Methodist Youth Fellowship group in October 1989.

Like the Sai Baba and ISKCON missions, the Assembly of God, Mormon, and Seventh-Day Adventist missions are relative newcomers to Fiji, though my impression is that all three antedate these two Hindu groups in the islands. As noted earlier, in Fiji all of these groups have mainly stuck to their own sides of the street, Hindus talking to Hindus, Christians to Christians. This was not true of all religious missions to Fiji during its colonial period, however, and the salient difference emerges clearly if we look back to the first religious missions to the islands.

Catholic and Methodist missionaries were among the first Europeans to take up permanent residence in the Fiji Islands. They came in the early nineteenth century, a time when the only South Asians present were a handful of "lascars," low-ranking sailors off of British ships who chose to stay in Fiji and blended almost unremembered into indigenous Fijian society (Clunie 1984). The missions coexisted with European commercial agents in Fiji for most of the nineteenth century. It was not until the American Civil War, and the waning of a gold rush in Australia, that substantial numbers of Europeans saw any promise in working Fiji's land. By the time of Fiji's cotton boom in the 1860s, and the beginnings of its sugar plantations in the wake of cotton's failure, the indigenous Fijian population was already Christian and almost all Methodist, the Methodist missions having been much better funded and organized than the Catholic.[3] Commercial debts to French and American traders led indigenous Fijian chiefs to see the wisdom of British royal protection, and sovereignty over the islands was ceded to the British crown by a group of Fijian chiefs in 1874. Not long thereafter the British organized these and other Fijian chiefs into a Great Council of Chiefs, and set about using this local aristocracy (as they saw it) to codify the local customs and land tenure, and control social life in the islands (see France 1969; Kaplan 1989a, 1989b). The first governor of Fiji, Sir Arthur Gordon, was impressed by the indigenous Fijians and their civil potential, especially because they had so quickly embraced Christianity and had such impressive chiefs. To the consternation of the settlers, he reserved all land in Fiji not already owned by Europeans for perpetual indigenous ownership, and this reservation of 83 percent of Fiji's land is still in place today. Gordon also strictly regulated the use of indigenous Fijians as plantation labor. But Fiji needed labor, and capital, to pay for itself, and Gordon, previously governor in Mauritius and Trinidad, knew the solution. He invited in Australia's leading sugar refiner, the CSR Company, and established a system for indentured labor immigration from India. The first Indian "coolies," as they were called, arrived in Fiji in 1879, and the system continued until nationalists in India forced its abolition in 1919. The result of this system was a thriving sugar industry and a twentieth-century Fiji almost evenly split in population: half indigenous Fijian and half Fiji Indian, or "Indo-Fijian."

In the late nineteenth century Fiji's Christian missionaries were quite apprehensive. They were proud of but not confident in their Fijian converts, and had been well warned by mission literature about the dangers of "backsliding." Calls for funding, especially in Australia and New Zealand, stressed the danger of the new, encroaching heathen race, and an aggressive Christian mission to the Fiji Indians was launched. Despite substantial and continued funding and the deployment of able missionaries, this mission was a near-total failure. Very few Fiji Indian Hindus and Muslims converted to Christianity. However, even fewer indigenous Fijians became Hindus or Muslims. Both in their assessment of the threat and in their efforts to deal with it, the Methodist missionaries underestimated the implications of colonial routinization of "racial" differences.

After years of failure to convert adults, the Christian missions to the Fiji Indians, like other colonial Christian missions that ran into trouble, turned to the young and became sponsors of schools and orphanages. As the Fiji Indians began to organize themselves on their own behalf, they called on Hindu and Muslim social organizations in India to remedy this situation. The Arya Samaj was the first organization to launch a substantial non-Christian religious mission to Fiji, with a focus like the Christian one on schools. By the 1930s opponents of the Arya Samaj's doctrinaire *nirguna* (God as formless, imageless) and socially Westernizing brand of Hinduism imported Sanatan Dharm preachers and teachers to found more schools. This movement, which quickly gained predominance among the Fiji Indians, stressed the devotional version of the *Ramayan* epic written by the saint-poet Tulsi Das, the *Ramcaritmanas,* as the crucial text to guide the simple, banished overseas Indians. Meanwhile the Muslim League sent lawyers as well as teachers for Muslim schools, and South Indians appealed to one of the leading educational orders in Madras, the Ramakrishna Mission, to supply religious and educational leadership for them. In 1939 a

Ramakrishna swami arrived, took up residence in Nadi, the South Indian center in Fiji, and shortly thereafter opened Sri Vivekananda High School. The government and the sugar company were happy to let the Indians assume the costs of building and maintaining their schools. Against Christian mission protest, the government appointed teachers to properly established Indian schools, and the last hopes of the colonial Christian mission to the Indians faded and died. For their part, the Indian religious missions, Hindu and Muslim, have always focused almost entirely on "their own." What then of the firebombs in 1989?

The Violence

On the night of October 14, 1989, a Methodist Youth Fellowship met for all-night prayers. After praying from 8:00 P.M. to 4:00 A.M., eighteen members of the group, ten men and eight women, left church, bought benzine at a gas station, and set out to burn down all the Indo-Fijian houses of worship in Lautoka, Fiji's second-largest city. They were arrested as they regrouped after setting fire to the four largest: the ISKCON Krishna-Kaliya Temple, the Sanatan Dharm's Vishnu Mandir, the Lautoka Sikh Gurdwara, and the Lautoka Mosque. Only one of the eighteen arsonists was a juvenile, sixteen years old; the oldest were in their twenties. A few had police records, not uncommon for urban indigenous Fijians. All confessed to the police, their confessions taken by indigenous Fijian police officers in the Fijian language, full versions in court records, then translated into English by the same police officers. All told the police that they acted because the Bible said to burn idols. One of the arsonists added that they wanted to make Fiji a Christian country, another that the Bible said that Indians prayed to goddesses and the idols must be destroyed. One cited 2 Exodus 14, but their prayer leader cited 2 Chronicles 14 (a passage that does indeed praise destruction of idols) and added that he did it because the holy spirit was in him. Two said that their work was not finished.

It would not be wrong to say that the crimes shocked and energized the nation, but what nation, and how? Four days after the attacks, a one-day stop-work protest led by Indo-Fijians shut down business in the major cities and towns. On the same day, a coalition of Hindu and related organizations — the Sanatan Dharm Pratinidhi Sabha, the Arya Pratinidhi Sabha (Arya Samaj), the TISI Sangam (a Tamil South Indian organization), the Andhra Sangam, the Kabir Panth, and the Sikh Society of Fiji —

announced that all public celebrations of Diwali for 1989 were cancelled. Acting President of the Sanatan Dharm, Harish Sharma, also a leader in the National Federation Party, explained the cancellation: "The experience of Indo-Fijians since the coup and in particular the sacrilege of temples during last weekend gives no cause for celebration for Deepawali"; as usual, Hindus would clean and pray at home, and "they will pray for the nation and ask God to give guidance to those who have chosen the evil path" (*Daily Post,* October 20, 1989). Before the coups in Fiji (which I discuss in greater detail later), Diwali was the preeminent Hindu public celebration there, celebrated especially after Fiji's independence as the day of Ram's return to righteous rule in Ayodhya. During the days of indenture and after, the trope of exile had been emphasized to connect the *Ramayan* narrative to the lives of Fiji Indians. By the late 1960s and 1970s the prospect of a peaceful, prosperous, and politically equal future — and not incidentally, a permanent future for Indo-Fijians in Fiji — had been marked by bright, happy Diwalis, holidays welcoming the goddess Lakshmi into Hindu homes and hearts and welcoming Ram back from exile to righteous rule (see also Kelly 1988a). All the Diwalis since the coups have been muted; in 1989 the muting was deliberate, but more mournful than provocative.

For the muting of Diwali to have been provocative, the target audience would have to have valued the ritual and the connections it worked out between Fiji, Lakshmi, and Ram. The "interim" postcoups government issued press releases on the day of the work-stoppage deploring the "fire incidents," and a team led by the Acting Prime Minister visited the sites and met with officials of each religious group. The groups "were given personal assurances by Major-General Sitiveni Rabuka, Minister for Home Affairs [and organizer of both of Fiji's coups] that the security forces would ensure that law and order was maintained," and afterward these messages were reaffirmed "in Hindustani" by the only Indo-Fijian member of the cabinet, Minister for Indian Affairs Irene Jai Narayan. Presumably the original speeches, like the daily newspapers and the press releases, were in English. But English, in postcoups Fiji, is no longer by nature the vehicle of a Eurocentric, colonial-continuant vision of the polity. Watch the play of "we" and "you" in the remarks made in English to the religious groups by the Acting Prime Minister, also released to the press on October 19:

> All of us in government are deeply saddened and shocked by the fire incidents of last Sunday. . . . We have come here today to let you know that we are deeply concerned about the welfare of people of all religions. We want to assure you that your individual religious freedom will be protected and you

will continue to have the freedom of religious worship and association which everyone has enjoyed in Fiji.

We ourselves deeply value our religious beliefs and therefore we understand and share your feelings of grief and shock at the desecration of your holy sites. . . . We know and accept that there are many paths to God and we fully respect your path. We will always ensure that in Fiji every man, woman, and child is given the right to follow the path of his or her choice.

The unpleasant actions which bring us here today are those of a few isolated fanatics and extremists. They do not in any way represent the behaviour of the majority of the people. The majority in this country have always practised religious tolerance, respect and goodwill towards one another, that too is the Fijian way—the way of Fiji.

Twelve days later, the day after Diwali, this same government issued a press release announcing that the Indian embassy to Fiji was officially down-graded to consular status, and that the current ambassador, who would not be replaced, had three days to exit the country. Before long even the Indian consulate was closed. Fiji since 1987 has had very little patience with any Indian or Indo-Fijian public voice. The "we" with "our religious beliefs" of the postcoups Fiji government officers was evangelicalized Methodist, in-digenous Fijian, and chiefly. The "majority" in this official imagination is first of all an indigenous Fijian community, with Indo-Fijians granted membership as guests when they too find their place within "the Fijian way—the way of Fiji."[4]

This smug official interpretation met little favor on either side of the street. Indo-Fijians were fearful, their leaders announced. Fiji was rife with rumors of a conspiracy to destroy Indo-Fijian places of worship all over the country.[5] New fences, locks, and other security systems went up around Fiji mosques and temples, and private security forces were posted. Meanwhile, pressure built on the courts and government to pardon and exonerate the arsonists. Crowds of indigenous Fijian sympathizers gathered outside the courts when the arsonists were arraigned and denied bail. Individuals wrote letters to the newspaper, organizations sent delegations. The Ba Province Women's Council together with the Methodist Youth Fellowship peti-tioned the Minister for Women, Culture and Social Welfare to arrange a pardon for the arsonists, who "should not be condemned for the act but should be loved and cared for in accordance with Christian belief" (*Daily Post,* October 28, 1989). The Minister, Adi Finau Tabakaucoro, agreed, and criticized the official Methodist Church, which had also condemned the act. " 'I disagree with the act,' she said, 'but the Methodist Church should have acted more responsibly by preparing something that was more remedial rather than outright condemnation of the act' " (ibid.).

Another indigenous Fijian politician went further. Sakeasi Butadroka, longtime indigenous Fijian nationalist spokesman and briefly a government minister after the first coup, challenged the government's portrayal of the sentiments of the indigenous Fijian majority. In the week after the Indo-Fijian work-stoppage, he announced, as the *Daily Post* summarized him,[6] that "the government must act and it should ignore the threats made by the Indo-Fijian community following the series of temple burnings but should pay attention to the Fijian silent majority who are behind the act" (October 25, 1989). The real issue, according to Butadroka, was "the Sunday Observance fight." If the government did not act on public wishes to enforce the observances more strictly, he said, "I'm warning everyone that the situation in the west could get ugly." He also announced, as the *Post* summarized him, that "whether threats by the Indo-Fijian community to retaliate are true or not, the Sunday Observance fight would continue" (ibid.).

The controversial Sunday Observance laws, prohibiting most business and other public activities (even picnics) on Sundays, were decreed after the second coup. We consider the coups themselves next, but first the end of the story for the arsonists. They finally came to trial in May 1990, and all but the leader received absolute discharges after pleading guilty. Their lawyer had argued broad political and religious themes on their behalf, to a packed and supportive courthouse (as reported in the *Fiji Times,* May 18):

> In mitigation for the 17, Mr. Bulewa told the court that the actions of the youths were inspired by their religious connections [convictions?] which called for the destroying of all idols being worshipped by people.
> Mr. Bulewa said according to the Bible, pagan worship was illegal and the primary aim of the youths was to destroy the idols being worshipped by the local (non-Christian) communities.
> He said the two military coups in 1987 were done to protect the land, customary rights and religious rights of the Fijian people and the transformation of Fiji into a Christian state.
> "But the new draft constitution before the government and the Great Council of Chiefs has fallen short of safekeeping Christianity and other Fijian people's rights. The shortcoming has also resulted in other offences."

The *Fiji Times* seems to have added "(non-Christian)" to the second paragraph here, and thereby muddied the theological waters, perhaps deliberately. Clearly the Christians do not worship idols, that was the whole point of the arson (never mind any quibbles about the Muslims). But *idol* is the term routinely used by the Fiji media for Hindu images, as in the *Post* headline of October 21, 1989, "Hindu Idols Disappear," above a story about vandalism and the theft of images from two temples in Nadi, six days after the arson in Lautoka. In any case the lawyer's point was to compare this crime with other controversial crimes that received "noncustodial sentences" in postcoups Fiji: indigenous Fijian roadblocks in support of Sunday Observances, the burning of Indo-Fijian shops in Suva, Indo-Fijian sugarcane harvest boycotts, and a gunrunning effort. In sentencing the next day, the Lautoka High Court judge condemned the arson, said it would have led to "anarchy if the victims were not tolerant," and in his most reported comment, said that the leader of the arsonists was "acting in the name of the devil more than in the name of the Lord" (*Fiji Times,* May 19, 1991). But if Mr. Justice Saunders thereby presumed a Christian set of options, he also accepted the argument for lenience in hopes of promoting harmony and announced the light sentences.

Amid such efforts to promote harmony, informal attacks on Indo-Fijian places of worship have been commonplace since this decision. At least one (unsuccessful) effort was made to firebomb a Methodist church in Lautoka two days after the original arson, but Christian churches in Fiji are still open structures, unguarded at night, many without locks. Hindu and Muslim structures struggle for better security. The Nau Durga Temple in a working class community outside of Suva (Narere 8 miles, where I have done field research since 1984) has been broken into at least five times since 1987. In January 1990, months after the arson, vandals removed the *Ramcaritmanas* from the temple, the Tulsi Das text used weekly by the local Ramayan Mandali (worship group), and burned it in a nearby rubbish dump. This incident was egregious enough to be reported in the press (see the *Fiji Times,* January 15, 1990, and February 5, 1990). Other events go unreported, even to the police, whose ranks have been sifted and inflated since the coups and are not entirely respected by everyone. In at least one case police themselves deliberately knocked over images in a Hanuman temple, during an investigation of violations of the Sunday Observance laws. But the attacks seem to have risen in frequency since enforcement of these laws was eased. As most of my informants see it, the principal goal of the temple break-ins is to find money. Still, defecation is sometimes involved (see, for example, the *Fiji Times,* September 11, 1987).

The Coups, the Nation, and Religious Discourse in Fiji

In 1987 the Fiji coups were portrayed by the perpetrators to the world media as disruptive and non-Western but necessary events, necessary to protect indigenous culture and property from the encroachments of out-siders, development, and modernity. This depiction played off the Pacific romance — the romantic identification of the Pacific with the innocence, natural luxury, and sensuality of paradise that has lured and oriented gener-ations of Europeans, now as tourists (see Kelly 1988b). But for internal consumption, the coups of 1987 in their aftermath are increasingly por-trayed as assertions about the scope and shape of the sacred in Fiji, as in the arson trial mitigation speech quoted earlier. Once upon a time, around the late 1960s, the British were under pressure from the Indo-Fijians and the world community to make Fiji self-governing, and they in turn had to pressure their allies in rule, the indigenous chiefs, to give up colonial privileges and accept some new form of government. To guarantee the chiefs their places in government, several steps were taken. Seats in the Senate were reserved for Great Council–nominated chiefs. In the lower house, some seats were racially reserved and others set up with racially restricted constituencies. In the racial reservation system, the Indo-Fijians, then comprising slightly more than 50 percent of the population, were given 40 percent of the seats, not a small difference in a democracy. A party called the Alliance Party, led by the Fijian chiefs, won the first elections. Committed to multiracialism, and under British scrutiny, the Alliance lead-ers appointed many Indo-Fijians to government posts. The British left Fiji in a shower of awards and honors. By my calculation, over 1 percent of the adult population of Fiji received some sort of recognition from the Queen on the occasion of independence, and everyone with intelligence and influ-ence was at least *offered* something. Privately and sometimes even publicly, Fiji Europeans were predicting violence, and, seeing little future for them-selves in the islands, 90 percent of them had emigrated from Fiji by the end of the 1970s.

The violence did not come until 1987, after a major election surprise. A new Fiji Labour Party succeeded in winning enough urban support among indigenous Fijians and the disproportionately empowered General Electors (mainly Europeans in 1970, now mainly "part-Europeans," other Islanders, and Chinese) to form a large majority in a coalition with the National Federation Party (the party by then known as the "Indian" party, actually Fiji's first political party, formed out of labor unions in the 1960s). The chiefs were out of office for less than a month. Then Col. Sitiveni Rabuka, third-ranking officer in the army, put them back into power on May 14, 1987. After rounding up the coalition leaders, Rabuka handed over power to the old Alliance Party leaders. Over the next few months, they worked out a plan with the coalition leaders for a government of national unity. The week this was announced, Rabuka led his second coup, on September 25, 1987. This time the ties to England were cut, a Republic of Fiji was declared, and Rabuka imposed his own vision on the country. In both coups, the exclusively indigenous Fijian military channeled the rioting and intimidated and controlled the people of Fiji using techniques learned from military service in United Nations peace-keeping forces in Lebanon and the Sinai. After the second coup, a new logic for restriction on public movement was announced. The Sunday Observance Decree, issued November 9, listed allowed and forbidden activities and declared that henceforth Sunday was legally to be "a sacred day," and that "all persons irrespective of whether or not they profess the Christian faith shall respect Sunday and shall . . . neither do nor omit to do any act that may undermine the significance of Sunday to the Christians in the Republic of Fiji."[7]

The question of how Methodist Christianity has articulated with the rest of indigenous Fijian culture has exercised the new generation of ethnographers among indigenous Fijians (see especially Kaplan 1990; Toren 1988). Clearly, indigenous Fijians do not feel the contradictions others see between their religion and their culture; as Martha Kaplan explains, the key mediating term is *loloma* or kindly love, the gift-bestowing relationship that characterizes the chiefs' service to the people they dominate, people's debts to chiefs, and, from the early mission days, Christ's grace. Indigenous Fijians clearly distinguish the way of *loloma* — which is the way of real Christians and was always the way of real Fijians — from the way of money, which is the way of all exploitative foreigners, including the Indo-Fijians as they see them.

How does this stuff of culture and religion enter into national politics? Peter van der Veer invites us to center our studies of the South Asian diaspora on, as he puts it, "the dialectic of religious and nationalist discourse" (see the Introduction). For Fiji, the dialectics are not only within the religious and nationalist sentiments of the South Asian-descended group but, as in some of the other cases van der Veer reviews, just as fundamentally in relations between groups: the dialectics are actually, and irreducibly, dialogics. To explain how the coups have increasingly been refigured and debated in Fiji as a matter of the scope and shape of the sacred, I would like to come at the question of "nationalist discourse" from another angle. Recent efforts have largely failed to establish the essential features of "nations," either in reality or as imagined. The real imagined communities of the world are a moving target: for example, van der Veer's account of the liveliness of nationalism in diasporic imagination seems to be evidence against Richard Handler's model of "entitivity," the nation as an intrinsically homogenous and bounded unit. Similarly, contemporary *hindutva* (Hindu-centered) nationalism in India, and the various forms of indigenous Fijian nationalism are bad news for models that insist on egalitarian citizenship as the core of the nation idea. Any number of cases provide counterexamples to the notion that nations are at root what they were for Johann Gottfried Herder: primordial, culturally particular, and enduring folk communities, or even imaginary projections of such communities. It seems to me that what "nations" have in common is that they control or want to control states, and more particularly that "nations" are the narratives that establish the connections between people and their rulers, and make state institutions "ours" rather than "theirs."[8]

In this light a recent analysis of indigenous Fijian political discourse in the 1980s becomes very interesting. Henry Rutz (n.d.) argues that three different visions of Fiji's history were in dramatic contention within the political debates of the indigenous Fijians, before and after the coups. The leaders of the Alliance Party and the Great Council of Chiefs have always pursued a Royalist line, linking their power, ironically, to the original cession of Fiji to the British monarchs. They tell the story of Fiji as a successful blend of colonial power and their own, their chiefly mediation delivering downward the benefits of the outside world and holding off its threats. The great antagonist of this political line was that first articulated after independence by radical nationalist Butadroka, a story of Betrayal of the Land. In this story, the cession of Fiji to Britain and a series of events since then are portrayed as the encroachment of foreign power onto Fijian heritage, abetted by greedy and turncoat chiefs. The lost election gave new salience to the story of the Betrayal of the Land, and the first coup was explicable within both models of the nation; it was the second coup that was truly devastating for the Royalist line, as it cut the links to the British Crown. Col. (now Brig.-Gen.) Rabuka took power to defend the land from the latest threat, but shied away from the logical conclusion of the betrayal narrative — rejection of the chiefs themselves. When the government he formed himself (including Butadroka among others in his cabinet) proved inefficient and unmanageable, on December 5, 1987, he returned paramount power to the old Alliance leaders, with "traditional" ceremonies of apology (*soro*) for any offenses he committed against their sacred standing. Rabuka could do this because, from the first coup onward, he had been promoting a third, different narrative of the Fijian nation. The chiefs owed their right to rule not to British respect but to God, who licensed them when they were wise enough to convert, brought the British and then the Indians to Fiji for the Fijians' benefit, and then prodded Rabuka to be the Fijians' defender when they needed defending. In the nineteenth century, the Christian missionaries had removed ancestral deities from control over Fijian politics. In the royalist vision, the British monarchs had filled the void at the top. Rabuka, a Methodist lay preacher, put the Christian god in their place, a very present, active, and Fijian Christian god, with definite plans and intentions. This particular vision of Fiji has a special implication: Fiji will truly be at peace, Rabuka has explained, only when it is a fully Christian nation. The Indians should be led to convert.

Religious discourse only occasionally resorts to the genre of historical narrative, and even when it does its points are more often allegorical than genetic. But narratives of historical genesis and/or destiny seem a particularly common vehicle of nationhood, often enshrined in public commemorations, such as Bastille Day or May Day, Thanksgiving, and the Fourth of July. Van der Veer observes a typical intertwining of religious and national discourse in migration situations, wherein groups realize themselves as the people who do, or have done, particular rituals, realize themselves as the people of a particular religious commitment and history. I think this model captures fairly well the forms of Hindu, Muslim, Sikh, Aryan, and Indian national identity claimed by Fiji Indians through most of their colonial history. But I also think that many contemporary Indo-Fijians are now reacting in a different mode, under leadership such as that provided by the Hare Krishna and Sai Baba organizations. They are reacting against nationalist claims that have attempted to weave religious identities and powers into national identities and powers in a different and more volatile mix than is common: claims to national religious destiny, as well as national religious origins. When the General Secretary of the Methodist Church Rev. Manasa Lasaro announced that he had joined a newly formed Fijian Christian Nationalist party, he quoted Joshua 24:15 and announced that Fiji's future would depend on which God it chose to serve.

> The Christian God, the God our forefathers had served, blessed and looked after Fiji for more than 100 years. . . . This God and his Son, Jesus Christ, have shaped our country into what it has been until now. Other parties, other associations and other groups deny and overlook Christian ideals. But with this party, God is its very base. Ladies and Gentlemen, this party is based on trusting and being loyal to God. (*Daily Post,* March 10, 1990)[9]

The contention between different visions of the nation among indigenous Fijians is intensifying in postcoups Fiji. The first elections were held in

May 1992, with over half of the seats reserved for indigenous Fijians. In anticipation, political parties proliferated for the first time. Even the Labour Party (the one party that still makes a point of denying that "race," as the locals call it, is the most basic feature of identity) has a place again, winning about half the Indo-Fijian seats. But most of the action lies in contention between Christian parties, betrayal-of-the-land parties, and a new Fijian People's Party, officially backed by the Great Council of Chiefs. Each of these parties tries to capture the rhetorical high points of the others; everyone seems to call for a multicultural, tolerant society and a Christian state, a better planned economy founded on a free market, more foreign investment with tighter controls on foreign investment, more rights and higher wages for labor and severer penalties for strikes. But while the pure products of political reason are going crazy, some points of clarity have emerged for Indo-Fijian contemplation. First, the "we" of the nation in postcoups Fiji, whatever the sharper outlines of its future, is indigenous Fijian and Christian in primary self-conception, and certainly wants no particular contribution from Hinduism or Islam. Its gamut runs only to toleration, and centers strongly on achieving and sustaining some form of indigenous paramountcy. Second, this new nation is clearly frustrated with its status quo — still far from mastery over marketplace relations despite political control — and is in the mood to experiment. In perhaps the most common articulation of this mood, it desires not simply to be, but some-how to become a Christian nation, something that would involve and establish (again) really proper social relations in the land.

With all this said, we can now understand better what the chargé d'affaires of the Indian embassy was talking about, not too long before he too was sent packing. At the ceremony putting the desecrated *Ramayan* text to sea, "he spoke of religious tolerance and world embracing kinship" (*Fiji Times,* February 5, 1990). He said, "India has never considered *dharma* (religion) to be a means of empire-building even though Indian religions have travelled far beyond the waves of its ocean waters" (ibid.).[10]

World-Embracing Kinship and Postcolonial Hindu Missions

The basic situation in Fiji is that the indigenous Fijian chiefs have taken control of the state and intend to perpetuate their own authority, and that the current plan seems to be to control capitalism by means of Christian grace. Economically, things are getting worse. Sizing this situation up, the

Indo-Fijian community has already selected a favorite coping strategy: emigration. They are getting out when they can, up to their quota limits in British Commonwealth countries and the United States. Almost everyone talks about emigrating, but only about five thousand a year (out of a population above three hundred thousand) actually manage to emigrate. These are mainly people from the middle class, including most of the lawyers and hundreds of doctors, teachers, and accountants.[11]

Otherwise, the Indo-Fijians can best be called careful in their politics. Able labor leaders, especially Mahendra Chaudhry, pick their spots to take stands, try to force the government to accept the idea of a bargaining table, and make deals when offered the chance. In the summer of 1991 Chaudhry forced the government to deactivate antistrike and anti-harvest boycott decrees with the threat of a national strike, and negotiated a new cane price while facing death threats. Hindu spokespeople have emerged from such organizations as the Sanatan Dharm to decry violence against temples, and have done more than mute public Hindu celebrations. At annual conferences and at national "summit meetings" of Indo-Fijian organizations, they have passed resolutions condemning discrimination against Indo-Fijians and condemning the new, discriminatory constitution in particular. The largest Hindu organization, the Sanatan Dharm, passed a resolution at its annual meeting in May 1990, two days after the sentencing of the arsonists, stating that "the Sanatanis believe in world brotherhood and the sabha sympathizes with and supports all those brothers and sisters throughout the world fighting for freedom and equality and justice and in particular lends its moral support to the people of South Africa for their struggle against apartheid" (*Daily Post,* May 21, 1990). But such resolutions were at best ignored by the interim government. Meanwhile, it was University of the South Pacific students and teachers who went further than anyone else in Fiji, in using Hindu vehicles to contest postcoups public order. In 1990, a student group celebrated the Hindu holiday of Holi by burning effigies of Irene Jai Narayan and other Hindu participants in the "interim" government on a Holi bonfire, as if they were the evil mythological figure Holika, with the press and photographers invited (*Daily Post,* March 13, 1990). On Diwali, 1990, physics lecturer Anirudh Singh led a burning of the draft constitution in a Hindu temple; this went too far. A few days later Singh was abducted and tortured, and later charged with sedition while still in a hospital bed. The sedition charges were later dropped, and five soldiers pleaded guilty to his abduction, were fined, and received suspended sentences. But Singh was not invited to identify them, and in any case, he says more than five were involved. He now lives, effectively in exile, in London.[12]

So, what does a respectable Hindu mission to Fiji say and do, under these circumstances? The Sai Baba group's politics, if they can even be identified as such, lie clearly with the soft-stepping Interfaith Council. This forum was started after the coups by "European" Presbyterian and Catholic clergy, long-term Fiji residents, hoping simply to create a space for inter-religious respect. The Interfaith Council is modeled on the Council of Churches, but casts a wider net. Members of the group meet mainly to exchange information about their faiths and to create a network of personal relationships among themselves.

Apart from this, each Sai worship group has simply done its best to keep going during the years of the coups aftermath. For one important group, the Gujarati-dominated center focused on the temple in Suva, this effort has proved particularly difficult, because so many of the leading members have emigrated. Other centers elsewhere in Fiji have been more successful. I discussed the political situation in Fiji with the leaders of one of the other centers, and they told me the following: Baba says that the place where you are born is your country and you should serve it. Therefore after the coups they tried to keep their Sai worship and welfare activities going. People told them not to drive around in their Sai center van, for fear that it would be confiscated, especially on Sundays, but they held *bal vikas* (school for children) and other Sunday programs as usual. One Sai leader went to the army barracks and got a letter from Rabuka himself permitting his center to drive on Sunday, and this letter was said to cover all of the Sai centers in Fiji. Even in the months after the second coup, some of the Sai groups violated the 8:00 P.M. curfew, had meetings in violation of a pro-hibition on meetings of more than ten people, and were never harassed by the police.

There is more to the Sai interview, but first a few comments. Babb (1986: 172) stresses the "persistent note of cultural nationalism of a kind that sometimes verges on nativism" in Sathya Sai Baba's teachings. This is evident in a Sathya Sai Baba lesson on patriotism, "Character is Life," in the front pages of *Golden Age 1980*, a Baba book highly praised by devotees in Fiji. There Baba teaches that "devotion to one's motherland is as important as devotion to God." What causes the problems in nations? "We find turmoil and trouble in several spheres of life because personal character, national character, and discipline are now at the lowest ebb. Only when these three are practised by all, will there be peace and security in the country." What then should one do? "Above all, a spiritual attitude must be steadily cultivated. . . . You must strive for your own uplift, remaining in society." He ends the lesson with five aphorisms:

Helping oneself necessarily leads to helping others
The fruit of envy is agony
Hate begets hate
If you torture, you shall be tortured
If you love, you shall be loved.

Basically, the Fiji devotees seem to be following Baba's instructions: trying to love their country of birth and trying to serve it, especially by being examples in self-development of character, faith, and charitable services.

In the interview, I asked, What about the fallen government, and anti-Indian discrimination? Let the indigenous Fijians run the government, one of the Sai leaders insisted, the other nodding in agreement. Let the Indians become a minority in Fiji, then no one will bother them, like the Chinese in Fiji now, or the Indians in Australia, New Zealand, or the United States, who have no need to be political. I asked again about discrimination. There was no need for Indians to be the top men everywhere. But here my two hosts were in a small disagreement. One argued that it was good for Fiji to have indigenous Fijian figureheads running every office, because they simply took bribes and otherwise never interfered in people's plans. The Indo-Fijian bureaucrats always interfered, and still demanded bribes. But the other Sai leader was more concerned about the quality of national planning—the lack, in postcoups leadership, of what Baba called "character" in the rulers.

These Sai leaders, I should stress, were only expressing personal views in a highly decentralized organization. And obviously, some of these claims were rationalizations at least partially concocted to deflect my dangerous questions. But I think they are consistent in the main with the lived responses of the Sai devotees to the political crisis. Immigration seems to pose the biggest dilemma: people leaving stress their duty to their children, and the lack of character of government leaders. More than once I was told that the visas were simply applied for, and the rest was left in Baba's hands. Those staying point to the need for love and service to homeland—but sometimes in a way that suggests that this is a spiritual teaching difficult to assimilate.

ISKCON in Fiji publishes volumes commemorating celebrations of

Sri Vyasa Puja, "a festival for devotees of the Lord to honour representatives of Srila Vyasadeva in disciplic succession." The volumes are principally collections of letters written in humble thanks and praise from devotees all over the world to Srila Tamal Krishna Goswami Gurudeva, who is the Spiritual Master for Singapore, the Philippines, New Zealand, Australia, China, Inner Mongolia, and Dallas as well as Fiji. But Fiji is accorded pride of place. The volumes begin with a praise letter to Gurudeva from a contributor who is not his disciple, but rather his "Godbrother," Prabhu-pada's wealthy Fiji initiate Vasudeva Dasa. In his letter in the 1989 volume, Vasudeva Dasa notes the troubles facing Fiji:

> Presently, people here have become distressed by the political turmoil and the intentions of those in power to convert everyone to Christianity. To spread Krsna consciousness at such a time is a great task and we are confident that Krsna will guide a pure devotee like you to achieve success. (ISKCON 1989: 4)

The same volume contains Gurudeva's prescriptions for dealing with the political crisis, in a reprinted letter sent to his Fiji devotees, dated July 13, 1987 (pp. 60–62), after the first coup, but before the second. Noting the political unrest, Gurudeva suggests that his disciples must feel "great anxiety regarding your individual futures," and the future of ISKCON in Fiji. The unrest will affect the movement but, he assures them, "Krsna consciousness is a transcendental process. . . . Although the harmonious atmosphere in Fiji may be disturbed, the transcendental atmosphere of our temple and our devotional lives should not be affected." Though we live in the Kali-yuga (dark age, lowest age), "our temples are actually in the Satya-yuga [age of truth, highest age]."

The later firebombing of the largest ISKCON temple in Fiji would not shake Gurudeva's commitment to this theme, which was as clear in his public discourse I heard in Lautoka in 1991 as it was in his 1987 letter, which continued: "The history of humanity shows that from time to time one race tries to dominate another," an outcome of divine illusory energy. "When one person or group predominates over another, it tends to develop pride. Normally, the reaction from the pre-dominated is to become angry. A Vaishnava, however, remains always humble." This is actually a great test of faith, and should be seen as a divine mercy to inspire newly determined pursuit of Krishna consciousness.

> If Fiji is no longer a paradise, at least we will not be deceived into thinking that Fiji can be a permanent home for the soul. . . . If now the atmosphere in Fiji is

less favorable, it is a blessing in disguise . . . Now there is no longer reason to be attached to the land of one's birth, and thus Krsna has severed one of the most difficult of all attachments.

The rest of Gurudeva's letter addressed dilemmas of migration. He advised staying in Fiji if possible. But "if for some reason one feels that it is essential that one migrate," then the most important thing is to choose a destination where there are ISKCON devotees to associate with. "If by migrating one improves oneself materially, but suffers spiritually, the plan was not properly conceived." And in any case, "My relationship as spiritual master to all of you is in no way jeopardized by the current events which have taken place in Fiji and will not be jeopardized under any circumstance. The relationship as spiritual master is an eternal fact and is not subject to change due to time, place, and circumstance."

The tone of Gurudeva's letter in 1987 was comforting but serious, and careful, in its references to local political realities, noting for example that "it is safe to say that the multi-racial harmony, which existed in Fiji, is a thing of the past." And security for the spiritual master's visit was very tight. Only one gate, with more than one guard, permitted entry into the temple compound. But in the 1991 lecture the main departure from the tone of the 1987 letter was *greater* confidence about Krishna consciousness in Fiji's future. Several references were made to how small a country Fiji was, and a visiting American sannyasi, asked to speak, said he was sure that Krishna consciousness would soon sweep the islands, and from there the other island groups of the Pacific, and then Australia and New Zealand. The line got a laugh, but a very nervous one.

The differences between the Sai Baba and Hare Krishna approaches to spiritual life are, I hope, quite clear. In 1991 I discussed all the Hindu missions in Fiji with Fiji's current Ramakrishna swami, who divided them into the "fundamentalist" groups, including the Arya Samaj and ISKCON, and the "liberal" groups, including his own and the Sai Baba followers. The fundamentalist groups, which also included the Muslims and the Christians in general, had exclusive visions of what God had to be and which texts were true. The liberal approach accepted all faiths, studied hard, lived cleanly, accepted the hard work and disinterested attitude toward the truth that also made up the best "scientific" attitudes, and was ready for the truth to reveal itself.

Whether or not we accept this particular characterization of the difference between these missions, I want to get past the differences to the similarities of response to a postcolonial political crisis — the threat to an overseas Indian community posed by what Hugh Tinker might call a "sons-of-the-soil" nationalism, unchecked by colonial overlords and invested with its own religious mission. Certainly Baba called for love of country, while the ISKCON master saw the strife as a blessing because it broke attachment to homeland. But both groups insulated their mission from any particular duty to respond politically. In contrast, Fiji's first "liberal" Ramakrishna mission leader, Swami Rudrananda, became a radical labor organizer, helped found a union, and spent part of World War II under house arrest. Fiji's first Hindu mission of any kind, the Arya Samaj, was openly committed to political as well as social uplift, promoting the formation of a commitment to Aryan self and nation, explicitly anti-Christian and clearly anticolonial as well. From the ranks of the Arya Samaj came most of Fiji's early Indian political leaders and the founders of the first sugarcane growers' union, the Kisan Sangh. (For more on the Arya Samaj mission to Fiji, see Kelly 1991.) The Sanatan Dharm group grows increasingly political in its voice in Fiji (though some of its once-active members are concerned about this turn). Why have the newer missions so carefully insulated their religious practices and plans from political attachments and controversy?

Several obvious explanations are at least partially true and cannot be neglected. I asked the current Ramakrishna mission swami why he was less politically active than his predecessor, and his answer was that with generations of educated people available, the politically inclined no longer want or need his help. But better division of labor cannot be the whole story, given the political potential of the religious voice. Are the new missions more naive, and/or less in touch with the histories and problems of the overseas communities they serve? Quite possibly the visiting American sannyasi knew as little, or less, about Fiji's social history than the early Arya Samaj missionaries. But there is nothing naive about the new security system, and in light of that, I think we should see at least some deliberation in the apparently careless political arrogance of the sannyasi's prediction of Krishna conquests: a shock to try to grip his audience, but to what end?

No doubt, to go to the other extreme, the Fiji military are intimidating, as they intend to be. The threat of crime in most South Pacific nations is now very real, a basic part of urban and rural life, and in Fiji even the police are not trusted. But if the point is that ISKCON and the Sai Baba committees have been intimidated into political silence, then why has the Sanatan Dharm not been intimidated into political silence?

A more subtle approach to the problem would begin with the difference between a colonial society, governed by self-distanced "liberal" over-lords, and the postcolonial scene where the "races," set into competition with each other, are no longer refereed. Clearly, through most of Fiji's colonial history, the great Fiji Indian politicians sought tactically to move the British overlords into policies more favorable to the Indians. The Aryan civilization of the Arya Samaj was clearly designed as a vehicle for standing up to European civilization. Now, simultaneously, it is the "sons of the soil" who must be cajoled or coerced, directly, and the "liberal," tolerant orienta-tion of the state is no longer guaranteed. From 1970 to 1987 the principal Indo-Fijian political efforts were to maintain and buttress the rhetoric of multiculturalism and development against growing calls for indigenous Fijian paramountcy; these efforts failed (see also Kelly 1988b). Such condi-tions not only explain why the political problems are large, but also account for the abandonment, in places like Fiji, of lines of political argument that were successful against the colonials, especially the Arya Samaj–style strat-egy of emphasizing the distinctness and virtues of an Indian civilization and heritage. In 1947, the Fiji Indians gained much more than they lost by celebrating India's emergence and the end of the Raj. At Fiji's inde-pendence, Indo-Fijian commentators began to criticize "cultural sabre-rattling" and called for a new emphasis on being fully Fijian. But if these conditions nullify the potential of *hindutva* nationalist-style counterargu-ments to indigenous Fijian nationalist assertions, do they really close off all potential for Hindu political commentary or contribution?

The piece missing so far is simply the transnationalism intrinsic to the projects and modes of practice of the newer Hindu missions. How likely is it, after all, that Sai Baba or Krishna have something particularly important to say about politics in Fiji? In fact, Prabhupada did allow the possibility that Fiji was somewhere in particular: the place of Ramnik Dwip, the island without predators to which Kaliya the serpent was banished after his defeat by Krishna. Because one of the senior Fijian ancestor gods was a serpent, the association was a natural, and long predates Hare Krishna presence in Fiji. The Hare Krishna simply named their temple for it. Indigenous Fijians are not impressed by the claim. Once it was put into a school folklore reader, but it was nervously removed more recently. In any case, it is not now the substance for any real political dialogue.

Colonial empires moved laborers wantonly, allowed others to move freely, and tried to teach all the colonized that it was a virtue not to be national or political. The dirty trick was especially on the displaced, in a century in which nations succeeded the empires. But in a place like Fiji, one can hear both colonial and postmodernist resonances when a Sai Baba leader denies the value and denigrates the rajasic virtues of political striving. If Vivekananda's and Gandhi's narrative of Hinduism, Hinduism as spiritually against Western materialism, is still alive in the new Hindu orders, perhaps its political valence has reversed, from the grounding for political mobilization to a place of retreat from political imperatives. For people whose practical best option seems to be moving when the going gets rough, in a world more or less organized against them, the newer forms of *bhakti* and spiritualism may provide ways to be real *without* being national, ways to find particular community while otherwise respecting, and requesting respect from, a world-embracing kinship of humanity (to recall the words of the soon-to-pack chargé d'affaires).

An allegory from the annals of American advertising is worth consideration. Hellmann's mayonnaise executives decided, following market research, that the reason why their share of the mayonnaise market was stagnant was that the average American tended overwhelmingly to use whichever mayonnaise his or her mother had used. To try to raise its market share, the company devised television commercials that showed motherly women using Hellmann's mayonnaise, trying to capture the imaginations of the viewers whose mothers had used no mayonnaise at all. Is this what the new Hindu missions are about, providing versions of a Hindu tradition to people with no real memories of Hindu practice? I doubt it. At least, I am sure that this is not the whole story.

My claim, then, is that the new Hindu missions are not (in contrast to the Hellmann's advertising campaign) an effort to sell a substitute tradition to a diasporic community somehow more threatened than Westerners seem to be by what the West has labeled "modernity." It has long comforted Westerners to imagine that they are uniquely "modern" — if I may speak as a Westerner, to imagine that modernity is more ours than theirs. This sensibility is what makes the substitute tradition theory of the missions seem plausible. No doubt the missions provide this ersatz Hinduness sometimes for some people, but I wonder whether this interpretation explains more about the historical and social sensibility of the migrants or of the scholars. To me, the missions seem also to provide something very different for their diasporic audience. They are a source of nonnational self-realization for people whose forms of self-consciousness we may not so easily encompass.

Let me finish with two ethnographic vignettes. Sai Baba's shakti (power) does flow transnationally. In Narere, outside of Suva, a demi-official Sai center focuses its weekly bhajans (devotional songs) on a taxi-driver's daughter who is overcome by Sai Baba, and dispenses advice, blessings, and prasad (divine food gifts). It used to be her older sister who received this grace, but she got married and moved to Modesto, California. Now it is the younger sister who is overcome, except during her monthly menstrual periods. Then the power is received, still, by her sister in Modesto, to the benefit of a Sai circle there.

Finally, the flamboyant and deliberate arrogance of the American ISKCON spiritual master is resisted, but also loved, by his audiences in Fiji. He comes to Fiji for speaking tours twice a year, and hundreds of people routinely turn out to hear him, perhaps eight hundred at the Sunday meeting I attended in Lautoka. But of course, many of these people were actually coming out for the lunch served after the prayers, a weekly event for the Lautoka Gujarati community, and as the program went on many of the late arrivals looked quite impatient. (In Nadi it is the Ramakrishna mission's Sunday retreat and lunch that is the focus of the Gujarati community. There a retreat that begins with less than a dozen people at 9:00 A.M. grows to a crowd of more than two hundred from between 11:30 and 12:00.) At the end of Gurudeva's discourse in August 1991, on karma, rebirth, suffering, and the benefits of the spiritual life (delivered in English), he asked the crowd for questions. One question, possibly intended to encourage further questions, came from one of the initiated devotees in front, and Gurudeva answered it. No one else raised a hand. "No questions?" he asked. He looked toward the women's side. "Any questions from the Mata Jis?" He sighed. "Gentlemen? Children?" No questions were forthcoming. "So no one has any questions," he said. In resignation he ended the program, and invited everyone to lunch. After lunch my wife and I gave a lift home to the widow of a movie-house owner, who had trusted fate to deliver her home, and she was full of praise for the prayers and discourse. Did she find Gurudeva abrasive? Not at all. It has been my experience that many in Fiji do; he is frequently criticized and jokes are told. But he also has his admirers, even among people who are convinced that he is far too dogmatic. I cannot prove it, and no one, least of all this widow, was impolite enough to point it out directly to *me*, but I think it likely that the dogmatism is understood, and accepted, as a consequence of his being an American. A limiting condition, even in a sannyasi.

Notes

1. Of course, both the ISKCON and Sai Baba organizations resist the label "Hindu" for their religions, but for different reasons indicative of their different styles. ISKCON (the International Society for Krishna Consciousness) seeks more specific labels, decrying "Hinduism" as a foreigners' depiction of Indian religious

traditions in general. ISKCON leaders will accept "Sanatan Dharm" as a name for their religion, and in certain circumstances will make the argument that all revealed religions are paths to the Godhead. However, they prefer their followers to delimit their religion more specifically as Vaishnava Bhakti, or better as Hare Krishna or ISKCON. When touring Fiji in 1985, ISKCON leader Gurudeva instructed his audiences not to write "Hindu" as their religion on census and visa forms, but rather to write "Hare Krishna." In contrast, the Sai Baba leadership presents Sai as the living synthesis of the world's religious traditions. The emblem for their organization embeds on the petals of a lotus the symbols for five world religions: a cross for Christianity, moon and star for Islam, fire for Zoroastrianism, wheel for Buddhism, and the syllable Aum for Hinduism. When a new Interfaith Council in Fiji prepared a book entitled *Faith in Fiji,* the chapter on the Sai organization was included in the Hindu section of the book; this categorization was criticized by Sai leaders in Singapore, a fact pointed out to me by a Fiji Sai Baba delegate to the Interfaith Council when I told him I was going to write a paper about Hindu missions to Fiji. I promised him I would note the organization's rejection of the delimitation "Hindu." On the other hand, he readily agreed that the Sai organization had a special relationship with Hindus, and when, at an Interfaith Council meeting, the Hindus gathered for a prayer, the Sai Baba delegates joined in, while the Sikhs, for example, did not. In *Faith in Fiji,* the Sikh chapter is found in the "Other" section. As far as I know, ISKCON had not yet participated in any way in Fiji's new Interfaith Council; there is no chapter on ISKCON in *Faith in Fiji.*

2. For a subtle and interesting discussion of Sathya Sai Baba's appeal among the middle class in India, see Babb 1986. Almost all of Babb's observations struck chords with my own experience among Baba devotees in Fiji, including his point that even the most serious devotees still treasure the miracle stories and rely on Baba's whimsical unpredictability to resolve the theodicy problem. But I am less convinced than Babb that this "reenchantment of the world" should be portrayed as "a Weberian reversal" (p. 200), since Baba's miracles and whimsy seem to inspire no similar whimsy or unpredictability among his most devoted followers, who strike me as just as earnest and methodical, and as frequently in business, as Max Weber's Protestants, if not for the same reasons.

3. The Methodists had no Protestant competition because the Protestant missionary groups had divided up the Pacific territories into different zones of responsibility. The Protestant mission to Fiji was run by the London Missionary Society, a Wesleyan organization. The Catholics did not abide by the deal and contested with the Protestants in many Pacific venues, usually losing out. For more on the conversion of indigenous Fijians to Christianity see Garrett 1982, Sahlins 1983, and Kaplan 1990.

4. A sharp contrast to the Acting Prime Minister's use of "we" and "you" is provided by the message sent by the Coalition leader and one-time Prime Minister, indigenous Fijian Timoci Bavadra, to the people of Fiji on the occasion of this Diwali. An excerpt:

> Our religions should not be used to divide us. Even if our places of worship are burned, no one can take away the religious beliefs and standards of goodness we set ourselves in our daily life.

Our different religious faiths are beacons which light up our understanding of the ideals we all commonly share as human beings.

Even if the ceremonial Diwali lights do not shine this year, I hope we will
all remember their significance — with a prayer that the lighted candle of
democracy will one day be rekindled. We hope its warm rays will nurture the
tolerance of Fiji's people, in their different religions, beliefs, ethnic groups and
social classes.

I continue to work and pray for a new dawn of peace and goodwill in our
country. God's light, at the beginning of every day, is among his greatest gifts.
Our faith in him — and in Fiji — must remain unshakable. I ask you to join me
in working and praying for the light to return to our country, not only during
Diwali, but at all times. (Bavadra 1990: 357)

Bavadra sent this message from a hospital bed in Auckland, and died four days later,
the day after the Indian ambassador was expelled from Fiji. The Fiji Labour Party
still seeks an able and indigenous Fijian successor as its permanent leader.

5. Many people both Indo-Fijian and indigenous Fijian, people whose judg-
ment I respect, believe these rumors, the gist of which is that the fervor of the
Lautoka group caused them to act prematurely and wrecked a plan to attack Indian
temples all over Fiji. True or false, the power of the rumor is a sign of current
alienation and mistrust and is probably itself a contributor to the ongoing attacks on
Indian places of worship as described below.

6. Many of the most important and inflammatory moments of recent political
rhetoric have come through the medium of the *Daily Post,* a newspaper that began
after the coups, rather than through the pages of the standby of colonial days, the
Fiji Times. The *Post* began, locals report, as an embarrassingly thin, promilitary
newspaper. But in the last three years, for reasons not clear to anyone I talked to
about it, the *Times* has become less willing to report things critical of or dangerous
to government, whereas the *Post* is simply more reckless and reports more extreme
views on many sides. Whatever else lies behind this difference, it has allowed the
fledgling, less established, and smaller-staffed paper to find a place for itself in Fiji's
marketplace, while the established paper, aware of the costs of the shutdowns of the
coup year, plays it safe.

7. This decree is reproduced in B. Lal 1988 (p. 119). For more detailed
accounts of the coups in Fiji, see B. Lal 1988, V. Lal 1990, and Howard 1991.

8. Homi Bhabha (1990) is perhaps the first to emphasize the connections
between nations and narration. Other interesting works on nationalism that have
influenced my views here include Lass 1988, Malkki 1992, and Borneman 1992, as
well as Anderson 1983, Corrigan and Sayer 1985, and Chatterjee 1986. For an excel-
lent review of current anthropological literature on nationalism, see Foster 1991. On
nation, narrative, and national ritual in Fiji, see also Kaplan n.d. (forthcoming).

9. Joining Lasaro as spokesman for this party was, ironically, Butadroka,
original spokesman for the betrayal narrative. As we have already seen in connection
to the Lautoka temple burnings, Butadroka quickly joined the Christian band-
wagon. "It's now time to stand as a party of Fijian Christians moving to serve God
who in turn will see to the future of our country," he argued. "God has called this
party at this specific moment for a purpose" (*Daily Post,* March 10, 1990).

10. If it is an irony in the life of this bureaucrat that he returns to the India of the Bharatiya Janata Party (BJP) and Vishva Hindu Parishad (VHP), it is not so amusing that news of events in Ayodhya and elsewhere in India have more recently provided the indigenous Fijian nationalists with ample evidence of imperial Hindu designs, despite the near complete absence of any Hindu nationalist on the Fijian scene. I have no concrete evidence, at present, of what role if any will be played by images of the BJP and VHP in Fijian politics. On the other side, I do not know whether any bricks for a new Ram temple in Ayodhya were ever sent from any Hindu groups in Fiji. More generally, very few Indo-Fijians express any interest in returning to India for more than pilgrimage and holidays, despite their intense interest in emigrating from Fiji. The common opinion seems to be that India is also a mess. In any case, reticence to return to India has been a general feature of Fiji Indian migration since the early 1930s, when the difficulties faced by outcasted returned emigrants were widely publicized by C. F. Andrews, Bhawani Dayal Sannyasi, and the Gandhians. In a campaign directed especially against South African efforts to push out its overseas Indian population, the exindentured laborers were explicitly and repeatedly advised to stay put.

11. These spaces in Fiji's economy are largely being filled by what the local (University of the South Pacific) academics have taken to calling "recolonization." New, temporary workers from Australia, New Zealand, and the United States Peace Corps fill the gaps. Accountants are frequently in Fiji on temporary transfer within the same corporation, such as Bank of New Zealand or Westpac. The Peace Corps' specialty is teachers. Although it is astonishing to see Fiji's elite suburbs full of white faces for the first time in my experience in Fiji, and though it is clear that indigenous Fijians are much happier working for "Europeans" (as they have been all along, especially in the tourist industry) than for "Indians," there are real limits to the notion of recolonization. One is reminded, in conversation with these guest workers, of Shiva Naipaul's comments in *North of South* (1979) about the lack of a sense of responsibility that is characteristic of the white "expatriates" in postcolonial Africa.

12. Dr. Singh has recently published a book in Fiji about his experiences and current politics, which I have not yet seen (Singh 1992). When one of Singh's confessed abductors was later posted to United Nations peacekeeping duties in the Middle East, protests caused the cancellation of this plum assignment and, it is said, created new resentment toward Singh in the Fiji military. An indigenous Fijian journalist told me, "I worry about that boy, if he comes back." Dr. Singh is forty years old.

References

Anderson, Benedict
    1983   *Imagined Communities: Reflections on the Origin and Spread of Nationalism.* London: Verso.
Babb, Lawrence
    1986   *Redemptive Encounters: Three Modern Styles in the Hindu Tradition.* Berkeley: University of California Press.

Bavadra, Timoci

1990   *Bavadra, Prime Minister, Statesman, Man of the People: Selection of Speeches and Writings 1985–1989.* 'Atu Bain and Tupeni Baba, eds. Nadi: Sunrise Press.

Bhabha, Homi, ed.

1990   *Nation and Narration.* London: Routledge.

Borneman, John

1992   *Belonging in the Two Berlins: Kin, State, Nation.* Cambridge: Cambridge University Press.

Chatterjee, Partha

1986   *Nationalist Thought and the Colonial World: A Derivative Discourse.* London: Zed Books.

Clunie, Fergus

1984   "Fiji's First Indian Settlers." *Domodomo* 2, 1: 2–10.

Corrigan, Philip, and Derek Sayer

1985   *The Great Arch: English State Formation as Cultural Revolution.* Oxford: Basil Blackwell.

Foster, Robert

1991   "Making National Cultures in the Global Ecumene." *Annual Review of Anthropology* 20: 235–60.

France, Peter

1969   *The Charter of the Land.* Melbourne: Oxford University Press.

Garrett, John

1982   *To Live among the Stars: Christian Origins in Oceania.* Geneva and Suva: World Council of Churches, and the Institute of Pacific Studies, University of the South Pacific.

Golden Age 1980

1980   Prasanthi Nilayam, Andhra Pradesh: Sri Sathya Sai Books and Publications, Sri Sathya Sai Central Trust. (No listed ed.)

Howard, Michael

1991   *Fiji: Race and Politics in an Island State.* Vancouver: University of British Columbia Press.

ISKCON

1989   *Sri Vyasa Puja: The Most Blessed Event.* Fiji: International Society for Krishna Consciousness.

Kaplan, Martha

1989a   "The 'Dangerous and Disaffected Native' in Fiji: British Colonial Constructions of the *Tuka* Movement." *Social Analysis* 26: 20–43.

1989b   "*Luveniwai* as the British Saw It: Constructions of Custom and Disorder in Colonial Fiji." *Ethnohistory* 36, 4: 349–71.

1990   "Christianity, People of the Land, and Chiefs in Fiji." In John Barker, ed., *Christianity in Oceania.* Lanham, Md.: University Press of America, 127–47.

N.d.   "Blood on the Grass and Dogs Will Speak: Ritual, Politics, and the Nation in Independent Fiji." In Robert Foster, ed., *Nation Making in Postcolonial Melanesia*. Ann Arbor: University of Michigan Press. Forthcoming.

Kelly, John

1988a "From Holi to Diwali in Fiji: An Essay on Ritual and History." *Man* (n.s.) 23: 40–55.

1988b "Fiji Indians and Political Discourse in Fiji: From the Pacific Romance to the Coups." *Journal of Historical Sociology* 1, 4: 399–422.

1991 *A Politics of Virtue: Hinduism, Sexuality, and Countercolonial Discourse in Fiji*. Chicago: University of Chicago Press.

Lal, Brij V.

1988 *Power and Prejudice: The Making of the Fiji Crisis*. Wellington: New Zealand Institute of International Affairs.

Lal, Victor

1990 *Fiji: Coups in Paradise*. London: Zed Books.

Lass, Andrew

1988 "Romantic Documents and Political Monuments: The Meaning-Fulfillment of History in Nineteenth-Century Czech Nationalism." *American Ethnologist* 15, 3: 456–71.

Malkki, Liisa

1992 "National Geographic: The Rooting of Peoples and the Territorialization of National Identities among Scholars and Refugees." In Roger Rouse, James Ferguson, and Akhil Gupta, eds., *Culture, Power, Place: Explorations in Critical Anthropology*. Boulder, Colo.: Westview Press.

Naipaul, Shiva

1979 *North of South: An African Journey*. New York: Penguin.

Rutz, Henry

N.d. "Rhetorical Tradition and the Making of the Fijian Nation." In Robert Foster, ed., *Nation Making in Postcolonial Melanesia*. Ann Arbor: University of Michigan Press. Forthcoming.

Sahlins, Marshall

1983 "Other Times, Other Customs, the Anthropology of History." *American Anthropologist* 85: 517–44.

Singh, Anirudh

1992 *Silent Warriors*. Suva: Institute of Applied Studies.

Toren, Christina

1988 "Making the Present, Revealing the Past: The Mutability and Continuity of Tradition as Process." *Man* (n.s.) 23: 696–717.

Young, John

1984 *Adventurous Spirits*. St. Lucia, Queensland: University of Queensland Press.

Madhavi Kale

3. Projecting Identities: Empire and Indentured Labor Migration from India to Trinidad and British Guiana, 1836–1885

This chapter considers issues relating to the creation of Indian communities and culture in Trinidad and British Guiana, British Caribbean colonies which, between 1845 and 1917, imported more than four hundred thousand workers from British India to work on sugar plantations. Both the primary and secondary literatures on these Indian communities have been vitally concerned with questions of cultural continuity: the degree to which Indians in Trinidad and British Guiana have retained or reproduced essential aspects of Indian culture, from notions of caste to preferences in food and clothing (Schwartz 1967; Moore 1977; Speckmann 1965; Cumpston 1953, 1956; Tinker 1974; Wood 1986; Mangru 1987; Birbalsingh 1989; Mishra 1979; Dumont 1974). This analytical tendency has contributed to reifying "Indian" culture and, in the process, has reduced the men and women who left India to work in the British Caribbean to mere carriers of this reified culture.

Clearly, traditions, practices, and values deriving from migrants' varied experiences in India were important to the emergence of distinctive "Indian" communities and cultures in these colonies. These processes, however, were also shaped by a constellation of distinctively imperial contexts in which indentured emigration from India could and did take place. These include, among others, the declining significance of the Caribbean to metropolitan fortunes and policy-making, consolidation and integration of empire and imperial administration in India, and bourgeois agitation for political and economic reforms in England (regarding suffrage extension and the elimination of protective tariffs, for example) (Bayly 1989; Kale 1992).

The first two parts of this chapter focus on the notorious and influential pilot project in importing Indian contract workers into British Caribbean sugar plantations proposed by John Gladstone in 1836. The underlying intentions of this project, outlined in the earliest letters proposing the scheme, continued to inform both representations of Indians in the Caribbean and policies for governing Indians, despite changed circumstances, relations, and contexts. The chapter's third and fourth parts illustrate how such representations and policies affected two aspects of community formation — the importation of women indentured laborers and the celebration of a public festival.

Gladstone's Experiment

In 1833, Parliament passed the Act of Abolition, which provided for the termination of slavery in British colonies as of August 1, 1834. Slavery was followed by a transitional period known as "apprenticeship," which was to last until 1840, and which was supposed to give both former slaves and former slave-owners the opportunity to adjust to "free labor" conditions. What this meant, in effect, was that former slave-owners were to have exclusive rights over the labor of their former slaves for six years after the end of slavery. Apprenticeship gave planters in the British Caribbean and Mauritius a chance to develop alternative strategies for controlling labor, and they made the most of it.

On January 4, 1836, barely two years after the abolition of slavery, John Gladstone, Liverpool merchant and father of William Ewert Gladstone, dictated a letter to his nephew at the Calcutta shipping agency Gillanders, Arbuthnot and Company (Tinker 1989; Checkland 1971). Gladstone explained that he had heard the firm had recently sent a number of Indian laborers to Mauritius, and that he was interested in exploring the possibility of making similar arrangements for certain colonies in the West Indies, where he himself owned sugar plantations (UK [HC] 1838 no. 232, encl. no. 1, John Gladstone to Gillanders, Arbuthnot & Co., January 4, 1836: 1–2; Geoghegan 1873: 2; Tinker 1974: 63). "You will probably be aware that we are very particularly situated with our Negro apprentices in the West Indies," he delicately explained, "and that it is a matter of doubt and uncertainty how they may be induced to continue their services on the plantations after their apprenticeship expires in 1840. This is a subject of great moment and deep interest in the colonies of Demerara and Jamaica." Gladstone further explained that, in anticipation of 1840:

It is of great importance to us to endeavour to provide a portion of other labourers, whom we might use. . . . [to] make us, as far as it is possible, independent of our negro population; and it has occurred to us that a moderate number of Bengalees, such as you were sending to the Isle of France [Mauritius], might be very suitable for our purpose.

Finally, Gladstone sketched out the terms under which he and his associates would import and employ such "Bengalees," about one hundred of whom he proposed bringing to Demerara from Calcutta. They should be, he stipulated, "young, active, able-bodied people," at least half of whom ought to be married, "and their wives disposed to work in the field as well as they themselves." They should enter into binding contracts for five to seven years. In exchange for their labor (which he described as "light"), the workers would get housing, food, medical assistance, either clothing or wages of no more than four dollars a month for the able-bodied (women and children would be paid according to a sliding scale based on this wage), and a free passage to British Guiana, where they would be distributed in groups of twenty to thirty people to participating plantations. Gladstone concluded by observing that already "several importations from the Madeiras and Azores have taken place into Demerara, and so far with good effects on the minds of the blacks" (UK [HC] 1838 no. 232, encl. no. 1, John Gladstone to Gillanders, Arbuthnot & Co., January 4, 1836: 1–2).

In their favorable response, Gillanders and Arbuthnot carefully assured Gladstone that, "in inducing these men to leave their country, we firmly believe we are breaking no ties of kindred, or in any way acting a cruel part." The "Hill tribes" in question, they explained, "known by the name of Dhangurs, are looked down upon by the more cunning natives of the plains, and they are always spoken of as more akin to the monkey than the man." In short, they implied, such people would be better off in the West Indies laboring under five-year contracts than they were at present in India (UK [HC] 1838 no. 232, encl. no. 2, Gillanders, Arbuthnot & Co. to John Gladstone, June 6, 1836: 2–4). By the late spring of 1837, government approval had been secured and final arrangements had been completed. A few months later, the ships *Hesperus* and *Whitby* left Calcutta for Demerara. They arrived in January, disembarking a total of 437 contract laborers.

Within a year, the system was suspended. The British and Foreign Anti-Slavery Society and affiliated groups in England, India, and the British sugar colonies in the Caribbean and Indian Ocean raised concerns that recruitment of indentured laborers in India was characterized by fraud, deception, and kidnapping — the very practices widely associated with the transatlantic slave trade from which British entrepreneurs had profited for generations, and which Britain was now attempting, at great cost, to suppress (Tinker 1974; Kale 1992). The governor of Bengal appointed a committee to investigate allegations of false representation and kidnapping brought against the traffic, while the House of Lords ordered that relevant papers, including Gladstone's correspondence with his Calcutta agents and with the colonial secretary, be published for formal consideration and debate on the system's future (UK [HC] 1838, no. 232: 1).

In addition, unfavorable reports on the condition of the workers who had left India on the *Hesperus* and the *Whitby* continued to appear, especially about those assigned to Gladstone's estates (*British Emancipator,* January 9, 1839). These estates became the object not only of Anti-Slavery Society investigations, but also of an official local inquiry, reluctantly ordered by the governor of British Guiana, Henry Light. In the short run, the result was that planters' attempts to resume importation of Indian indentured workers were unsuccessful for nearly four years. Only in 1843 was it allowed again, and then only to Mauritius. Two years later, British Guiana, Trinidad, and Jamaica were allowed to participate, although under conditions less favorable to planters than those that Gladstone had secured in 1837. It was not until 1860 that five-year contracts were again sanctioned by the Indian government for Indian workers bound for selected colonies in the British Caribbean. By then, the system of indentured labor importation had become permanent, and the concerns of colonial elites and administrators had expanded to problems of governing not only indentured Indian workers, but also Indians whose indentures had expired, and who appeared to be preparing to settle in the colony (Kale 1992).

Gladstone's Purpose

Gladstone's first letter to Gillanders and Arbuthnot reveals the motives behind the scheme: Indian workers were to be the medium through which sugar planters would reassert their control over Afro-Caribbean workers. This was an end toward which the planting interests mobilized many strategies and resources, ranging from individuals' attempts at enticing workers away from neighboring plantations (or even colonies) to legislative efforts to criminalize freedpeople's mobility through restrictive antivagrancy and antisquatting laws. Schemes for importing laborers from overseas were part of these labor control strategies (Green 1975: 164–65;

Bolland 1981: 594; Foner 1983: 24–26; Adamson 1984: 47; Scarano, 1989: 59; Blackburn 1990: 441–42). In their efforts to challenge Afro-Caribbean workers' position in local labor markets and undercut their ability to bargain effectively for higher wages and better conditions, planters sought workers from neighboring colonies, from the United States, Madeira, Ireland, and Sierra Leone as well as from India. Like them, Indian workers were recruited to be "scabs."

This purpose was never again stated as frankly as it was in Gladstone's first letter to Gillanders and Arbuthnot. Over the course of the next five years, planters' claims that labor available to them was inadequate numerically and morally became orthodoxy: claims that black workers were lazy, unreliable, untruthful, and unable or unwilling to understand or honor a contract were reproduced and sanctified in the reports of parliamentary and royal commissions appointed to investigate the condition of the sugar colonies almost every decade into the twentieth century. Historians of Indian indentured labor migration have not adequately considered the significance of the genealogy of these unfavorable representations of black workers either for the introduction of contract workers from India or for the subsequent emergence of distinctive communities among them. This is unfortunate, because disparaging characterizations of Afro-Caribbean workers were critical to the emergence of official characterizations of Indian workers in the British Caribbean.

As planters like Gladstone saw it, Indian workers were recruited and introduced into British Guiana and Trinidad for the "benefit" of Afro-Caribbean workers: to alarm, but also to "educate" and inspire them. As the latter's performance and potential as "free" workers were devalued, Indian working men were extolled for their docility, industriousness, and respect for the sanctity of contracts. Planters and other supporters of indentured labor immigration piously and pointedly wished that Afro-Caribbean men would follow Indian working men's example.

But this was only one side of the storytelling. Once Indian workers were on the plantations, planters' and administrators' praises were leavened with distaste and dissatisfaction. Indians, they observed, were steadier workers than those of Afro-Caribbean descent, but they were also avaricious, jealous, less robust, and given to killing their women, not to mention dishonest, idolatrous, filthy, and so on. In 1884, L. A. A. de Verteuil, a leading member of Trinidad's French-Creole elite, noted approvingly that, "The Hindoos, such as I have been able to observe them in the colony, are a mild and timid race, obsequious, wanting in firmness and perseverance, more prudent and wily than energetic and straightforward. They are intelligent, rather industrious and saving." He added, however, that "a distinctive trait in the character of the Coolie is insincerity; one cannot depend upon what he says. The private life of those who have not yet been influenced by civilization is, generally, depraved and disgusting" (de Verteuil 1884: 160–61).

Greater experience of Indian workers led to further refinement and elaboration of these characterizations; thus Trinidad planters could eventually ask that the agents in India send fewer recruits from Madras. As one visitor to Trinidad explained in his travelogue, the indentured workers from Calcutta proved to be, "valuable, steady labourers, while those from Madras are for the most part useless. . . . the scum and refuse of the city of Madras — stray waifs who have sunk very low in their lives before they find their way into the hands of the shipping agent" (Gamble 1866: 33–34). Although colonial plantation owners and managers recognized that Indian laborers were enabling them to become independent of Afro-Caribbean workers, they were not altogether satisfied with Indian workers, either.

In fact, planters and the governors who represented them were sufficiently dissatisfied with all Indian workers (whether from Calcutta or Madras) to send their agent, James T. White, to China in the early 1850s to look into opportunities for recruiting workers there, at colonial expense. As White wrote in 1851, Chinese workers were "fully alive to the necessity of authority for their regulation and control . . . generally tractable and manageable," strong, tough, and "not averse to foreigners" (P.R.O., C.O., 885/1, xvi, White to Barkly, August 21, 1851). They were also, as de Verteuil noted three decades later, "highly intelligent and discerning, steady labourers, and well versed in the tillage of the soil" (de Verteuil 1884: 160).

This was not the first time that people interested in British Caribbean sugar had turned to China. In fact, a parliamentary committee had investigated the possibility of recruiting Chinese workers for British Caribbean plantations as early as 1810, although the colonial assemblies had not been notified of their efforts (Higman 1972: 21–44). The 1810 parliamentary committee's report noted that, at the time, regular immigration from China would be impracticable. Among other things investigators were convinced that it would be difficult to get Chinese women to emigrate, and that, given prevailing social conditions in the British Caribbean, allowing Chinese men access to local women would be awkward. In any case, such emigration was illegal in China, and at the time it was felt that pursuing the matter on behalf of West Indian sugar planters would jeopardize trading prospects for British firms in China (UK [HC] 1810–11, II no. 409).

Efforts to recruit Chinese men resurfaced in the aftermath of emancipation and the Gladstone debacle. In 1843, the colonial secretary, Lord Stanley, received a delegation of West Indian sugar planters desperate for access to overseas contract workers. Stanley informed them that Britain's ongoing crusade against the slave trade made it difficult for his government to sanction emigration of free laborers from Africa, and that, for the moment, emigration from India was still banned and could not yet be contemplated. He added, however, that he and his government had no reservations about his guests trying to recruit a work force in China, provided their efforts were confined to territories under British control. Anticipating antislavery activists' — and others' — concerns about sexuality and race, Stanley noted that recruiting women would be difficult, if not virtually impossible, but he conceded that this need not be an insurmountable obstacle, as prospective employers could invoke recent precedents involving exclusively male emigration from the Kroo coast of Africa. He noted also that because labor emigration was well-established and routine among some Chinese communities, elaborate protocols to protect them from fraud and abuse would be unnecessary. Soon after, the Colonial Office granted licenses to four planters in British Guiana to import five hundred laborers each from China. Included among the four prospective employers were the Gladstones (*Reporter,* December 13, 1843: 326–28).

By 1851, when British Guiana and Trinidad sent White to China, British subjects' relations with the Chinese government had changed; though the latter still frowned on emigration of Chinese, the British felt they could ignore the proscriptions at less risk to their individual and imperial interests. In his reports to Governor Henry Barkly of British Guiana, White explicitly and exhaustively described ways of getting around the prohibitions. White was also explicit in urging the superiority of Chinese workers to those from India. He discredited Bengali workers, in particular, in terms suggesting he was not alone in his disapproval and that he had a receptive audience at home. He sent Governor Barkly a copy of an article from the Bengal *Hurkuru,* which he felt vindicated the West India planters' costly quest for Chinese workers. According to the article, a local planter had

employed a number of labourers from different parts of the country, Bengalees, Dangars, and Chamars, in addition to whom he had a gang of 20 Chinese. The rate at which each of these classes were employed was Rs 2.12 per month to the Bengalees, Rs 2 to the Dangars, and Rs 4 to the Chamars, the Chinese being engaged at Rs 8 each. . . . he began to make comparisons, the land and labour generally that was allotted to each being precisely similar; and the result showed more exactly than he could have well conceived that the Dangars did as much as 2 Bengalees, the Chamars equal to the Dangars, and the Chinese overran 2 Chamars; the result fully proving the greater economy of the higher-paid [Chinese] labourer, his 8 rupees a month being equivalent to 12 rupees to the Dangars, or 38 rupees to the Bengalee.

The author concluded that Chinese laborers "would be found very useful on the sugar plantations of the West Indies" (P.R.O., C.O., 885/1 xvi, White to Barkly, August 21, 1851).

Characterizations of Indian migrants were directly linked to the role they were to play in the sugar colonies, in relation primarily to Afro-Caribbean workers, over whom planters were determined to reassert authority. If India became the primary recruiting field for British Caribbean planters, it was not because Indians' characters, as laborers or otherwise, had made them ideal immigrants; rather, it was because Indian workers were, for political reasons, more readily accessible than workers from other parts of the world. The primary documents on Indian indentured labor migration are full of claims that Indians were innately suited to agricultural labor, to taking direction, and to working hard for low wages. These arguments, however, were justifications for seeking and securing Indian indentured workers, especially once other areas proved inaccessible and importation of contract workers from India had become a permanent strategy for producing sugar on plantations. Once Indians had been integrated into the colonial economy and had become permanent fixtures in the colony generally, attitudes toward them seem to have hardened.

Women Indentured Laborers

The proportion of men and women among passengers on immigrant ships and among indentured laborers on Caribbean sugar plantations was determined not by nature, kinship, or custom, but rather by planters' and imperial administrators' prejudices and preferences. Identities projected onto Indian laborers, then, had a profound impact on the laborers' opportunities to create distinctive "Indian" communities and culture.

As far as British Caribbean planters were concerned, Indians were not intended to stay, initially: they were supposed to play the role of scabs and then leave. Until the 1880s, when this attitude changed, planters had little interest in encouraging Indians to settle in their colonies, and no interest in recruiting women. They wanted male laborers, and grudgingly accepted women only when the Indian government insisted, as a condition for allowing the system to start again, that women account for about one-fourth to one-fifth of the recruits sent to the colonies. Not that the planters gave up; throughout the century they complained loudly of the difficulty of recruiting women, in an ongoing effort to get the Indian government to reduce or even eliminate its requirements regarding these unwanted laborers. As we have seen, Gladstone's first letter to Gillanders and Arbuthnot indicated that he had initially been open to hiring equal numbers of men and women from India, provided the latter would also enter into indentures and work in the fields. His abandonment of this position illustrates the degree to which the legacies of slavery and abolition movements, profit margins, and competition dictated sex-ratio policies regarding indentured labor migration.

Gladstone's willingness, professed in January 1836, to hire Indian women suggests that he anticipated and wanted to preempt hostile criticism of his new labor scheme. Mobilizing bourgeois gender ideologies and family values, antislavery activists had argued, effectively, that in their pursuit of profit, slave-traders and slave-owners violated the sacralized institution of family — not only by separating husbands and wives, parents and children, but also because overvaluation of male labor-power led to unnatural demographic conditions among slave populations and, by extension, allegedly depraved sexual practices. Although Gladstone was willing to hire women, he clearly shared the assumption that they would be less productive than men. He negotiated this potential difficulty by proposing to pay Indian women less for their field labor than he would pay their male counterparts, even though they would work the same hours, on the grounds that the labor itself (classified as "light" work, or "women's" work) was of less value or less onerous than that performed by men.

Furthermore, it was Gillanders and Arbuthnot who asserted — for the record — that cultural conservatism regarding women in Indian society would make recruiting women for indentured emigration difficult and expensive. They also indicated that Gladstone's sugar-producing competitors in Mauritius had been importing Indian laborers in ratios of ten men to each woman for some years, without Indian government interference or objection. Given Gillanders and Arbuthnot's authoritative, experienced, and on-the-spot assessment of the challenges and expense involved in recruiting women, and given the precedents allegedly established by his Mauritius rivals, there was little reason for Gladstone to insist that the firm send him equal numbers of men and women laborers, even if he had shared abolitionists' concerns about sex ratios, sexuality, and the sanctity of the family.

Assumptions that women were inferior agricultural laborers (less productive, less efficient, weaker, and more prone to illness than men) articulated with engendering imperial wisdom about both "Indian" culture and the condition of India's women, and enabled prospective employers and their agents to secure from India primarily male workers. They also, however, enabled critics of indentured labor migration to invoke the antislavery rhetoric and passions of earlier years in their new crusade against labor practices they deemed unfair to both Indian and Afro-Caribbean workers, and in defense of family values. Indian women in colonies that imported indentured labor from India were not only presumed to be less productive than men and accordingly assigned lower wages, but also excoriated for provoking instability on the plantations, where they reportedly excited all manner of passions in Indian men, and where they were often murdered for their pains. In some colonies, notably Fiji and Trinidad, murder and suicide rates on plantations employing Indian indentured workers were allegedly unusually high, and in the case of murder, the victims were predominantly women (Reddock 1985; Lal 1984, 1985; Sheperd 1989; Kelly 1991).

Explanations given by contemporaries for this violence generally reflected their roles in this imperial labor reallocation scheme. Colonial authorities and employers tended to attribute it, tautologically, to Indian men's allegedly characteristic possessiveness and jealousy, and to the venality of those low-class Indian women who could be recruited to work on overseas plantations. In their turn, critics of indentured labor migration and Indian government officials tended to blame planters for creating a dangerous paucity of women on colonial sugar plantations, up-country agents of licensed recruiters in India for enlisting and thus introducing "immoral" women to plantation work forces, male indentured laborers for their ill-controlled jealousy, and indentured Indian women for the violence. When colonial employers compared Indian indentured workers with Afro-Caribbean workers, they continued to celebrate the former as models of industrial docility. At the same time, however, and with little tension, Indian men's violence, especially against Indian women, was eventually duly included among the list of characteristics believed to distinguish Indians (Wood 1968: 154; Gamble 1866; de Verteuil 1884; Comins 1893; UK [HC] 1910, XXVII: I–II).

Few of the people whose opinions are found in government reports, minutes of evidence collected by various committees of inquiry, and contemporary histories attributed the violence to work and living conditions on the plantations, where Indian indentured workers were isolated and unable to leave, even during free time, without a pass: where, in short, thanks to the contracts they had willingly entered, Indians were systematically deprived of control over their labor and lives for the duration of their indentures. Indian women were generally the only women on the estates, and competition over them was not limited to Indian men (drivers, interpreters, laborers of high and low caste), but also involved predominantly white managers and plantation staff (Reddock 1985; Lal 1985). In this context, the struggle to assert control over Indian women, primarily over their sexuality (violently or through efforts to influence marriage and divorce ordinances), was an important dimension of the process by which distinctive communities and cultures developed among Indians on and off the sugar plantations (Kelly 1991).

Hosay

The limits and possibilities that migration and life as plantation laborers presented to overseas Indians can be discerned in official representations of Trinidad's so-called Coolie Disturbances that occurred in 1884 during celebration of Muhurram, or Hosay — or the "Madrassee Festival" — as it was locally and popularly known (Trinidad Ordinance no. 9 of 1882).

On October 30, 1884, troops near San Fernando fired on a procession of Indians, mostly indentured and "free" plantation workers apparently, who were celebrating Hosay by carrying torches and *tazias* or *tadjahs* (representations of the tombs of the Prophet's grandsons) to the sea. According to the official report on the incident, an ordinance had been passed recently expressly forbidding the celebrants from entering the town carrying lighted torches; the celebrants appeared to have ignored the proclamation. When stopped outside the town by police, they refused to put the torches out and disperse, even when the Riot Act was read; confronted with this mutinous behavior, the authorities present ordered the police to open fire. Twelve people were killed, and 107 were treated for injuries from buckshot wounds (P.R.O., C.O., 884/4 no. 55, Norman, 1885: 45).

Whether the celebrants had violated the prohibition against carrying lighted torches into the city deliberately or because they had not heard of it is not clear. Some newspaper accounts and some of the witnesses examined in the course of the official investigation of the incident asserted that the celebrants were unaware of the ordinance, and unprepared for the confrontation that befell them. Like J. E. Andre, who brought the incident to the attention of Charles Allen, president of the British Antislavery Society, such authorities condemned the police action as an "atrocious massacre" (P.R.O., C.O. 884/4 no. 55, Norman, 1885, encl. 3 in no. 10, J. E. Andre to Charles Allen, November 7, 1884; Charles Allen to the [London] *Times,* November 28, 1884: 74–75). However, others asserted, and the official investigator concluded, that the police had reacted responsibly and properly in response to provocative behavior on the part of the celebrants (Singh 1988).

The official investigation and report were commissioned by the Colonial Office. The imperial government had been obliged to take this action, not least because of Andre's and Allen's efforts to publicize the incident in Britain and India. In addition, news that the Trinidad authorities had tried to regulate celebration of Hosay in the first place might have led to problems with the Indian government, since it had made protection of Indians' rights to practice their religion a condition for colonial participation in the indentured labor scheme. In short, news that Trinidad police had fired on and killed Indians celebrating a religious festival threatened to increase opposition to the entire system of indentured labor migration in the British Caribbean, in Britain, and in India.

The investigator the Colonial Office chose was Sir H. W. Norman, Governor of Jamaica, a former officer in the Indian Army who still spoke some Hindi and who, as a subaltern in the Indian Army had, as he himself explained, "commanded a detachment of native soldiers, mainly Hindoos, regulating and escorting a procession of Mahomedan soldiers, which passed through crowds of Sikhs and Hindustani Hindoos" (P.R.O., C.O., 884/4 no. 55, Norman 1885, encl. no. 10: 45). Norman's report endorsed the actions of the Trinidad authorities, from their attempting to regulate celebration of Hosay in 1882, to the order to open fire on the processioners on October 30, 1884. He argued that the processions as they had developed in Trinidad were no longer religious in character, and that in attempting to regulate them, the Trinidad authorities had not violated the terms of their labor agreements with the Indian government. He explained:

> Care had been taken in framing the rules that no part of them should interfere in any respect with the religious obligations of the Mahomedans, but I may remark that of the Indian immigrants in Trinidad, barely a fifth are Mahomedans, that some of the most respectable Mahomedans in the Island hold aloof from the procession, either because they consider it unsanctioned by

their faith, or because of the boisterous nature of the procession; in fact, the
ceremony, although it is purely appertaining to the Mahomedans, is one in
which most of the persons engaged are Hindoos.

And he added, "the whole celebration has in Trinidad long been regarded as
a sort of national Indian demonstration of a rather turbulent character"
(P.R.O., C.O., 884/4 no. 55, Norman 1885, encl. no. 10: 42). Norman
went on to explain that this aspect of the celebrations was both a result of
and exacerbated by growing self-confidence among Trinidad Indians. He
wrote:

> After a residence of some time in Trinidad the Coolie not only becomes a man
> of a more independent spirit than he was when in India, but according to some
> reliable evidence, he often becomes somewhat overbearing. . . . There can be
> no doubt that the Coolies feel their power, or rather, I should say, have an
> exaggerated idea of that power.

In fact, on the strength of his experience with Indians in their native land,
Norman concluded that the disturbances occurred partly because, as he put
it, the "Coolies" had been too "indulged." He noted that often "bodies of
Coolies" had come to the Immigration Office to communicate their griev-
ances, "carrying their cutlasses and other agricultural implements." This had
"encouraged among them the notion that they were powerful and could do
what they pleased." Norman noted that

> an officer of Indian experience, accustomed to a position of control over
> natives, would have quietly insisted upon the Coolies quitting the office, and
> would have told them that when 1 or 2 of their number come back in a quiet
> respectful way, and without their implements or sticks, they would be attended
> to. I do not doubt that they would have complied, and thus learned to behave
> properly in future. (P.R.O., C.O., 884/4 no. 55, Norman 1885, encl. no. 10:
> 46, 48)

In celebrating Hosay (which Norman insisted on calling Muhurram),
Trinidad Indians were indicating that they were not merely laborers, however much their employers and governors sought to confine them to that
role. By developing a celebration in which not only the Muslim minority
but also Hindus and Afro-Trinidadians could participate, indentured workers in Trinidad were breaking with traditional forms of Indian cultural
expression known to Norman, an old India hand with specific experience of
supervising "Native" troops overseeing religious processions. In developing Hosay, Indian workers had become not only "overbearing," but also

unpredictable, possibly ungovernable. When the stipendiary Magistrate for San Fernando, together with the Inspector Commandant of Police (who had apparently gone to that town from Port of Spain for the occasion), ordered that the police fire, they were aiming at the celebrants' pretensions to self-definition.

This intention is even clearer in the decision, made by the Colonial Office, to send Norman, an imperial civil servant with experience in the Indian Army, to investigate and report on the incident. Thanks to his experience in the Indian Army, Norman could credibly address and, as it turned out, refute any implication that, in interfering in the procession, the Trinidad authorities had interfered with Indians' right to engage in their traditional religious practices. His background lent authority to his final recommendation to the Colonial Office regarding the government of Trinidad: namely, that in future, Protectors of Immigrants be recruited from among former Indian Army or administration officers, who would know how to "attend to" Indians in Trinidad effectively without indulging them, and so preclude the possibility of future confrontations. He established that Hosay in Trinidad was a deviant and largely nonreligious celebration attended mostly by plantation laborers, and that official interference was appropriate — perhaps, his report implies, even necessary.

Norman had known and supervised Indians in India; he was governor of Jamaica, a British Caribbean colony which had imported Indian indentured workers and had a small Indian population. In short, he probably appeared to most people — from administrators in the Colonial Office and in the Indian and Trinidad governments to opponents of indentured labor migration in Britain, Trinidad, and India — to be well-qualified to judge what was authentic Indian practice, and what was not: better qualified, at any rate, than the Indian indentured workers themselves (Freitag 1989).

Conclusion

The fact that academic discussions of Indians in the British Caribbean have centered on questions of cultural continuity is perhaps not surprising given the extent to which people of Indian descent in the British Caribbean seem to share some practices and values with people in India itself. Academic preoccupation with cultural continuity is not surprising on other grounds as well. Trinidad Indians themselves are, by most accounts, proud of the persistence of "Indian" culture in Trinidad; like historians, social scientists, and some politicians who study these immigrants, they interpret this persistence as evidence of the resiliency of Indian culture, and of the people who preserved cherished practices of their homeland under conditions of exile, exploitation, and marginalization. Although the first migrants from India arrived in Trinidad in 1845, Indians continue to be considered, and to consider themselves, isolated, to varying degrees, from "mainstream" Trinidad culture, society, and politics (Birbalsingh 1989; Mishra 1979; Lamming 1981).

Twentieth-century political developments, ranging from the independence of former colonies in Asia, Africa, and the Caribbean between the 1940s and 1970, to Black Power movements that emerged in the Americas (including Trinidad and other parts of the British Caribbean) in the 1970s, have only heightened some Caribbean Indians' identification both with contemporary India as a modernizing nation, and with India as a civilization of great antiquity and complexity. In the process, Indians have further distinguished themselves from mainstream black Caribbean society (Jagan 1989; Ryan 1972).

In short, conditions in contemporary Caribbean countries are the context for academic and popular interest in questions of cultural continuity among their Indian populations. To a large degree, affirmation of persistence and resiliency of Indian culture is intended to dignify and empower people of Indian descent whose participation in the political life of their countries is often marginal and uneasy. As Eric Williams and George Lamming have pointed out, however, it should be remembered that cultural persistence can and has been interpreted negatively, as evidence of barbarism, underdevelopment, backwardness. Like slavery and indentured migration, such disempowering associations, made and normalized in nineteenth- and early twentieth-century British Guiana and Trinidad by missionaries, colonial administrators, employers, and working people alike, were legacies of colonialism and imperialism (Williams 1963: 109–12; Lamming 1981: xxiv).

To question the nature and extent of cultural continuities, then, need not involve either rejection of overseas Indians' cultures or further marginalization of Indians' communities in the Caribbean. Rather, the point is to move beyond those terms, values, and frameworks bequeathed us by nineteenth-century British imperialism in the form of immense mountains of carefully preserved official documents. To understand the nature and extent of Indian cultural continuities, and to explain the way indentured labor communities formed in the way they did, the instrumental dimension of indentured labor migration to Trinidad and British Guiana has to be considered fully. Not to do so is to miss a central principle in the development of laws, regulations, and attitudes governing Indian migrants' labor and lives, and, by extension, to miss a factor critical to the emergence of distinctive "Indian" cultures and communities in Trinidad, Guyana, and elsewhere in the British Caribbean (Lamming 1991: 53–54). Geographic distribution of Indians in Trinidad and Guyana, and cultural distinctiveness in gender relations and in festivals (and by extension, in the retention of caste notions, food and clothing preferences, and practices) must be framed in terms of the purposes for which Indians were introduced to British Caribbean colonies, and that shaped their relations with others in these multiethnic societies: as "scabs" hired in the aftermath of the British abolition of slavery.

Acknowledgments

Research for this chapter was supported by a Social Science Research Council doctoral dissertation research grant (South Asia Program, Summer 1991), and by Mellon Dissertation Fellowships (University of Pennsylvania, 1990–91 and 1991–92), and was conducted primarily at the Public Records Office and the India Office Library and Records, London; the Institute for Commonwealth Studies, University of London; and the Rhodes House Library, Oxford University. Versions of this chapter appear in my dissertation, "Casting Labor: Empire and Indian Indentured Labor in Trinidad and British Guiana, 1837–1945" (University of Pennsylvania, 1992), and were given at a panel on indentured labor for the conference "Production and Coercion: Unfree Labor in Comparative Perspective," University of Pennsylvania, November 13–14, 1992. My thanks to Peter van der Veer and David Ludden for the opportunity to participate in the South Asia Regional Studies Seminar in 1991, to Rob Gregg, Peter van der Veer, and Aisha Khan for reading and commenting on drafts of this paper, and to Nikhil and Nadia for cooperating.

References

PRIMARY SOURCES

PUBLIC RECORDS OFFICE

   C.O. 884/4 no. 55, January 13, 1885. "Correspondence Respecting the Recent Coolie Disturbances in Trinidad at the Mohurrum Festival, with the Report thereon by Sir H. W. Norman, K.C.B., C.I.E.

C.O. 885 / 1 xvi, confidential, printed December 22, 1851. Correspondence of James T. White to Governor Henry Barkly, British Guiana, on "Emigration from China to the West Indies."

PARLIAMENTARY PAPERS

(House of Commons) 1810–11 II no. 409. "Report of the Select Committee appointed to consider of the practicability and expediency of supplying our West India Colonies with free Labourers from the East."

(House of Commons) 1838 no. 232. "Copies of all Orders in Council for Colonial Ordinances for the better Regulation and enforcement of the relative Duties of Masters, Employers, and Articled Labourers in the Colonies of British Guiana and Mauritius; and of Correspondence relating thereto."

(House of Lords) VII no. 101. "Correspondence between the Secretary of State for the Colonies and the Governors of British Guiana, respecting the Immigration of Labourers."

SECONDARY SOURCES

Adamson, Alan
    1984   *Sugar without Slaves: The Political Economy of British Guiana, 1834–1904.* New Haven: Yale University Press.

Bayly, C. A.
    1989   *Imperial Meridian: The British Empire and the World, 1780–1830.* New York: Longman.

Birbalsingh, Frank, ed.
    1989   *Indenture and Exile: The Indo-Caribbean Experience.* Toronto: TSAR.

Blackburn, Robin
    1990   *The Overthrow of Colonial Slavery, 1776–1848.* New York: Verso.

Bolland, O. Nigel
    1981   "Systems of Domination After Slavery: The Control of Land and Labor in the British West Indies after 1838." *Comparative Studies in History and Society* 23: 591–619.

British Emancipator.
    1839   London, January 9.

Checkland, S. G.
    1971   *The Gladstones: A Family Biography, 1764–1851.* Cambridge: Cambridge University Press.

Comins, D. W. D.
    1893   *Note on Emigration from the East Indies to Trinidad.* Calcutta.

Cumpston, I. M.
    1953   *Indians Overseas in British Territories, 1834–1854.* Oxford: Clarendon Press.

1956   "A Survey of Indian Immigration to British Tropical Colonies to 1910."
        Population Studies 10, 2 (November 1956): 158–61.
De Verteuil, L. A. A.
    1884   *Trinidad: Geography, Natural Resources, Administration, Present Condi-
            tion and Prospects.* New York: Cassell and Co.
Dumont, Louis
    1974   *Homo Hierarchicus: The Caste System and Its Implications.* Chicago:
            University of Chicago Press.
Foner, Eric
    1983   *Nothing But Freedom: Emancipation and its Legacy.* Baton Rouge: Loui-
            siana State University Press.
Freitag, Sandria
    1989   "State and Community: Symbolic Popular Protest in Banaras's Public
            Arenas." In Freitag, ed., *Culture and Power in Banaras: Community,
            Performance, and Environment, 1800–1980.* Berkeley: University of Cal-
            ifornia Press, 203–28.
Gamble, W. H.
    1866   *Trinidad: Historical and Descriptive: Being a Narrative of Nine Years'
            Residence in the Island with Special Representatives to Christian Missions.*
            London: Yates and Alexander.
Geoghegan, J.
    1873   *Note on Emigration from India.* Calcutta. (India Office Library and
            Records.)
Green, William A.
    1975   *British Slave Emancipation: The Sugar Colonies and the Great Experiment,
            1830–1865.* New York: Oxford University Press.
Grierson, George A.
    1883   *Report on Colonial Emigration from the Bengal Presidency.* Calcutta. (In-
            dia Office Library and Records.)
Higman, B. W.
    1972   "The Chinese in Trinidad, 1806–1939." *Caribbean Studies* 12, 3: 21–44.
Jagan, Cheddi
    1989   "Indo-Caribbean Political Leadership." In Birbalsingh, *Indenture and
            Exile,* 15–26.
Kale, Madhavi
    1992   "Casting Labor: Empire and Indentured Migration from India to the
            British Caribbean, 1837–1845." Ph.D. dissertation, University of Penn-
            sylvania.
Kelly, John D.
    1991   *A Politics of Virtue: Hinduism, Sexuality, and Countercolonial Discourse in
            Fiji.* Chicago: University of Chicago Press.
Lal, Brij
    1984   "Kunti's Cry: Indentured Women on Fiji Plantations." *Indian Economic
            and Social History Review* 22, 1 (January–March): 55–72.
    1985   "Veil of Dishonour: Sexual Jealousy and Suicide on Fiji Plantations."
            Journal of Pacific History 20, 2–3 (July–October): 135–55.

Lamming, George
    1981   Foreword. In Walter Rodney, *A History of the Guyanese Working People,*
            1881–1905.
    1989   "The Indian Presence as a Caribbean Reality." In Birbalsingh, *Indenture*
            and Exile, 45–54.
Mangru, Basdeo
    1987   *Benevolent Neutrality: Indian Government Policy and Labour Migration to*
            British Guiana, 1854–1884. London: Hansib Publishing.
Mishra, Vijay C., ed.
    1979   *Rama's Banishment: A Centenary Tribute to the Fiji Indians, 1879–1979.*
            Auckland: Heinemann.
Moore, Brian L.
    1977   "The Retention of Caste Notions among the East Indians in British
            Guiana During the Nineteenth Century." *Comparative Studies in Society*
            and History 19, 1 (January): 96–107.
Reddock, Rhoda
    1985   "Freedom Denied: Indian Women and Indentureship in Trinidad and
            Tobago, 1845–1917." [*Indian*] *Economic and Political Weekly* 20, 43
            (October 26): 79–87.
Reporter
    1843   December 27.
Rodney, Walter
    1981   *A History of the Guyanese Working People, 1881–1905.* Baltimore: Johns
            Hopkins University Press.
Ryan, Selwyn D.
    1972   *Race and Nationalism in Trinidad and Tobago: A Study of Decolonization*
            in a Multicultural Society. Toronto: University of Toronto Press.
Scarano, Francisco
    1989   "Labor and Society in the Nineteenth Century." In Franklin W. Knight
            and Colin A. Palmer, eds., *The Modern Caribbean.* Chapel Hill: Univer-
            sity of North Carolina Press, 51–84.
Schwartz, Barton M., ed.
    1967   *Caste in Overseas Indian Communities.* San Francisco: Chandler Pub-
            lishing.
Sheperd, Verene
    1989   "Indian Women in Jamaica, 1845–1945." In Birbalsingh, *Indenture and*
            Exile, 100–108.
Singh, Kelvin
    1988   *Bloodstained Tombs: The Mohurrum Massacre, 1884.* Macmillan Carib-
            bean: University of Warwick.
Speckmann, J. D.
    1965   *Marriage and Kinship among the Indians of Surinam.* Assen, Holland:
            Van Gorcum.
Times of India
    1991   "Archives." July 2.

Tinker, Hugh
    1974   *A New System of Slavery: The Export of Indian Labour Overseas, 1834–1920.*
        New York: Oxford University Press.
    1989   "The Origin of Indian Migration to the West Indies." In Birbalsingh,
        Indenture and Exile, 63–72.
Williams, Eric
    1963   *History of the People of Trinidad and Tobago.* London: André Deutsch.
    1987   *Capitalism and Slavery.* London: André Deutsch.
Wood, Donald
    1986   *Trinidad in Transition: The Years after Slavery.* London: Oxford University Press.

Aisha Khan

4. Homeland, Motherland: Authenticity, Legitimacy, and Ideologies of Place among Muslims in Trinidad

Introduction

Along with other areas of inquiry in anthropology, studies of population movements, the construction of identities, social conflict, and group relations have been increasingly turning away from unified representations of culture toward the viewing of social phenomena as multicultured, multivoiced, and variously empowered. Diaspora studies — the study of population movements and displacements and the creation over time of literal and symbolic communities — similarly reflect the recognition that stability in points of origin, finality of destinations, and coherence of identities are notions that have all been questioned and reassessed in recent scholarship (Breckenridge and Appadurai 1989: i). In embracing new themes and premises, diaspora studies address social identities as multiply inflected and continuously reproduced. They also take issue with the various ways that culture is conceptualized — in both emic and etic terms — as these have influenced our understanding of particular localities and the populations within them (e.g., Scott 1991; Segal 1993; Khan 1994).

In this chapter my aim is twofold. By focusing on discourse relating to issues of authenticity and legitimacy in religious and cultural expression among Muslims of Indian and African descent in Trinidad (West Indies), I explore ideas about history, displacement, belonging, and identity. In so doing, I also address the question of how we approach transnational identity formation within diaspora populations, particularly in the Western Hemisphere. My interest is in considering how particular ideologies of identity are shaped and marshalled in struggles over representation, both in the sense of symbolic imagery and in the sense of political access to material resources. To this end I offer an ethnographic glimpse of religious ideology among Afro-Trinidadian and Indo-Trinidadian Muslims — specifically, regarding the authenticity and legitimacy of Islamic belief and practice. Although immediately concerned with religious matters, Trinidadian Muslims' discourse is also indicative of how Islam in diaspora is interpreted, deployed, and transformed. Reflecting Muslims' respective group histories as well as their daily lives, this discourse addresses other, broader arenas of social interaction, including, significantly, class and ethnic conflicts.

The relationship between religious idioms and processes of identity construction in Caribbean "plural societies" has been relatively under-researched, compared to other foci in this part of the world. Yet looking into the minutiae of everyday beliefs and practices, we are able to see the ways in which a particular religious idiom articulates with and expresses power relations among competing groups in multiethnic, postcolonial nation-states. What the following discussion ultimately suggests, among other things, is that discourse concerning the "purity" or the "correctness" of Islam in diaspora contains, in this Caribbean example, vital imagery and a subtext of struggle and negotiation that figure in the cultural politics and uneasy ethnic group relations among Indo-Trinidadians and Afro-Trinidadians.[1] This imagery and subtext are also part of the deployment of notions about locality, region, and community in identity construction and in the plasticity of group boundaries.

In their recent discussion, Akhil Gupta and James Ferguson remind us that both the changing world and changing academic perceptions have led to increasing appreciation of the "disjuncture of place and culture" (1992: 7). Yet diverse local populations and communities create new or different ideologies about junctures of place and culture, as discrete or essential(ized) loci of customs or traditions, which serve as an integral part of how these groups make sense of their condition of displacement or feelings of (dis)connectedness. Gupta and Ferguson note that the blurring of "here" and "there" disturbs the certitudes in the center as well as in the colonized periphery (ibid.: 10). Speaking primarily of contemporary diasporas, they imply a dichotomy between the displaced population of a locality and the "people remaining in familiar and ancestral places" (ibid.). The Caribbean region's very foundation is in many ways a precarious one in conceptual terms, however, because the whole notion of "familiar and ancestral" is problematic (e.g., Lewis 1983; Price 1985; Trouillot 1992; Segal 1993; Khan 1994). Therefore, a clear-cut division demarcating the displaced from those defined as the long-entrenched, so to speak, is not a framework best applied to a situation where the genesis of the entire entity derives from a series of diasporas, the nature of these histories and ancestries being an ongoing matter of discussion and debate.

For Afro-Caribbean and Indo-Caribbean peoples, the passage of approximately 400 years and 150 years, respectively, lends a particular nuance and depth to their experience as well as to interpretations of their cultural and social displacements, which are distinct from far more recent emigrations. For example, Gupta and Ferguson point out that

> remembered places have often served as symbolic anchors of community for dispersed people. This has long been true of immigrants, who . . . use memory of place to construct imaginatively their new lived world. "Homeland" in this way remains one of the most powerful unifying symbols for mobile and displaced peoples, though the relation to homeland may be very differently constructed in different settings. (1992: 11)

When dealing with diasporas that long precede contemporary postindustrial migration waves, however, "memory of place" must be analytically refined. One obvious point is that length of time can render information about one's "homeland" that much more scant or inaccessible, as well as creating greater space for re-visioning it. A second point is what we might call the thematic dimension of displacement, which concerns the way people define their diaspora. What is remembered varies, being charged with diverse sorts of "reminders," as is the case, for example, in the Indo-Caribbean: missionaries, pilgrimages, films, sacred texts, pedagogical treatises on practice interpreted by specialists, and so on. Third, what people remember is characterized in part by how they remember. Oral or written traditions about the emigration can depict, for example, heroism (Indians as rescuers of empire),[2] liberation (from oppressive or debilitating conditions such as those existing in mid- to late nineteenth-century India), predicament (betrayal of ancestral Indo-Trinidadians as deceived indenture "volunteers"; persecution of ancestral Afro-Trinidadians as slave captives).[3]

In looking at diasporic processes, we must specify dimensions, contexts, idioms, and mechanisms that constitute a particular diaspora, lest "diaspora" become an abstruse, macrolevel rubric that insufficiently conveys the "vitality of bricolage" that local diaspora communities constantly exhibit (Breckenridge and Appadurai 1989: iii) — the cultural, political, and economic developments and events that evolve in microlevel contexts of ethnographic experience, everyday life. Indian diasporas in the Caribbean encompass both a transnationalism in literal terms — in the forms of labor migrations, kinship ties, pilgrimages, and peripatetic missionaries and spiritual leaders — and symbolically in the creation and re-creation of "imagined communities" (Anderson 1983; cf. Cohen 1985). Within these creations, the way individuals and groups envision an identification with another place includes manifold "inventions of tradition" (Hobsbawm and Ranger 1983) as well as diverse "nostalgias without memory," Arjun Appadurai's phrase for looking back on worlds never lost (1990: 3).

In reconsidering the duality between "here" and "there," I explore some key dimensions of Trinidadian Muslims' constructions of sacred and secular space, and their significance for the relationship between local ideas about cultural origins and religious tradition. In positing an ideological tension, I hope ultimately to demonstrate that the concept "diaspora" actually includes many referents, both connected and disjunctive. In other words, the place to which one returns is not necessarily the place from which one came.

The Past as a Foreign Country[4]

In his discussion of the social uses of the past, David Lowenthal associates the fluid (time) with the concrete (territory), creating a poetic contrast in his claim that "during most of history men scarcely differentiated past from present . . . the past seemed not a foreign country but part of their own" (1985: xvi). Differences among Muslims, particularly Indo-Trinidadians, regarding the connection between culture and place and the webs of belonging between past and present shape the ways the past is literally and figuratively conceived as either "foreign" or familiar country. Spatial geographies overlap with a temporal terrain, where distance (in terms of time and miles) is mediated by emotion, whether strident or ambivalent. What constitutes the past for the Muslims I discuss here is not confined to ideological simulacra or abstract visions of linkages — primordial, genealogical, historical. The past is also embodied in a physical locality, a land — that is, what I will distinguish for present purposes as homeland and motherland.[5] Land certainly has metaphoric dimensions, but actual places have actual characteristics, however they may be construed and debated. Historical and contemporary India, Arabia, and Africa (and occasionally Pakistan) all figure as reference points, and sometimes touchstones, in religious discourse, and partly represent particular "cultural" or "religious" qualities.

In his work on Muslims in Indonesia, another postcolonial multiethnic society, John Bowen employs the notion of "frontiers." In power struggles over the meaning and significance of particular details of religious practice, he says, "it is in the frontiers of Islam that such diacritic meanings ('indexing authority') are most prominent" (1989: 613). Bowen's own examples of frontiers range from geographic to discursive. I think we can view *non*-Muslim societies as another kind of Islamic frontier for diaspora Muslims. As an example of what Dale Eickelman refers to as "dispersed, transregional 'minority' Islamic groups" (1984: 11), Caribbean Muslims' concern with depth of belief and correctness of practice gains salience through their perception that they lack a deep cultural history of Islam such as exists in Asia, Africa, and the Middle East. Hence, the nature of contemporary Islam is a source of animated discussion.

Further complicating is the historical development of Islam, that is, the course of its "Indianization." Indian indentured laborers' heritage, brought with them from India to the Caribbean, existed under conditions of oppression and discrimination by a colonial apparatus not terribly concerned with cultivating the cultural forms of its workers. And the contemporary conditions under which Indo-Trinidadians' cultural forms are cultivated (or not) by the postcolonial state constitute the arenas in which ethnic politics and their contests of visibility occur. In social contexts of non-Muslim majorities and state apparatuses that exercise non-Islamic political and cultural hegemony, frontiers can be seen as ambiguous territory, as interstitial spaces that are arenas of religious, political, or economic power to be secured by competing factions among minority communities. For Muslim minorities in Christian states (whether officially labeled as such or not), such as those of the Caribbean, frontiers are both literal and metaphoric. They are literal in the sense of being at the geographic, communication, and cultural edges of population diasporas out of "home" countries (the importance of the globalization of cultural flows, particularly in the form of the media, notwithstanding [see Appadurai 1990]). They are metaphoric in the sense of being uncertain and insecure domains of the negotiation and manipulation of identities in the face of quite distinct and powerful cultural, religious, and political-economic forces. In Trinidad, different interpretations of identity are struggled over by ethnic and ethnoreligious minority communities for various forms of power, using the details of religious observance that denote difference in order to define and defend determined meanings (Bowen 1989). The ability to determine the prevailing interpretations is, to a significant extent, what empowers an individual or group.

By looking at the specific messages that people want to convey to those perceived as "like" themselves as well as to "others," and by considering the larger domains of meaning that encompass these messages, we can elicit the points of tension and ambiguity that political and cultural struggles among frontier diaspora populations both contend with and express.

The creation of homelands (or the notion of motherlands) does not necessarily require literal memory or knowledge on the part of those who are harking back to a place of belonging or origin (which are not the same thing). Moreover, people can construct the ties binding select aspects or dimensions of their experience without entirely committing themselves to a particular place. In other words, the relationship between "here" and "there" is a continuous and dialectical process of the transmission of knowledge, information, beliefs, and practices rather than a trajectory of customs or values proceeding from one place to another at a particular point in time. As Ulf Hannerz points out, although "there is surprisingly little of a post-colonial ethnography of how Third World people see themselves and their society, . . . and its place in the world [,] a cultural analysis of their fantasies and of what they know for a fact," Third World cultures are "involved in an intercontinental traffic in meaning" (1987: 347). Constructing identity in the Indo-Caribbean diaspora is decidedly an "intercontinental traffic in meaning," where fact and fantasy are shaped by historical and contemporary political and social experiences and are continuously promulgated, recollected, and talked about.

Considering Context: Islam in Trinidad

Although my observations are based on fieldwork with Indo-Trinidadians,[6] it is necessary to incorporate Afro-Trinidadian Muslims' discourse for a fuller consideration of the significance of context (historical, contemporary) regarding displaced communities and transnational processes. To grasp the complexities of diaspora populations (particularly in postcolonial, ethnically heterogeneous societies), sufficient consideration must be given to the other local communities with whom overseas populations interact. This is particularly important when similar idioms of cultural expression are common among them, obtaining from long and intimate association. Considering an Afro-Trinidadian Muslim voice is also necessary because "argument and conflict over the form and significance of practices are . . . a natural part of any Islamic tradition" (Asad 1986: 16).

Hinduism is characterized by a fluidity that invites scholarly comment when "homogenized" into uniformity in overseas contexts (see, for example, van der Veer and Vertovec 1991). In contrast, Islam presupposes, at least ideally, a coherence that renders actual or possible variations in practice a matter of discussion on the part of clerics, lay practitioners, or scholars. While never completely determining social relations, orthodoxy, or the "correct model," is pivotal in Islamic traditions (Asad 1986: 15). It is, as Talal Asad points out (ibid.), more than merely a body of opinion; it is a distinctive relationship of power, through discourse and debate about what is "correct" and what must prevail.

A necessary point of departure in addressing these issues is the question, What factors are critical to an exploration of diasporic processes as they are manifest on the micro, or ethnographic level? For Islam is shared by both Indo-Trinidadians and Afro-Trinidadians, but in contested and negotiated ways that reflect two important and interlinked dimensions: their contemporary relations with each other vis-à-vis the Trinidadian state, and their relation to their respective social and cultural pasts.

The historical conditions of British colonial ventures in African slavery and Indian indenture in the Caribbean brought these two subjugated populations together in a plantation-based economy. Establishing an ethnically segmented labor market, where Indians and Africans and their descendants were initially relegated to distinct sectors of the production system (see Wood 1968; Brereton 1979), colonial policy and practice fostered competitive and at times antagonistic relations among laboring sectors. The hierarchical organization of both occupation and production in the Trinidadian colony established to a great extent the basis on which contemporary and subsequent social groups would coalesce and interact.

With respect to the contemporary conditions of the postcolonial state, after independence from Britain (1962), control of the political apparatus was assumed by the People's National Movement political party (PNM), comprised predominantly of a middle-class Afro-Trinidadian leadership. In a system of patron-clientelism (see Stone 1980), the state has been the primary distributor of resources such as civil service positions, sponsorship of the arts (which are often ethnically identified), funding for denominational schools, government contracts, access to formal education, and so on. It also continues to be generally imbued with Afro-Trinidadian and middle-class associations on the part of the majority of Indo-Trinidadians and Afro-Trinidadians. As Cecilia Karch observes, "perhaps, the PNM's greatest success has been the forging of a Trinidadian identity and culture; but it remains to this day an Afro-Trinidadian culture and identity" (1985: 130). As a consequence of its activities and internal composition, the state serves as an interlocutor of ethnic identity construction among Indo-Trinidadians and of class identification among sectors of the Afro-Trinidadian population. Moreover, through its various ministries and sponsorships, the state also has functioned as an important arbiter of national identity; the discourse of Trinidadian nationalism partially involves debate as to which specific ethnocultural groups best represent, and hence comprise, the nation (see Williams 1990). Thus, the state serves as an interlocutor for ethnic identity among Afro-Trinidadians as well, through its symbolic association with things Afro-Caribbean. For Indo-Trinidadians, however, this cultural construction of the state is not an affirmation of their ethnocultural identity, but a challenge to it.

Within the arena of nation building and questioning both the basis on which resources are distributed as well as their actual distribution (Williams 1990), Afro-Trinidadians and Indo-Trinidadians historically have pressed the state for rights and recognition in an idiom of cultural distinctiveness based partly on attributed qualities and capabilities. These attributes can serve as the basis for legitimating a deservedly recognized and rewarding position in the social hierarchy, authenticating a group's identity, and justifying its claims to various positions of power (Williams 1989, 1990). Invoked in these processes are self-conscious and at times rhetorical conceptualizations of culture, tradition, heritage, and/or roots. Empowerment by Afro-Trinidadians and Indo-Trinidadians is attempted, in part, through asserting their own, and challenging each other's, claims to specific cultural characteristics and traits that demarcate and distinguish them as a group. These characteristics and traits can be envisioned ethnoculturally or with respect to class position in the social structure. The claims involve debates whose subjects range from government sponsorship of African and Indian arts or organizations, to alleged ethnic discrimination in employment or provision of infrastructure, to the quality of a group's particular cultural or religious practices and morality.

Pervading this discourse are two simultaneous modes of thought, or ideologies. One is that authenticity of identity and legitimacy of social positioning are themes resonant in Trinidadian society as a whole. As Brackette Williams (1989, 1990, 1991) has theorized, in multiethnic nation-states certain cultural forms are validated as "real" or "authentic" culture and are compared unfavorably with devalued, "inauthentic" cultural forms that are categorized as "mere adaptive strategies," as superstitions, or as deviant behavior (1990: 112). As reified notions, these attributed cultural qualities and capabilities function in Trinidadian society as diagnostic emblems for establishing ethnic, religious, or class identities, and are descriptive of group identity insofar as the quality and boundaries of a group's identity are assessed: how much culture, what kind of tradition, how grand the heritage, how attenuated the roots. Among Trinidadian Muslims of Indian and African descent, pivotal to these issues is how the definitions and interpretations of culture, tradition, heritage, and roots are expressed in religious arenas. As indicators of distinctions they mark not only religious boundaries but the authenticity of the practices or characteristics they encompass. Religious interpretation and expression serve as important contested domains of authenticity of identity and legitimacy of social place, where questions about culture and tradition are framed and spelled out.[7] Religious expression is subject to the scrutiny of what is real, what is pure, and hence what is effectual in guiding people's actions and empowering their lives both spiritually and socially.[8]

In Trinidad, authenticity and legitimacy essentially involve notions of purity. Among Trinidadian Muslims, *authentic* implies originating from a source — untampered, untainted, and unabated. Also implicit is a sense of timelessness: what served then does so now. In addition, authenticity suggests conscientiousness, which in Trinidad is read as correct and sincere practice and belief. These qualities must be managed, however, because overzealous correctness has the danger of conveying intolerance or exclusivity, which are contrary to social ideals of acceptance and "living good with people." Similarly, seemingly effusive sincerity has the danger of appearing to be what is locally decried as "hypocritical" (a false, excessive protesting that is presumed to mask self-serving and hence unreligious motives) and/or irrationally "fanatical" (not discerning the appropriate degrees, expressions, and arenas of religious practice).

These characteristics act as filters for defining and assessing not only the immediately relevant religious significance of these issues but also the wider domains of meaning that refer to definitions and assessments of cultural practices, traditions, historical heritage, and the play of these in ethnic identity and group competition. There is always a fine line separating an egalitarian from a hierarchical ethos. *Religious* purity that emphasizes distinctions must reconcile with the social imperative of "living good with people." This resonates with what I believe is a larger trope of purity operating in Trinidad, where *racial/ethnic* purity must reconcile with the need for equality and cooperation, and where *cultural/traditional* purity aids resistance to colonial and postcolonial hegemony yet must reconcile with the pursuit and incorporation of modernity and "progress" (Khan n.d.). These issues are precariously negotiated by Indo-Trinidadian and Afro-Trinidadian Muslims, mediated to a large extent through their distinct ethnic identities, though purportedly transcending such distinctions as religiously irrelevant.

A second mode of thought or ideology that is significant in the local context also relates to issues of authenticity and legitimacy. As such, it is both related to and articulates with the politically and economically engendered discourse of authenticity discussed earlier. It consists of the historically characteristic aspect of Islam that concerns identifying and eschewing certain practices deemed inappropriate to the basic tenets of Islam. Potentially inappropriate acts and beliefs characterized as "cultural," "traditional," or "innovations" are those that have accreted through social and cultural influence rather than through demonstration by or dictum of the Prophet Muhammad. These concerns are certainly not unprecedented or unique to Trinidad. The effort to define and eschew practices deemed inappropriate to the basic tenets of Islam, and the identification of such practices as cultural or innovative, characterize diverse Islamic reforms throughout history in a variety of Muslim societies or communities. Yet, while religious discourse is in itself interesting, it generally also points to other forces or currents in daily life not always considered by practitioners as being directly within the domain of "things religious." Thus, the Trinidadian case goes beyond an inquiry into Islam per se, focusing instead on a window into the convergence of several social issues addressed within a religious idiom.

Islam, in the Trinidadian context, is interpreted by Muslims as a model for realizing harmonious interethnic social relations; its practice is seen as a model for Muslim group unity. Its practice is also seen by practitioners as potentially revealing qualitative differences between Muslims. These differences not only indicate the diversity of expressions of Islam in local contexts (compare, for example, Asad 1986; Eickelman 1984). They also tell us about wider social and political processes in the societies in which they are embedded.

Although my research encompassed Indo-Trinidadian communities throughout several districts, the Afro-Trinidadian Muslim data were gathered primarily from members of the only large Afro-Trinidadian–dominated *jamaat* (congregation) in the island. Afro-Trinidadian Muslims associated with other *jamaats* or mixed Indo-Afro Muslim organizations would undoubtedly have some ideas that contrast with those raised here.[9] The issues of religious and cultural authenticity and legitimacy are a common area of interest to most practicing Trinidadian Muslims of all ethnicities, however, and similar concerns are evident in diverse discussions.

Exploring religious ideology among Indo-Trinidadian and Afro-Trinidadian Muslims requires an examination of the ways that conceptualizations of culture and religion are reified on the local level and set in contrast with each other in the formation of ethnic divisions and coalitions. By *reification* I mean the process whereby any social grouping or community seizes upon particular practices or traits that they have defined as cultural, symbolically extracts them from the routine, habitual, or unconscious actions of daily life, and ideologically deploys them as various kinds of indexes or descriptive metaphors in establishing their identity.

In his useful discussion of culture, nationalism, and cultural reification, Bruce Kapferer states, with regard, for example, to Sinhalese Buddhists, that in nationalism, culture "becomes an object, a reified thing, something which can be separated or abstracted from its embeddedness in the flow of social life" (1988: 1–2). This partly involves a "process of symbolic disarticulation or decontextualization that removes ideas embedded in the fabric of social practices and symbolically idealizes them" (1988: 97). Kapferer is referring to processes where culture becomes something sacralized and acts as a unifying force in ethnic identity (ibid.: 98), in contrast with the Trinidadian case. In the Sinhalese context, "culture, its artifacts, texts, or ideas, separated from any concrete situation of social interaction, made freely abstract, is placed beyond or outside any specific social contextual limitation on its meaning" (ibid.). The process of reification among Trinidadians, however, places "culture" — as abstract concept and concrete traits or customs — not beyond any limitations of its meaning but directly within the confines of group discourse, shaped accordingly in debates over the authenticity and legitimacy of each group's religious practices. For each, "religion" both represents "culture" and denies it.

Religious discourse among Indo-Trinidadian and Afro-Trinidadian Muslims, then, fundamentally involves several constellations of associated symbols. Each of these speaks to simultaneously imagined and geographic localities, the debated sacred or secular spaces of origin and return.

According to Trinidad's 1980 census data, approximately 6 percent of the total population of 1.2 million identify themselves as Muslim, and about 15 percent of the approximately 42 percent Indo-Trinidadian population state adherence to Islam. The proportion of Muslims is not reliably disaggregated for the Afro-Trinidadian community: verbal reports vary anywhere from 1,000 or 2,000 to 10,000, depending on the source. Some Africans, as slaves or free immigrants, arrived in the New World as Muslims (Warner-Lewis 1991). An active African Muslim presence in Trinidad was evident at the turn of the nineteenth century and continued for several decades (Campbell 1974); the legacy of this presence is seen today in such place names as Mandinga Village, a small community in the southwestern part of the island. By the mid-nineteenth century, however, "an effective, vibrant Black Muslim presence in the Caribbean had disappeared" (Samaroo 1988: 6; Campbell 1974). Relations between African and Indian Muslims in the nineteenth century likely were minimized by the early geographic separation of African and Indian laborers. Moreover, the forces of creolization and Christianity were influential in shaping Africans' religious expression as they arrived in the Caribbean (Warner-Lewis 1991). This should not be taken as conclusive evidence, however, that interaction between African and Indian Muslims was necessarily nonexistent in nineteenth-century Trinidad. Far more historical research is required, both on early African Muslims in the New World and on Afro-Indo Muslim relations.

Among non-Muslims, local knowledge of Islam by far has been associated with Indo-Trinidadians.[10] This association derives from Indians consistently having been the Muslim majority in Trinidad as well as from the influence of South Asian forms of Islam historically predominating on the island. Brought by the indentured immigrants to the Caribbean, these forms were influenced by Hinduism and the Indian cultural patterns of the subcontinent, as opposed to those of the Middle East. As Brinsley Samaroo (1988: 7) remarks, "In modern-day Trinidad and Guyana, where there are substantial Muslim populations, there is much confusion, often conflict, between these two types of Islam."[11] As observers have noted (e.g., Ryan 1991; Samaroo 1988; Kasule 1986) and as is empirically evident, there are diverse expressions of Islam among both Indo-Trinidadian and Afro-Trinidadian adherents. Besides the expected differences in degree of observance among individuals, there are variations in interpretation on the part of Muslim leadership and religious organizations. These include an "orthodox" Sunni majority (primarily Indo-Trinidadian and whose national organization has state recognition), minorities of Ahmadiyya, and reformist or other Sunni bodies that have evolved locally, as well as those who have recreated in Trinidad dimensions from other Islamic traditions such as Shia (for example, those who commemorate Hosay, or Muharram).[12]

Some modes of interpretation have become "institutionalized" (Kasule 1986: 202) by the various Muslim organizations in Trinidad (if they were not already in India), each more or less representing a particular ideology of practice. While all of these factors make it difficult to treat Trinidadian Muslims in homogeneous terms, not all interpretations have equal weight. In South Asia, for example, the position of the Ahmadiyyas in the debate about orthodoxy has more sustained intensity than it does in Trinidad. This is due largely to the relatively small numbers of followers in Trinidad and their lack of islandwide influence, such as is achieved through state recognition, political office, particularly wealthy or prominent community leadership, and so on. Interestingly, because Indo-Trinidadian and Afro-Trinidadian Muslims are similarly concerned with issues about the nature and role of cultural traditions in religious observance (rather than, say, about the identity of the last prophet), their multiple discourses bring them into each other's focus as sharply, if not more so, than with those Muslims who have other, perhaps even more profound kinds of ideological or doctrinal differences.[13]

A number of international developments have significantly shaped the character of Afro-Trinidadian Islam. Along with the growth since the late 1950s of ethnically mixed Indo-Afro Muslim organizations within Trinidad and the rise since the early 1960s of an international Black Power movement and North American Islam, Afro-Trinidadian Muslims — in local parlance "returnees" (through their African roots) rather than "converts" — began gradually to increase their numbers and the force of their presence on the island. North American influences notwithstanding, another source has gained historical and symbolic significance in this florescence, and that is Africa. As one Indo-Trinidadian Muslim who is well-versed in Trinidad's history of Islam put it,

> When the African states began to achieve independence . . . the people of African origin [in Trinidad] also began to look at what was happening in the African continent. . . . "What about the African culture? Islam was the religion of the African forefathers." . . . The more people became conscious of African culture . . . they had to realize that Islam is part of Africa.

The Afro-Trinidadian Muslims with whom I spoke did not necessarily invoke Africa as a particular kind of cultural space in discussing their ideas about Islam as much as Indo-Trinidadian Muslims tended to do when referring to them. Yet Africa does figure as a symbolic point of reference in the discourse of authenticity among Afro-Trinidadian Muslims. An Afro-Trinidadian Muslim informant explained,

> The African people who came to Trinidad basically were from West Africa, and more specifically from the Mandingo and Fulani tribes. And all these people who came here were Muslims, so the African presence of Islam has been here from the inception, four hundred years ago, and not twenty years ago.

Here the significance of (West) Africa and its indigenous peoples anchors a supralocal religion to a historically profound commitment to it on the part of peoples of a specified geographic entity. The point here, as expressed by this Afro-Trinidadian Muslim, is not about (African) cultural influences on Islam but addresses both the legitimate presence of a non-Indian–influenced Islam in Trinidad and the authenticity of claim to it by Afro-Trinidadians.

Among Afro-Trinidadian Muslims, at least with reference to the largest and most active of the *jamaats,* interpretations of the nature of Islam combine with perceptions of Africans' history in the Caribbean to create a Muslim identity. That distinction is construed in terms of resistance to political and economic oppression, and as a challenge to state power and distribution of resources and opportunities. Contrasting with what they see as concessions on the part of Indo-Trinidadian Muslims' religious enervation as well as innovation, many Afro-Trinidadian Muslims view an authentic Islam as challenging the structural inequalities of the society that go against the grain of Islamic egalitarianism.[14] Afro-Trinidadian Muslims are largely from the urban "grass-roots," that is, the poor and working classes (what I call the "precarious" working class, as distinguished from the "secure" working class [Khan n.d.]).[15] Among them Islam is seen as a way toward social as well as moral and spiritual uplift. Espousing resistance to hegemonic Christianity, Euro-American colonialism, and social inequality, these Afro-Trinidadian Muslims identify the state with a set of values and priorities associated with elite interests. Somewhat ironically, given Afro-Trinidadian control over the postcolonial state and its stance (implicit or otherwise) of offering patronage to the Afro-Trinidadian population, intra-ethnic class distinctions help to hinder realization of the communal unity that the PNM called for. Afro-Trinidadian Muslims are, in part, posing a critique of a state not reliably attending to those whose claims it purported to endorse: the grass-roots Afro-Trinidadians. The state is seen as antithetical to grass-roots classes since its orchestration by particular ruling interests makes it synonymous with the injustices of market relations. These relations not only promote a distracting and corrupting materialistic preoccupation, they also foster a system of stratification where the dispossessed are economically powerless and dependent on at best insecure conditions (compare Ryan 1991: 11).

For many Afro-Trinidadian Muslims, then, practicing Islam in an authentic, noninnovative way ideally provides not merely an alternative life-style but a corrective to the class and race inequalities perpetuated by the state. Ideally, by strengthening moral fiber, the practice of Islam will strengthen the position of the community in terms of the political culture of Trinidad. For many Indo-Trinidadian Muslims, however, practicing Islam is an instructive critique whose direction is focused more toward their own communities. This is so, in part, because of the concern for proper religious practice in itself as well as because the construction of intracommunity authenticity is directly germane to ethnic groups' claims to particular identities and positioning in the larger structure of patron-clientelism. A moral imperative is aimed at shoring up "correct" (but temperate) religious practice in a "Western" environment that is inherently rife with distracting temptations as well as with an "Eastern" history of non-Islamic influences — issues equally if not more pressing than directly challenging the state. The development of inappropriate intracommunity hierarchies requires as much attention as the existence of extracommunity interethnic inequalities. The perception is that a significant reflection of the incursions of either creolizing (Afro) and Western (Euro) or Hindu influences into Islamic practice is the elaboration of hierarchies of prestige based, respectively, on the superficial (and irreligious) accomplishments of materialistic endeavors or on ascribed status.[16] As one Indo-Trinidadian Muslim informant (referred to as a "Wahabi"[17] by more "traditional" — that is, India-bound — Indo-Trinidadian Muslims) told me,

> Islam got away from the slaves in Africa. But the indentured slaves [Indians] tried to keep it, with these little functions [commemorative ritual events]. But people today keep up the functions and leave off the rest. . . . People believe in too much functions. The Koran tells us, "Do not forget the needy," and in functions you only see the strong and wealthy ones. They are the people that are the most invited in functions, some sort of recognition of high, big personalities.

The more uniform class composition of Afro-Trinidadian Muslims vis-à-vis Indo-Trinidadian Muslims is certainly a contributing factor in underscoring class inequality and social injustice in the ideology of Afro-

Trinidadian Muslims.[18] As one Afro-Trinidadian Muslim, very active in community-based social welfare programs among black, urban grass-roots communities, told me:

> For them [Indo-Trinidadians], Islam is a private thing, to keep in their bedrooms [i.e., endogamy] or in the mosque. But . . . Islam has *all* social, political, economic requirements for life, but they [Indo-Trinidadians] didn't project this. Islam was just a private thing, they just go in the mosque, in their own small group. The *arrogance* of the British and Christians and the *impunity* in which they treated those people — they never reacted to that, while *we* have reacted. We say, "No, you can't put that on us at all, we're Muslims and we're going to live like Muslims." We want full respect, dignity, what is ours. They [Indo-Trinidadians] never did that, so now the contradiction comes between us and them. . . . Also, for the most part, a lot of the people who were becoming Muslims . . . in the African community were poor people, and the East Indian Muslims had in the last twenty years accumulated a fair amount of wealth.

Evident in this commentary is the subtext of a larger conflict between Afro- and Indo-Trinidadians, couched in terms of religious purity and authenticity, as we see in his continuing narrative:

> When the African [Muslim] presence came to Trinidad, all these innovations became clarified and that began a sort of ideological friction in the community . . . a lot of ideological conflicts because the African community saw it [Islam] in other places in the world and know the Koran.

Indo-Trinidadian ideologies of Muslim identity are formed with some attention to Afro-Trinidadian Muslim discourse, and the cultural images and social assumptions it contains. One Indo-Trinidadian Muslim explained:

> The Africans in this country always feel they have been a subjected race, with a slave background. They have been searching for a different philosophical approach to life, which they seem to have seen in Islam . . . this urge to develop themselves from the iniquitous past seems to be the focal point in their interest in Islam as a way of life. Islam, in fact, advocates freedom of thought, human rights, human dignity. And Trinidad's Africans may have been attracted to this, a new release from the perception of bondage. . . . This . . . has developed among them, like in American Black Power, shades of militancy. This leaving of their past, the psychological handicap, helps distinguish them from Indian Muslims. . . . Indians were exploited, but never *slaves*.

This theme of the historical oppression of these two ethnic groups is a factor in Indo-Trinidadian Muslim orientation to the state, insofar as political lobbying and organization is accomplished largely through general claims to equal representation and opportunity. Indo-Trinidadian Muslims certainly petition the state for freedom of religious expression, such as through recognition of sacred or special periods of the calendar and resources for denominational schools. Yet the configuration of Islam is not a militant one challenging the social system of stratification per se. One Indo-Trinidadian Muslim said:

> It's the same Islam, but there's a greater militance among the Muslims of African origin. . . . The Muslims of Indian origin, born in Muslim homes, having grown up . . . , [are] taking the religion for granted . . . not practicing it to its full extent, and they are just pedaling along. Here you have [Afro-Trinidadian] people who have returned to Islam. They feel they have now caught on to truth, and they accept it, so to speak, with both hands. [They ask] . . . "Why is the world so lopsided?, Why is the society so unfair?" The majority of the people who are embracing Islam from the African community come from the lower rungs of the socioeconomic ladder.

Just as class variation exists across the wider Afro-Trinidadian and Indo-Trinidadian populations, so too it exists within the Indo-Trinidadian and Afro-Trinidadian Muslim communities. I do not want to imply that the latter are homogeneously grass-roots and the former homogeneously middle class or "secure" working class. The ratio of middle-class or "secure" working class Afro-Trinidadian Muslims to grass-roots Afro-Trinidadian Muslims, however, is significantly unequal. Although I do not have precise statistics, it is locally accepted that the numbers of grass-roots Afro-Trinidadian Muslims are disproportionately large compared to other Afro-Trinidadian Muslims, partly for reasons presented in this chapter. Class differences also transect the Indo-Trinidadian Muslim community. Different strata likely would engage the discourse of authenticity with somewhat distinct ends in mind or in a different form. But a simple class-based dichotomy does not therefore obtain: that is, like class position does not ensure like interpretations of religion and culture. Grass-roots Indo-Trinidadian Muslims, for example, do not predictably mirror all the views of grass-roots Afro-Trinidadian Muslims, owing to the mitigating factors of history, culture, and the multivalent ways that groups can create and perceive their common interests. Still, some broad patterns of distinctions are conspicuous.

The middle-class and the "secure" working-class position of many Indo-Trinidadian Muslims does not foment among them a discourse of Islam that expresses concerns with oppression and resistance to the extent that it does with many Afro-Trinidadian Muslims. It is not that Indo-Trinidadian Muslims are unaware or unconcerned with class distinctions among themselves, or unequal relations of power in the wider Indo-Trinidadian population or in the society as a whole. But for Afro-Trinidadian Muslims, Islam addresses issues of alternatives to the legacies of their historical oppression within a discourse that addresses Western colonial and postcolonial (British, North American) power as well as reflecting their African cultural majority status in Trinidad. For many Indo-Trinidadian Muslims, Islam addresses issues of constructing and asserting a distinct identity — in the face of a cultural minority's concern both with absorption or overshadowing by Afro-Trinidadians and with the genealogical and historical proximity of Hindu Trinidadian brethren.

Ethnicity, as a particular kind of defining identity, is more pronounced in a greater variety of arenas among Indo-Trinidadians, whose cultural minority status no longer has as its most forceful influence a concern with British colonial domination but with the realization of postcolonial Afro-Trinidadians' preeminence in the Trinidadian state. This has highlighted notions of Indian cultural coherence or ethnic "groupness" more so than among Afro-Trinidadians, whose cultural-ethnic claims have been directed toward an Afro-Euro counterhegemonic discourse. Their claims address a European presence and may valorize that which is (culturally, historically) African-derived rather than European-derived. Afro-Trinidadian Muslims may emphasize that which is African through the idiom of religion (i.e., Islam), but not solely as an expression of their relations as an ethnic group with Indo-Trinidadians as an ethnic group. Their quest is more for legitimacy as a religiously enlightened and empowered disenfranchised class.

As discussed earlier, although claims to ethnocultural authenticity form part of groups' identity construction and competition for state patronage in Trinidad, the particular configuration of power relations among Afro-Trinidadian and Indo-Trinidadian Muslims gives rise to the salience of class interests among many Afro-Trinidadian Muslims as they address the state and ethnic-religious interests as they engage Indo-Trinidadian Muslims. For Indo-Trinidadian Muslims, the salience of interests expressed in ethnic-religious terms is more pronounced when they address Afro-Trinidadian Muslims; class distinctions tend to be acknowledged more obliquely, in terms of hierarchy.

Hence, Islam is politically significant for both Indo- and Afro-Trinidadian Muslims, but is interpreted and becomes meaningful in distinctive ways. We might phrase this as each, Indo and Afro, being immediately (though not exclusively) concerned with different interlocutors in their relations with the postcolonial Trinidadian state: respectively, Afro-Trinidadian ethnocultural hegemony and Afro-Trinidadian bourgeois class hegemony. For many Afro-Trinidadian Muslims, Islam addresses issues of alternatives to the legacies of their historical oppression. Among Indo-Trinidadian Muslims, Islam addresses issues of constructing and asserting a particular kind of ethnic identity. For both, however, Islam is a matter of rights. Some Trinidadians posit that Indo-Trinidadian Muslims are "assimilationist" and Afro-Trinidadian Muslims are "separatist." Although there is a difference in the general political orientation of the two groups, the distinction between them, irrespective of labeling, is that each sees their interests differently, in cultural-ideological as well as material terms — terms that marshall notions of homeland and motherland in the service of identity construction and political-economic empowerment.

As local, regional, and international forces influence social and ideological changes, Muslim organizations and leadership in Trinidad have prompted in recent years an increasing awareness of and religious discourse about "correct" interpretation. Such discourse is associated with debates over authenticity of practice, the purification of Islam from customs or expressions deemed un-Islamic, and the location and significance of original lands. The religious practices of Muslims, it is felt, were couched in, if not subsumed by, the histories and traditions of these literal and metaphoric places.

At the broadest level of religious discourse among Afro-Trinidadian and Indo-Trinidadian Muslims, there exists a fairly clear dichotomy with regard to religious claims. It must be remembered that these debates are, in the strict sense of Islamic egalitarian ideology, not appropriate comparisons: all practicing Muslims are equal in the eyes of God. But within the parameters of Trinidadian ethnic and class relations, contrasts such as the following do get posed. To summarize in broad strokes: as adherents of Islam, Afro-Trinidadians can claim group legitimacy through a heritage of Islam from their African origins; Indo-Trinidadian Muslims can claim they are more legitimate insofar as they, as indentured, never "lost" their religion (as allegedly did the African slaves), and hence deserve the credit for "keeping Islam alive" in the New World. Afro-Trinidadians, as purveyors of Islam, can claim to be more authentic insofar as they putatively have an unadulterated, more pure, noninnovative form of Islam; Indo-Trinidadians can claim to be more authentic insofar as Islam is embedded in their indigenous culture.

Interestingly, legitimation by African roots does not seem to be for Afro-Trinidadian Muslims a problematic claim in terms of the issue of cultural and traditional "innovations." This may, however, be a reflection of the implicit perception that Afro-Trinidadians did not retain sufficient "culture," owing to the onslaught of slave plantation existence, to sustain their indigenous religion. In addition, the historical experience of Africa serves now as metaphor more than as actual recollection or even current representations for Afro-Trinidadians. Yet contemporary conditions enhance the symbolic role of Africa. As an Indo-Trinidadian Muslim very active in one of the mixed Afro-Indo Islamic organizations commented:

> What we want to project [to potential returnees] is a Muslim from Mother Africa. . . . So African Muslims here get a pride and firsthand information, and greater interest in Islamic faith.

The notion of indigenous culture figuring in the authenticity of Islam among Indo-Trinidadians creates a two-pronged complication. If culture is an authenticating vehicle for Indo-Trinidadians in historic terms — that is, it is part and parcel of the cultural heritage of India — in contemporary terms it is that which threatens the perpetuation of Islam through the incursions of cultural practices and traditions (notably from Hinduism), innovations of pure form that render practice at best incorrect and at worst potentially ineffectual. Therefore, within the Indo-Trinidadian Muslim community there has been and continues to be a great deal of debate about the form and content of practice. Yet India looms large in the Indo-Trinidadian worldview. Whether a place to go on pilgrimages, a holiday spot, or the "old country" of one's parents or grandparents, India is a vivid image, even if, in some contexts, a less than admirable one. For some Indo-Trinidadian Muslims, Pakistan and Mecca (though not necessarily Arabia per se) are taking the place of India as sites of heritage identification, at least in symbolic terms. Yet ethnically speaking, in an arena of ethnic group conflict, India is a difficult entity to dispense with completely, as it is the consummate Indo-Trinidadian symbol of the group's arrival, survival, and force of presence. We may see India as a cultural mooring in ethnic identity construction and Arabia as a religious locus in ethnic identity construction.[19] Given the nature of ethnic politics in Trinidad, a strict choice between one or the other gives rise to troubling existential questions.

Contrasts in the definitions of correct religious knowledge through the newly revitalized fervor on the part of returnee Afro-Trinidadian Muslims or through the longevity and constancy sustained by Indo-Trinidadian

Muslims frames a good deal of the religious discourse among Muslim groups. At the heart of this discourse is an ambivalence about the definition and place of culture in religious expression (and hence, I would reiterate, ultimately in ideas about the "nation" and national life). For example, an Indo-Trinidadian Muslim observes,

> Islam started in Africa, and they [Afro-Trinidadian Muslims] are 100 percent African, Islam is in their roots. Yet you have this separation between Indians and Africans. Our country is a kind of race business [has racial prejudice]. And it is a fact that the converted Negro Muslims are learning more than the Indians. Some of them realize [by doing so] they [are] going back to their roots.

It is partly in this "race business" that the tenor of religious discourse between Afro-Trinidadian and Indo-Trinidadian Muslims is shaped. Although racial-ethnic divisions and ideologies color most dimensions of Trinidadian social relations, only in particular contexts are they confronted as problematic issues to be probed. These contexts, or arenas of discourse, include political rhetoric, genealogical reckoning, and people's assessments of social status. Otherwise, Trinidad's "race business" is more likely to be talked *around* than directly addressed. Indirection of speech is a cultural style in this part of the world (see, for example, Brenneis 1987) that tends to diffuse pointed commentary in everyday life as well as to discourage, at least ideally, confrontational behavior.[20] Occasionally, formal conferences and programs are sponsored by Muslim organizations that specifically address issues such as racial tension in Trinidad. In talking with me about social relations, however, Trinidadian Muslims tended to emphasize the unifying and egalitarian precepts of Islam and the benefits these offer toward alleviating conflict.

Yet reaching the goals of religious axioms is complicated by the nature of daily interaction. Although both Afro-Trinidadian and Indo-Trinidadian Muslims asserted to me that they have a vital bond and a significantly better relationship than with any others embracing different faiths, group boundaries are rarely fixed and unequivocal, for a number of reasons. First, the question of group unity in Trinidad is best seen as situational, and coalescence is established and reestablished in myriad ways depending on the contexts, issues, and actors in question. Second, the contemporary florescence of Afro-Trinidadian Islam is relatively recent, only twenty to twenty-five years old. There has not been sufficient time for the establishment of a large enough community of ethnically distinct (i.e., Afro-

Trinidadian) fellow Muslims. Third, the still comparatively small number of Afro-Trinidadian Muslims does not force the issue of unambiguously defined loyalties. For example, Indo-Trinidadian Muslims can, if they wish, continue to draw the line at intermarriage without necessarily jeopardizing the fundamental canons of egalitarianism and unity advocated in Islam. As an Indo-Trinidadian Muslim explained, "The fact of having a close religious bond does not negate other cultural feelings." This informant added, "But I would expect that people who educationally have a better grasp of Islam will come to terms with an interracial marriage much more readily than people who just follow Islam traditionally."

We have seen that, for the most part, then, Indo-Trinidadian and Afro-Trinidadian Muslims address what are in part ethnic group issues through a religious idiom that is concerned with authenticity and legitimacy of practice. Among the most common practices that foment ideological divisions among Trinidadian Muslims are saying prayers over food, celebrating the Prophet's birthday and *meeraj* (ascension), singing *qaseedas* (traditional devotional songs, usually in Urdu) during rituals, and standing for the *tazeem* (praise sung for the Prophet). Although the debate over these rituals gains greatest intensity within the Indo-Trinidadian Muslim community (revealing its internal variations), the activities of the Afro-Trinidadian Muslims pose other questions about which set of interpretations will prevail as a kind of Islamic touchstone, and throw into relief the forms of interpretation among Indo-Trinidadian Muslims. There is, moreover, not a neat dichotomy between Afro-Trinidadian and Indo-Trinidadian Muslims, for these processes also stimulate the ethnically mixed *jamaats* and religious organizations that crosscut the two groups.

These issues have given rise to, among other things, three intriguing concerns. First is the contrast of traditional and/or innovative (Indian) interpretations of Islamic practice versus a nonlocalized adherence (by implication, Arabian or African). The second concern is, according to some Indo-Trinidadian Muslims, the presence of so-called Wahabi fundamentalists (who are rarely individually identified and thus remain often invisible interlocutors, against which "orthodox"-but-not-"fanatical" forms of Islam are posed), as well as a qualitative distinction made between "Muslim" and "Islam." For those who employ this distinction, "Muslim" comprises a combination of individual idiosyncrasy, the particular cultural and social context of the environment, and the level of religious awareness and practice. A Muslim in this discourse is either one whose belief and practice reflects Indian influence *or* one who is not sufficiently or at all observant and is therefore a "Muslim in name only" (a common and not complimentary refrain in Trinidad). In keeping with the distinction, one who professes Islam, on the other hand, seeks that which is purer, more literal and less cultural, more conscientious, and less Indian in form. Whether Indian-influenced or not, sincere observance renders a person a "practical Muslim" (that is, one who practices), as opposed to being one "in name only." The third concern is the debated and unequally valorized differentiation between the formal or informal acquisition of Islamic knowledge. In the discussion that follows we will see how these themes are reflected in the construction of religious, ethnic, and class identities and in notions about homeland and motherland, places of origin and return.

Addressing Afro-Trinidadian Muslims' assertions about their authenticity of claim to and legitimacy of adherence to Islam, some Indo-Trinidadian Muslims create and refine their own claims, assertions, and ideologies of Islamic identity. Others construct an Islamic identity that eschews Indian associations and is in keeping, consequently, with Afro-Trinidadian Muslims' depictions. Although Indo-Trinidadian Muslims have engaged in these debates for much of the entire 150-odd years they have been in the Caribbean, the burgeoning of the Afro-Trinidadian Muslim presence in Trinidad not only evokes visions of an African motherland but also contributes to the invocation of the authority of an Arabian homeland for Indo-Trinidadian Muslims, in contrast with India and Pakistan, which are respectively motherland and homeland for many. As we will see momentarily, however, the distinction between motherland and homeland seems to have different implications for Afro-Trinidadian and Indo-Trinidadian Muslims with respect to the place in religion of culture, tradition, heritage, or roots.

Diagnostic Emblems of Group Boundaries

Categories and dichotomies posed for analytical or descriptive purposes are rarely as neat in ethnographic reality. It is certainly accurate to generalize about Afro-Trinidadian Muslim and Indo-Trinidadian Muslim group distinctions. When we take a look at religious discourse, however, it becomes apparent that the interpretation of and tensions around notions of culture and tradition make for crosscutting allegiances between Afro-Trinidadian and Indo-Trinidadian Muslims. These, in turn, create other kinds of group boundaries — and have implications for the construction of ethnicity.

What follows are examples illustrating the foregoing discussion concerning the conceptualizations of culture and tradition in Indo-Trinidadian Muslims' religious discourse. These are deployed locally to critique stratification and hierarchy and to debate the various diagnostic emblems of a group's boundaries. Other examples might also be appropriate, but those presented here are particularly encompassing, and thus revealing. The character of these critiques and debates is a product of both transformations over time within the Indo-Trinidadian Muslim community—which are affected by transnational, regional, and local processes and developments—and the history and activities of other Muslim communities, in this case notably Afro-Trinidadian. Understanding the meaning and expression of Islam in terms of conflicting ethnic groups highlights the complex articulation between purity requisites, piety symbols, and power struggles.

The theme of historical oppression becomes prominent in Indo-Trinidadian Muslim identity because the colonial experience figures in ideological struggles with Afro-Trinidadian Muslims over the relative value of Indians' bringing a vital Islamic presence to the Caribbean and preserving it for five generations. In contrast is the theme of Africans being the original adherents of Islam in the Caribbean and, despite an initial inability to retain it, learning it anew and, hence, more correctly—what we can refer to as formal acquisition as opposed to enculturated legacy. As one Indo-Trinidadian Muslim saw it,

> The African people [in Trinidad] *accepted* Islam so they had to *learn* about it. The Indian people, who, two generations before, were illiterate, they only knew some measure of their religion. But they weren't scholars, so a lot of innovations, traditional Islam, is what they knew. They brought innovations from India that was a part of their *cultural* traditions and not the purity of Islam.

And one influential Afro-Trinidadian imam asserted that, "'traditionally, . . . certain members of the Indian community had what they viewed as a hegemony on Islam and they felt themselves threatened by the emergence of a defiant group of African Muslims who were really practising the true tenets' of the religion" (quoted in Smith 1990: 9–10). In a similar vein was the comment made to me by an Afro-Trinidadian Muslim that "the Indians felt threatened that there'd be an invasion into the privacy of their *race*-religion." This tension between so-called Islamic and so-called racial identities forms the matrix for debates about the manner of ritual observance. Put succinctly by one Indo-Trinidadian Muslim man whose leanings are toward a "purified" reforming of Indo-Trinidadian Islam,

Way back in the fifties and sixties I just thought I was Muslim, because I was *born* in a Muslim family, and that made me Muslim. The practices in my environment, though, were different from what I later read. . . . I hadn't any idea of Islam then except to go to mosque on Fridays or prayer once in a while. . . . We had in the past, and we still have, a lot of the practices that we got from our foreparents in India. We are grateful for them keeping up Islam, but people are not trying to *learn* more. They are just *listening* to what is said. They go to functions and sit but they do not educate themselves.

And another Indo-Trinidadian Muslim defined a "traditional Muslim" as

one who has followed the practice of religion which he has found in his home and in his family and who has not taken the time or who has not managed to study the religion. . . . He is merely a member of the crowd . . . and does not have any *personal, deep* conviction on the principles of the faith, which you get through being educated.

Here we can see the convergence of two streams of thought: habituated life-style versus formal study, and enculturated traditions versus purified practice.

At the heart of the distinction between the legitimacy of customary or "traditional" religious practice and tutored religious practice guided by religious authority is the high value placed on self-conscious, achieved knowledge — in essence, doing something correctly and understanding its significance, thus heightening its personal meaning and therefore its effectiveness. Indo-Trinidadian Muslims are concerned to actively seek out greater knowledge and direction in the practice of Islam. Hence their interest in visits from missionaries and other religious figures, in attending lectures and related events, and in consulting texts. To paraphrase various informants, the argument goes that when certain ways of doing things have lasted for a long time, we lose connection to the ideas that fuel them because we become complacent; the old days were an age of faith where beliefs were blind and filled with superstitious ideas which must be distinguished from more appropriate ways of thinking. In fact, forty years ago an observer commented that the early Muslim indentured immigrants from India were living in an

age of faith and, as such, their beliefs were also blind. They made no scholarly research but followed the prescribed form of ceremonials in which they had been brought up in their homeland . . . though they had woven many strange and superstitious ideas around its fundamentals, they maintained the cardinal doctrines with unadulterated purity. (Rafeeq 1954: 22)

This perspective also brings to mind scholarly theorizing about the changes over time of meaning and comprehension of rituals for participants (e.g., Tambiah 1981; Block 1974). One of the primary agendas of religious revitalization among Trinidadian Muslims (and Hindus, for that matter) is to understand the meaning of ritual practices and not be a prisoner of blind faith. Unschooled belief can result in only superficial religious blessings and enlightenment, as well as being one more unpleasant indication of the historical betrayal experienced by Indian indentured immigrants, who were "fooled" by British colonial projects.[21] The concern with correct knowledge and its comprehension resonates with local ideas about upward social mobility, achievement, modernity, and progress, but is also significantly about empowerment through clarity of purpose and precision of enactment — both of which indicate the possession of knowledge. This is why, according to the Muslim Trinidadians with whom I spoke (particularly Indo-Trinidadians), Islamic forms of worship should not be seen strictly as "rituals." Although the anthropological identification of worship practices is most succinctly labeled as "ritual," on the ethnographic level, for many Trinidadian Muslims, rituals are defined as what Hindus or Christians do; rituals are actions that are intentionally bracketed and held distinct from the wider totality of social life, and thus may obfuscate through unfamiliar or incomprehensible *simi-dimi* (hocus-pocus).[22] An informant echoes a familiar sentiment: "Ritual is when you just believe in something because someone else does and have the priest just do it for you, save you."[23] Islam, Hinduism, and most forms of Christianity in Trinidad all define themselves as "a total way of life," yet the differing perspectives on the place of ritual in daily life, as well as how to view and refer to it, speak to an underlying concern with the meaning, as much as the practice, of religious worship.

In the debate over diagnostic emblems of Islamic practice and Muslim identity, religious and ideological agendas are formulated. In the process, associations between certain Afro-Trinidadian and Indo-Trinidadian constituencies are forged. Ever-resonant in Indo-Trinidadian claims to and interpretations of "Indian" Islam are Afro-Trinidadian claims to and interpretations of "African" Islam. In addition, there is the significance "Arabian" Islam holds for all Trinidadian Muslims. Affirming the attachment of Hindus (or Muslims) to India in a sense renders more flexible any association between Islam and a particular locality. For example, two Indo-Trinidadian Muslims remarked, respectively, "In the case of Hinduism, there is a much deeper bond between Hinduism and India than between Islam and any other area. We look upon Saudi Arabia because of Mecca and

Medina, as the two holy shrines are there and that is the bond. But it [Islam] is . . . a religion of the world"; "If I want spiritual enrichment, where do I go, to see the Taj Mahal or Mecca? Hindus always try to stick to Mother India."

As Jonathan Friedman aptly notes, colonized peoples' history can free itself "from Western dominance by projecting a value system produced in the modern context onto an aboriginal past. . . . Values are projected onto the past as the essence of cultural traditions that can be brought back to life by breaking with the present" (1992: 207). Indo-Trinidadian and Afro-Trinidadian Muslims are reaching toward the authenticity of the past (e.g., by recalling the historical duration of a religious practice, or stipulating "in the time of the Prophet") for not merely alternative but oppositional values of Islam that contrast with and thereby challenge the allegedly superior and correct Western modes of thought and domination, as well as state power and activities. But these retrospective searches for values and templates are shaped by the needs, opinions, contingencies, and hindsight of the present, and, for Indo-Trinidadians, are largely directed toward proper religious practice, holding "functions," and so forth.

In their own defense, some Indo-Trinidadian Muslims contrast the profundity of their belief with that of an Arab population who, it is implied, take their religion for granted. To quote another Indo-Trinidadian Muslim:

"The Asian Muslims, unlike their Arab counter-parts, are very fervent in their Islamic belief. . . ." He goes on, however, to say that Asian Muslims "tend to *ethnicize Islam by incorporating numerous ethnic traditions which are indeed foreign to the religion and as such have created and continue to create the impression that this is an Indian affair from the sub-continent of India and Pakistan.*" (Quoted in Ryan 1991: 87–88; emphasis in original)

Yet the incorporation of "numerous ethnic traditions" is not always deemed problematic and can serve as an important part of the ideological foundation in the construction of ethnic identity, as seen in this quotation from the *Muslim News* (July 1983; cited by Ryan [1991: 100–101]):

The African will cut or "brand" his face, but that does not mean he cannot be a good Muslim. Why do they condemn the customs of the Indians? [Some] want to impose an Arab type Islam in this country. Why must the Indian Muslim follow that?

So, although "ethnic" traditions deriving from the subcontinental mother-land can be perceived as an undesirable aspect of Trinidadian Islam, Arabia as a homeland of authentic Islam is distinguished from its local inhabitants, who are, to an extent, seen as fortuitous inheritors. A place and its people are not necessarily clearly distinguished, however, and when they are, it is not always of consequence. One elderly Indo-Trinidadian Muslim asserted,

> In Arabia everybody is a qualified Muslim. . . . You are what you eat and the butchers [there] are Muslims in the right sense of the word, performing the right duties. The wrong kind of food can block your spiritual progress. The person slaughtering the meat must be a *practical* Muslim.

The predominantly Indo-Trinidadian Muslim groups are at various degrees of reinterpreting "Islamic" injunctions and "Muslim" expressions of them. For example, one reformist imam illustrates this in his comment,

> *Traditional* practices are different from the handed-down practices of the Prophet. . . . *Traditional* means practices of old. . . . But the reforms were found through *research,* like [in] the *Hadith* [traditions — recorded words and deeds — of the Prophet]. . . . We don't make *niaj* [prayers] over *sirni* [ritual sweets]. We question putting food for the dead, the dead cannot eat. . . . And this was never done in the days of the Prophet. This was brought in as a innovation from India, influence from Hindu practice, a Hindu relic.

Here, the innovations of "tradition" are not merely distracting or diluting, they are a mark of backwardness through ignorance. Yet even this issue is rife with competing stances. For example, one of the founders of the oldest Muslim organization in Trinidad (and Indian-dominated), in a critique of the dominant, state-sanctioned Muslim organization (also Indian-dominated), said of them,

> [They] go in a lot for tradition, in their garb and in certain religious practices, in the mood and manner of life generally. . . . This is very narrow. . . . In this day and age, searching for the moon before you start your fast, this is very retrograde, very backward. When it's overcast you have to go to your watch to see when it's time for *namaaz* [daily prayer]. . . . But these *mullahs* still adhere to these traditional practices. . . . We don't like to *subjugate* people so that life is [merely] working, eating, and reading. Why limit things like music and song?

Here, traditions such as music and song are clearly within the domain of the cultural (Indian) but legitimately so, rather than being that which is antithetical to proper religious practice.

Images of identity are objectified or concretized in everyday terms in a number of ways; among the more important is clothing, which has both literal (i.e., immediately recognizable) and symbolic value. Through the means of what is variously defined as "Muslim" clothing, women, and to a lesser extent men, give public demonstration of piety, which has wider implications for indicating one's morals, values, and ultimately personhood. The ethnic group to which one belongs, the *kind* of clothing one adopts, and the extent to which it is worn, however, raise larger issues of allegiances and priorities.

For example, it is not uncommon for Afro-Trinidadian Muslim women to cover their faces in public. Furthermore, Afro-Trinidadian Muslim women generally wear a *hijab* (full head covering), along with a loose, ankle-length shift. An Afro-Trinidadian Muslim noted, "As far as the *visual* presence of Islam or the *awareness* in Trinidad is concerned about Islam, I would say that to a great extent the African community has been responsible for that." In contrast, virtually no Indo-Trinidadian Muslim women cover their faces (that I am aware of, at least), which many deem "fanatical," but wear what are locally known as *shalwar* (*shalwar chemise*) or occasionally *saris*, and tend to don the *orhni* (veil) as head covering rather than *hijab*. In addition, Afro-Trinidadian Muslim women are more likely to wear their distinctive garb routinely, whereas Indo-Trinidadian Muslim women more often confine these clothes to special or religiously marked occasions, such as personal celebrations, weddings, or festivals. These various objects of clothing might be seen in their entirety as "discursive," insofar as they communicate a much larger debate that includes concern with authenticity and legitimacy: fanaticism versus orthodoxy; the cultural "purity" of Islamic traditions versus the cultural "innovations" of Indian traditions; and the suggestion of proclivities toward political conciliation and social assimilation versus a more resolute stance of alternative loyalties.

These associations are, of course, not isomorphic with a particular item of clothing. For example, in the past decade or so, a number of Indo-Trinidadian Muslim women, as a show of revitalized faith and seriousness of intention, have adopted the *hijab* in place of *orhni*, while keeping the *shalwar* and *sari*. This shift in head-covering is interesting, on one hand, insofar as it is meant to demonstrate a heightening of both purity of religious practice and piety of life-style. On the other hand, and only implicitly, it presents contrasting notions of tradition — what is seen as religious tradition as distinct from cultural tradition. Although *orhni*-wearing is alive and well in Trinidad, it signifies the epitome of Indian roots, one item of timeless womanhood, if you will; an artifact of heritage shared by both Muslims and Hindus that distinctly conveys a sense of the authentic. That older women general wear *orhnis* (when in public) also reinforces the association between the past and the present. It also poses questions, however, about contemporary relics of Hindu influence, untutored and hence less legitimate Islamic practice, or even influences from Christianity that raise bigger issues of Westernization and creolization. For example, an Indo-Trinidadian Muslim woman suggested that

> the strict African wear is closer to the Islamic concept . . . it is almost total covering. Indians have given up the Indian wear for un-Islamic Western wear. The Africans here have thrown away their Christian wear and the Indians have adopted it. This is a complete turnaround.

In her comment, Indian tradition per se is not at issue as much as the alleged loss of it for a way of life even "less Islamic" (i.e., Christian, Western) than a religiously innovative Indian way of life.

In Indo-Trinidadian Muslim critiques of Afro-Trinidadian Muslim apparel, the Arabian and the African can become conflated, and the African cultural influence ultimately elides with the Arabian-Islamic qualities that connote purity. According to one Indo-Trinidadian Muslim man,

> In terms of being practicing Muslims [Afro-Trinidadians] are no different from Indian Muslims. There is no difference in their religious persuasion. But in terms of the cultural presentation of Islam there is certainly a difference between African and Indian outlook. There are certain groups of African Muslims here which have introduced certain African culture into their wear and even in the calligraphy in which they write certain slogans and texts in Arabic. They also have introduced the African incense and oils in wide circulation among their folks, as distinct from the incense used by the Indians. . . . And women converts of certain African sects here [use] the Sudanese African wear. Their face is completely covered. While that is so [correct practice], that [it] has its root in early Arab history, it seems to be an exaggerated interpretation of the law of *purdah* that the Koran enforces. . . . This is a version of the *burqa,* the African version. . . . They have brought in their African culture into their way of life, as distinct from the Islamic faith. Just as the Indians brought in their culture. This demonstrates, in my view, not an Islamic but a *racial* identity.

Visibility in dress is not merely a statement about asserting tradition, because "tradition" can signify either innovation for many Afro-Trinidadian Muslims or backwardness and blind faith (which veers uncomfortably close to superstition) among Indo-Trinidadian Muslims. Visibility for many Afro-Trinidadian Muslims shows both desire for acquiescence to a higher (sacred) authority and resistance to an at best questionable and at worst objectionable imposed (secular) authority. Visibility for Indo-Trinidadian

Muslims is also about clothing as symbolizing depth of belief and the implications for comportment that correct attire has. But by considering their own *hijab, orhni,* or *shalwar* as sufficiently pious and correct, and, as many have it, more extensive covering as going "fanatically" overboard, they also make a statement about the contemporary appropriateness and rational nature of Islam in a modern world.

Conclusion

Rather than simply serving to create inclusive-exclusive group boundaries in the Trinidadian population, Islam is variously interpreted, expressed, and transformed among Indo-Trinidadians and Afro-Trinidadians in their everyday lives to empower other, larger arenas of struggle — an effort that is articulated with spiritual enrichment. Trinidadian Islam's emphasis on practice and its correct interpretation raises both conspicuous and slight distinctions among its adherents. Significantly located on the level of organizational structure and relations with the state as well as on the level of individual experience and community relations, this emphasis reflects local debates about the nature and role of cultural practices and historical traditions in practicing Islam. Afro-Trinidadian Muslims have an Islamic heritage of the returnee who had historical claims to Islam (African "Mandingo") but who "lost" knowledge of indigenous religion and culture through the alleged erasures of the plantation experience. Indo-Trinidadian Muslims have cultural claims on Islam through their South Asian roots and (implicitly) the relative recentness of their diaspora.

Perhaps we can characterize for some Indo-Trinidadian Muslims an ideological shift from a motherland — the undisputed place of *cultural origins* — to a homeland — the authoritative locus of *religious tradition* (read "Islamic culture") and contemporary identity. In contrast, I suggest that my distinction between motherland and homeland does not obtain in as marked a way among Afro-Trinidadian Muslims, probably because (1) their more recent and formally pedagogically instilled religious beliefs would tend to emphasize the universality, the supralocalized nature of Islam; (2) the issue of innovative cultural practices and traditions that lead to impurity of practice is presumed to be not so problematic among Afro-Trinidadian Muslims (as among Indo-Trinidadian Muslims), given the larger question of the extent of retained indigenous African culture in the New World; and (3) African Islamic culture is perceived, I think, as not that different from Arabian Islamic culture, partly through Afro-Trinidadian Muslims' conceptions of the greater purity of African Islamic practice.[24]

The often conflicting definitions of correct religious practice, authentic knowledge, or traditional influences that bestow legitimacy confound any uniform expression or consequence of Muslim identity. The questions for diaspora studies are, first of all, how and why (historically, contextually); what, if any, definitions and interpretations prevail; and, what the social and cultural consequences are of this multidimensionality. One key domain of investigation is the significance of hegemonic cultural and political-economic structures in the construction of ethnic and religious identities at the local level. Another critical area of inquiry is the ways in which the leitmotifs of authenticity and legitimacy are infused in local conceptualizations of culture or tradition, serving in part to bifurcate culture and religion conceptually into separate entities. Thereby, ideologies are created of exclusivity and distinction as well as their being avenues for unity in competitive relations of power in "frontier" contexts, where sacred space is recreated in new, alien, or contested territories. The notions of motherland as a metaphor of kinship (Malkki 1992) or origin and homeland as a metaphor of home or return both convey the idea of a natural, genealogical tie to a nation which elicits a "temporal continuity of essence and territorial rootedness" (ibid.: 27–28). In the case of Trinidadian Muslims, homeland and motherland are complex metaphors whose referents are simultaneously contemporary and ancient localities that both serve and challenge competitive and accommodative relations of power.

Acknowledgments

I am grateful foremost to my Trinidadian friends and informants who graciously took their time to share with me their knowledge of and feelings about Islam and Muslims in Trinidad. In addition, I would like to thank Vincent Crapanzano, Brinsley Samaroo, Maulana Dr. Waffie Mohammed, Peter van der Veer, Allyson Purpura, David Maynard, Kevin Yelvington, and Chandana Mathur for their comments on various drafts of this chapter. Any shortcomings are entirely my own. I would also like to thank Frank Southworth and Peter van der Veer for inviting me to participate in the University of Pennsylvania's Department of South Asia Regional Studies colloquium series, 1991–92. Finally, this chapter received invaluable editing suggestions from Silvie Khan and the copy editors at the University of Pennsylvania Press. The fieldwork on which this chapter is based was part of a larger research project funded by Fulbright, Wenner-Gren Foundation, and Sigma Xi Society grants. I undertook writing this chapter while holding an Andrew R. Silk Dissertation Award (1990–91) and a Joyce-Knight Pre-Doctoral Fellowship (1992–93).

Notes

1. This is not to imply a simplistic model of ethnic conflict — Indo versus Afro. Indo-Trinidadians' and Afro-Trinidadians' relations with each other (as well as with the rest of Trinidadian society) are complex, running the gamut from intermarriage and community cooperation to overt accusations of "racialism" — at times simultaneously. The point here is that religious ideologies are embedded within local contexts and reveal broader social tensions.

2. A common theme in Indo-Trinidadian discourse about their presence in the New World is that they were brought after emancipation by the British to save the sugar economy.

3. The notion of a "diaspora of betrayal" for the Indo-Caribbean was initially suggested to me by Vincent Crapanzano (personal communication, 1992).

4. This is my paraphrasing of Lowenthal (1985).

5. My use of the terms *homeland* and *motherland* is intended as a means to examine Indo-Trinidadian and Afro-Trinidadian Muslims' ideologies and religious discourse. Although occasionally people do make reference to the terms *homeland* and *motherland* in their discussions, they do not do so with consistency, nor necessarily with reference to the same geographical entities — India, Arabia, or Africa are not invariably correlated with either concept, which shows there is not a patterned way of thinking. My use of these terms, however, enables me to highlight issues that are significant in Trinidadian Muslims' sense of religious and cultural space.

6. From 1987 to 1989 and in 1991, largely in southern Trinidad.

7. Although no absolute measure can be established regarding "actual" changes in Trinidadian Muslim practice vis-à-vis "perceived" changes, we must not give short shrift to the forces of gradual assimilation among Indo-Trinidadians — that is, what is commonly subsumed under "creolization" (in this context, the process of incorporation within mainstream or dominant culture). These processes are extremely persuasive on a variety of levels (e.g., economically, psychologically) and certainly have played a role in the transformation of Indo-Trinidadian culture over time. Hegemony by definition is never complete, and various forms of resistance prevent any inexorable march toward incorporation. However, state sponsorship of religiocultural or aesthetic forms, for example, is not merely a unilateral provision of support; some conciliation and accommodation must be made, as well, on the part of religious and other organized bodies. Moreover, for the PNM's first thirty years, the few high-profile, upper-echelon Indo-Trinidadians in the party tended to be Mus-

lim, which also may be relevant to creolization processes among Indo-Trinidadian Muslims.

8. See Bowen's (1989) elegant distinction between historical, diacritic, and iconic discourse in the public discussion of worship among Indonesian Muslims.

9. Indeed, because my circumscribed research sample reflects the particular way I approach these issues, a full sense of the diversity of Islamic groups in Trinidad is not immediately apparent here (e.g., the University of the West Indies Islamic Society, Muslim Credit Union, Islamic Dawah Movement, Islamic Funeral Service, and so on). Moreover, common cultural and ideological positions are created in formal educational institutions such as the Muslim primary and secondary schools. Therefore, this discussion should not be seen as representative of the entirety of Islamic activities in Trinidad.

10. This likely has been modified since the July 1990 coup attempt by the *Jamaat al Muslimeen* (see, for example, Ryan 1991).

11. Most Trinidadian Muslims today follow the Hanafi school of Sunni Islam.

12. I use the phrase "recreated dimensions" with reference to Shia practices because there is not a significant number of strictly observant Shia Muslims in Trinidad. Furthermore, the majority of indentured immigrants to Trinidad were Sunni Muslims. However, Uttar Pradesh, Oudh, and Bihar, from which most Indians came to Trinidad, were regions where religious heterogeneity flourished. Hinduism and Islam were mutually influencing (though Hindus were the majority population) and both Sunni and Shia forms of Islam coexisted. The Muharram commemoration in Trinidad, or Hosay as it is called (after Hussein, one of the Prophet Muhammad's martyred grandsons), is one of the few (if not the last) large-scale reflections of Shia influence on Sunni practice in this local context. Although most Indo-Trinidadian Hosay participants are aware of its Shia origins, it is not observed as something Shia. (Indeed, Hosay reflects significant Hindu influences and, to a lesser extent, ideology from Christianity, as well as having multiethnic participation and an early history in political resistance in Trinidad [see, for example, Kale, this volume].)

13. In contrast with the Ahmadiyyas' political importance in Pakistan after partition and their publicity after being barred from making the hajj (pilgrimage to Mecca), Trinidadian Ahmadiyyas are not prominent on the island. As far as I was able to ascertain, Ahmadiyyas are more likely to be Indo-Trinidadian; there are at least two Ahmadiyya *masjids* (mosques) and their associated *jamaats,* as well as some Ahmadiyya imams (two of whom I have interviewed). Yet instead of sharing center stage, they seem to be peripheral in the eyes of other Trinidadian Muslims; however, when Ahmadiyyas from other localities visit Trinidad, there may be overt friction. One reason for this distinction is, I believe, generational (Khan n.d.). The "older head" (elder) Ahmadiyya and Sunni Indo-Trinidadian Muslims may have close kin ties with each other. These bonds can in some respects override doctrinal differences, at least in terms of everyday life and relations. It is likely that less tolerance of Ahmadiyyas would be on the part of those Muslims (Indo or Afro) who are most concerned with the traditional and the authentic in Trinidadian Islam and/or who do not have a lifetime's experience of these emotional bonds of kinship.

14. Compare, for example, Bakhash (1993) and Lewis (1991).

15. *Grass-roots* is a local Trinidadian term and is used across class and ethnic groups. For purposes of my analysis, I refine "grass-roots" into two intraclass divisions (cf. Stuempfle 1990), because it is more than merely synonymous with "working class." By "precarious" working class I mean those with access only to earned (wage or nonwage) income. By "secure" working class I mean those who have what I refer to as quiet, or potential, assets such as land and other property, or access to resources such as uninterrupted and highest quality formal education for progeny, which allows the possibility for upward class mobility.

16. For reasons of limited space I can only briefly indicate that among Indo-Trinidadian Muslims, Hindu and Christian communities are important interlocutors in identity construction (as are Islam and Christianity for Indo-Trinidadian Hindus). How Hindus and Muslims devise boundaries among each other while they have cultural and political-economic relationships is discussed elsewhere (Khan n.d.).

17. Lansine (1974) explains, "The Wahhabiyya, . . . derives from the name of Muhammad Ibn Abd-al-Wahhab, a religious leader born in AD 1703 in Ayaina in the Najd Province, Central Arabia" (1974: 3). He and his associates were concerned with the "religious and moral laxity of the Central Arabian people" (ibid.: 3), and circa 1744 they engaged in a "revivalist campaign" to return to the "purity of Islam" (ibid.: 4–5; cf. Al-Azmeh 1993: 104ff; Hodgson 1974: 152). Two Indo-Trinidadian informants defined *Wahabi:* "The Wahabis is the name applied by those who don't think of them so well to those people who follow the interpretations of a leader called Imam Abdul Wahab, who was born in Saudi Arabia"; and "Wahabi-ism [is] raised from Arabia from *Najd,* from Abdul Wahab. That is why the religion is called Wahabi-ism or Wahabis. And it is a religion [that] fall and rise up, fall and rise up [comes and goes]. In the days of the Prophet these Wahabis give the *Sunna jamaat* people a *lot* of trouble. Until they catch up with Abdul Wahab and slay him for his wickedness. This is Islamic history. . . . Wahabis are a byproduct of Islam. They are trying to *change* Islam. . . . They do everything contrary to the *Sunna jamaat.* . . . Wahabis do everything in a cut short [short cut]."

18. It should be noted, however, that in certain circumstances or contexts, Afro-Trinidadian and Indo-Trinidadian grass-roots sectors are bound by political or moral issues that both see in common.

19. Mazrui (1990) also makes an interesting distinction between the religious and the cultural, though his point differs from my own. He argues that non-Muslim Afro-Caribbeans see Islam as Indian rather than African or Arab. They are, in contrast to North American African-Americans, unlikely to see Mecca as "a spiritual port of call on the way back to the cultural womb of Africa. . . . Mecca is more likely to be perceived as a stage of cultural refuelling on the way to the Indian sub-continent" (1990: 158). In other words, he posits that for the majority black population in the Caribbean, Mecca is associated with India and/or Indian Muslims, not with Africa and/or African Muslims.

20. "Everyday life" would not include such stylized cultural-linguistic forms as the calypsonian's craft or *picong* (verbal teasing that relies partly on ridicule in a contest of one-upmanship), because although these are hallmarks of the Trinidadian

ethos, they are culturally marked as constituting specific—i.e., specialized aesthetic—kinds of expression and communication.

21. That is, they embodied a diaspora of betrayal.

22. Although Hindus are also concerned with the issue of superstition and correctly understanding the meaning and significance of their own worship practices, they do not have similar debates over identifying these as rituals. Rituals, for them, are sites with the "intrinsic symbolic richness" (Bowen 1989: 615) of heritage and meaning that authenticate the Hindu way—the *sanatan dharm*—and legitimate as well as territorially map out the Hindu community. Hence, the importance of ritual and "keeping up ritual" is emphasized by pandits and other religious leadership. I should add that "hocus-pocus" is my translation of *simi-dimi*, a definition interpreted from fieldwork rather than that given by informants.

23. He is using *priest* in a generic sense to mean religious leader, not to indicate Christianity per se.

24. The complexity of these issues for Muslims outside of Trinidad, however, was thoughtfully remarked on by an Afro-Trinidadian Muslim informant: "That problem doesn't only exist in Trinidad. That problem exists in West Africa, too, where young Muslims are learning Islam and are coming up against old, old traditions. I mean, Islam has been in Africa since the eighth century and people have sat *down* on Islam, and a lot of traditions have grown over it. Many young people are trying to cut across the traditional underbrush and are having the same kind of problems."

References

Al-Azmeh, Aziz
    1993   *Islam and Modernities*. London: Verso.
Anderson, Benedict
    1983   *Imagined Communities*. London: Verso.
Appadurai, Arjun
    1990   "Disjuncture and Difference in the Global Cultural Economy." *Public Culture* 2, 2: 1–24.
Asad, Talal
    1986   "The Idea for an Anthropology of Islam." Occasional Paper Series, Center for Contemporary Arab Studies. Georgetown University (March).
Bakhash, Shaul
    1993   "Intimate Enemies." *New York Review of Books*, October 7: 43–45.
Bloch, Maurice
    1974   "Symbols, Song, Dance, and Features of Articulation: Is Religion an Extreme Form of Traditional Authority?" *European Journal of Sociology* 15: 55–81.
Bowen, John
    1989   "*Salat* in Indonesia: The Social Meanings of an Islamic Ritual." *Man* (n.s.) 24, 4: 600–619.

Breckenridge, Carol, and Arjun Appadurai
   1989   "On Moving Targets." *Public Culture* 2, 1: i–iv.
Brenneis, Donald
   1987   "Talk and Transformation." *Man* (n.s.) 22, 3: 499–510.
Brereton, Bridget
   1979   *Race Relations in Colonial Trinidad, 1870–1900*. Cambridge: Cambridge
           University Press.
Campbell, Carl
   1974   "Jonas Mohamed Bath and the Free Mandingos in Trinidad: The
           Question of Their Repatriation to Africa 1831–1838." *Pan African
           Journal* 7, 2: 129–52.
Cohen, Anthony
   1985   *The Symbolic Construction of Community*. New York: Tavistock.
Eickelman, Dale
   1984   "The Study of Islam in Local Contexts." *Contributions to Asian Studies*
           17: 1–16.
Friedman, Jonathan
   1992   "Myth, History, and Political Identity." *Cultural Anthropology* 7, 2: 194–
           210.
Gupta, Akhil, and James Ferguson
   1992   "Beyond 'Culture': Space, Identity, and the Politics of Difference."
           Cultural Anthropology 7, 1: 6–23
Hannerz, Ulf
   1987   "The World in Creolization." *Africa* 57, 4: 346–59.
Hobsbawm, Eric, and Terence Ranger, eds.
   1983   *The Invention of Tradition*. New York: Cambridge University Press.
Hodgson, Marshall G. S.
   1974   *The Venture of Islam, Vol. 1: The Classical Age of Islam*. Chicago: Univer-
           sity of Chicago Press.
Kapferer, Bruce
   1988   *Legends of People, Myths of State: Violence, Intolerance, and Political Cul-
           ture in Sri Lanka and Australia*. Washington, D.C.: Smithsonian In-
           stitution Press.
Karch, Cecilia
   1985   "Class Formation and Class and Race Relations in the West Indies." In
           Dale L. Johnson, ed., *Middle Classes in Dependent Countries*. Beverly
           Hills, Calif.: Sage, 107–36.
Kasule, Omar Hassan
   1986   "Muslims in Trinidad and Tobago." *Journal: Institute of Muslim Minor-
           ity Affairs* 7, 1: 195–213.
Khan, Aisha
   n.d.   Tradition, Piety, and Power in Diaspora: Ethnic Identity among Mus-
            lim and Hindu Indians in Trinidad. Ph.D. dissertation, City University
            of New York Graduate School. Forthcoming.
   1994   "*Juthaa* in Trinidad: Food, Pollution, and Hierarchy in a Caribbean
           Diaspora Community." *American Ethnologist* 21, 2: 245–69.

Lansine, Kaba
    1974   *The Wahabiyya: Islamic Reform and Politics in French West Africa.* Evanston, Ill.: Northwestern University Press.
Lewis, Bernard
    1991   *Islam and the West.* New York: Oxford University Press.
Lewis, Gordon
    1983   *Main Currents in Caribbean Thought.* Baltimore: Johns Hopkins University Press.
Lowenthal, David
    1985   *The Past Is a Foreign Country.* New York: Cambridge University Press.
Malkki, Liisa
    1992   "National Geographic: The Rooting of Peoples and the Territorialization of National Identity Among Scholars and Refugees." *Cultural Anthropology* 7, 1: 24–44.
Mazrui, Ali
    1990   "Religious Alternatives in the Black Diaspora: From Malcolm X to the Rastafari." *Caribbean Affairs* 3, 1: 157–60.
Price, Richard
    1985   "An Absence of Ruins? Seeking Caribbean Historical Consciousness." *Caribbean Review* 14: 24–29, 45.
Rafeeq, Muhammed
    1954   "History of Islam and the Muslims in Trinidad." *The Islamic Review* (September): 22–24.
Ryan, Selwyn
    1991   *The Muslimeen Grab for Power: Religion, Race, and Revolution in Trinidad.* Port of Spain: Inprint Publications.
Samaroo, Brinsley
    1988   "Early African and East Indian Muslims in Trinidad and Tobago." Paper presented at the Centre for Caribbean Studies, University of Warwick, Coventry, England.
Scott, David
    1991   "That Event, This Memory: Notes on the Anthropology of African Diasporas in the New World." *Diaspora* 1, 3: 261–84.
Segal, Daniel
    1993   "'Race' and 'Colour' in Pre-Independence Trinidad and Tobago." In Kevin Yelvington, ed., *Trinidad Ethnicity.* London: Macmillan; Knoxville: University of Tennessee Press, 81–115.
Smith, Keith
    1990   "Conversations with the Imam." In The Daily Express, ed., *Trinidad under Seige: The Muslimeen Uprising. 6 Days of Terror.* Port of Spain: Trinidad Express Newspapers Ltd., 8–10.
Stone, Carl
    1980   *Democracy and Clientelism in Jamaica.* New Brunswick, N.J.: Transaction Books.
Stuempfle, Stephen
    1990   "The Steelband Movement in Trinidad and Tobago: Music, Politics,

and National Identity in a New World Society." Ph.D. dissertation, University of Pennsylvania.

Tambiah, Stanley
    1985   "A Performative Approach to Ritual." In Stanley J. Tambiah, *Culture, Thought and Social Action.* Cambridge, Mass.: Harvard University Press, 123–66.

Trouillot, Michel-Rolph
    1992   "The Caribbean Region: An Open Frontier in Anthropological Theory." *Annual Review of Anthropology* 21: 19–42.

van der Veer, Peter, and Steven Vertovec
    1991   "Brahmanism Abroad: On Caribbean Hinduism as an Ethnic Religion." *Ethnology* 30, 2: 149–66.

Warner-Lewis, Maureen
    1991   *Guinea's Other Suns: The African Dynamic in Trinidad Culture.* Dover, Mass.: The Majority Press.

Williams, Brackette
    1989   "A Class Act: Anthropology and the Race to Nation Across Ethnic Terrain." *Annual Review of Anthropology* 18: 401–44.
    1990   "Nationalism, Traditionalism, and the Problem of Cultural Inauthenticity." In Richard Fox, ed., *Nationalist Ideologies and the Production of Cultures.* Washington, D.C.: American Anthropological Association, 112–29.
    1991   *Stains on My Name, War in My Veins: Guyana and the Politics of Cultural Struggle.* Durham, N.C.: Duke University Press.

Wood, Donald
    1968   *Trinidad in Transition: The Years after Slavery.* London: Oxford University Press.

5. Hindus in Trinidad and Britain: Ethnic Religion, Reification, and the Politics of Public Space

It is now widely accepted that "Hinduism" is a rather spurious category, constructed over the past 150 or so years by orientalist scholars and Indian leaders alike (see, for instance, W. C. Smith 1964; Frykenberg 1989; Hardy 1990). It follows that descriptions of the nature and breadth of phenomena to which "Hinduism" refers have been open to interpretation and change among foreign and indigenous subcontinental academics, and among Indian sages, nationalists, and communalists. For members of these latter categories, whose formulations amount to ideologies often having considerable potential for social and political mobilization (witness the Hindu Mahasabha, Rashtriya Swayamsevak Sangh, and Vishva Hindu Parishad), the constructed concepts, meanings, and uses surrounding "Hinduism" are especially prone to historical and contextual conditioning (Thapar 1989; Freitag 1989; van der Veer n.d.). It is not surprising, then, that within Indian communities outside of India, quite different contextual variables should also affect concepts, meanings, and uses of the term.

This chapter examines the development of "Hinduism" within two overseas Indian populations, in Trinidad and Tobago (henceforth Trinidad, especially as the latter island has negligible numbers of Hindus) and in Great Britain (henceforth Britain). Although there is no overwhelming difference in the actual size of the Hindu populations in question — Trinidad Hindus number around 265,000 (which is 63 percent of the country's Indian population, or 25 percent of the national total of 1.2 million), whereas in Britain there are some 387,360 Hindus (30 percent of all Asians, 0.6 percent of the total population of over 54 million) — several factors have effected contrasting trajectories of development in the two. In each case the focus here is on (1) the background and nature of Hindus' general place within an encompassing, evolving social structure, (2) how that place and structure have affected Hindus' engagement with what can be called "public space" (generally meant here as a sociopolitical arena of interaction and discourse historically varying in source and range as well as content), and (3) how all of these elements have conditioned the meaning of "Hinduism" — its formulation and place in ethnic consciousness, organization, and mobilization — by way of processes involving the reification of religious and cultural traits.

Hindus in Trinidad

The history of Hindus in Trinidad, spanning nearly 150 years, can be characterized by four successive stages of social and cultural development (Vertovec 1989, 1990b, 1992a). The first refers to the period of migration and settlement, when a heterogeneous population of individuals effectively constructed a new culture of everyday life in an alien environment. Next there occurred a period of increasing religious institutionalization, mainly due to intracommunal rivalries. The years surrounding decolonization and independence can be seen to represent a third, key stage, during which Hindu communal aspirations crystallized in party politics. The fourth stage broadly refers to the period from independence to the present, a time all the while marked by African (also locally called "Creole") political and cultural hegemony, during which the salience of Hindu ethnicity initially attenuated and then was rapidly revitalized. In each stage a different level or kind of public space was engaged by Trinidad Hindus.

MIGRATION AND SETTLEMENT
Following the abolition of slavery in the 1830s, administrators of Trinidad's colonial plantation economy sought a cheap, controllable labor force to replace the newly freed Africans (who the plantocracy quickly had come to disfavor when these ex-slaves became wage laborers). After relative success in Mauritius and British Guiana, a new system of importing indentured labor from India was introduced to Trinidad in 1845. The system was based around five-year contracts for the supply of agricultural labor in return for passage and maintenance in the colony. This satisfied the planters' economic needs while it provided opportunities, of a kind, to Indians predominantly from the impoverished rural countryside. Indentured migration lasted until 1917, by which time over 143,000 Indians — some 85 percent of whom were Hindus, mostly from what is now Bihar and Uttar Pradesh — came to Trinidad.

Initially, the Hindu population of Trinidad was characterized by great diversity in terms of language, regional custom, caste, and religious tradition. This was because the immigrants had been taken as individuals from across a large area of India, which itself was characterized by significant linguistic, economic, political, sociocultural, and religious differences between regions, districts, towns, and villages. In Trinidad the migrants were thrust together on the same plantation estates where, in addition to their difficult labor, they had to negotiate among themselves — both consciously and inadvertently — new, common forms of social, cultural, and religious practice.

This process of constructing new forms of practice continued, and probably accelerated, after the Indians finished their indenture contracts and settled in their own villages on the edge of the plantation sphere. By the end of the nineteenth century, most Indians in Trinidad were living in their own settlements rather than on estates, having opted to stay in the colony where land and work were readily available rather than return to the dire economic conditions from whence they came in India. In the nascent Indian villages of turn-of-the-century Trinidad, a common, creolized Bhojpuri came to function as an Indian lingua franca (while a creolized English had been adopted for interaction with whites and Creoles). Caste-based identities and systems of interaction or exchange were largely inoperative owing, among other reasons, to the fact that the corporate statuses, roles, and relationships that had held locally specific meanings in India could not be effectively recreated among migrants drawn from geographically sporadic caste origins. This was especially so in such a radically different context — an island, plantation colony with large, distinct, and stratified ethnic segments — where caste status consequently bore no implications for occupation, social mobility, or resource control (see Schwartz 1967; Jayawardena 1971; Vertovec 1992a: 25–50).

As common features of speech, modes of behavior, patterns of social interaction, aesthetics, and other related forms of everyday culture took shape among Indians in Trinidad, Brahman priests — who maintained their ritual status among Hindus because they were deemed repositories of sacred knowledge — formulated and propagated a virtually casteless, "lowest common denominator" Hindu tradition which catered to the religious needs of a diverse community (Vertovec 1989, 1992a; van der Veer and Vertovec 1991). Such a tradition, for the most part, took shape in homes or at village shrines (*kutis* or *shivalas*) through rites conducted on behalf of a kin group or settlement cluster by a nearby resident Brahman (who simultaneously served as individual guru or religious teacher, family priest, and ritual practitioner at the shrine). This process was occurring throughout Trinidad, taking place in a parallel manner at numerous settlements on the island. In the sense, then, that "Hinduism" was being constructed in a public space, we must describe that space—or better, those numerous parallel spaces—as very limited or small, each circumscribed by an immediate physical vicinity, engaged by a local Hindu group, and dominated by a central religious figure.

INSTITUTIONALIZATION

By the 1920s, the locally practiced tradition of Hinduism that emerged in Trinidad Indian settlements was taking institutional shape by way of the establishment of local organizations in larger villages and rural towns. In the late 1920s and through the 1930s it became nationally institutionalized as orthodoxy, largely through Brahmanic reaction to the mission work of the Arya Samaj.

Originally established in the Punjab in 1875, the Arya Samaj came to have pervasive impact throughout north India and in most overseas Hindu communities. The movement called for a Hinduism based solely on monotheistic Vedic principles, thereby rejecting all Brahman-controlled, idol-focused ritual propitiating a pantheon of gods and goddesses—that is, rejecting all the fundamental features of the Hinduism that had taken shape in Trinidad. The vehemence and eloquence of the Arya Samaji missionaries from India, who spoke throughout the island, sparked much controversy within Trinidad's Hindu population during the 1920s and 1930s. In response to doubts raised among Hindus all over the country and in opposition to the Arya Samaj (and unfortunately, to each other), two national Hindu organizations were established in 1932, each intent to standardize and bolster the "mainstream" tradition, increasingly called *Sanatan Dharma*.

Both organizations were formed with a view toward all Trinidad Hindus. Among its goals, the Sanatan Dharma Association sought "to propagate Hinduism, teach the tenets of Hindu Dharma and establish branches in various centres in the colony," "to establish Mardassars [schools]," "to settle disputes among Hindus," and "to seek religious rights from the Government" (in Kirpalani et al. 1945: 61). The Sanatan Dharma Board of Control stated, "The registration of this society is regarded by the Hindu community as being an important step in the direction of the unification of Hindu interests under purely Hindu control" (in Forbes 1984: 60). Priests and laypeople throughout the country affiliated themselves with one or the other organization (the latter had branches in thirty-two towns and villages by the late 1930s). Through these bodies Brahmans formally consulted one another on matters of orthopraxy, and large-scale religious events were organized, advertised, and undertaken. In the early 1950s these organizations merged to form the Sanatan Dharma Maha Sabha, which rapidly built dozens of Hindu schools, affiliated almost all of the Hindu temples throughout the island, and produced prayer books and a catechism declaring a singular Hindu "Creed." With such increasingly effective institutionalization, the public space for the ongoing construction of Hinduism had shifted from wholly local communities to that of the entire, islandwide Hindu population.

HINDU PARTY POLITICS

By the 1930s and through the postwar years in Trinidad, Indians in general had the lowest incomes, least education, poorest representation in civil services, and worst chances of upward socioeconomic mobility; Hindus, in particular, were relegated to the absolute lowest position in the society's status hierarchy (Crowley 1957). It is with these characteristics in mind that one must begin to understand the launch, in 1953, of the People's Democratic Party (PDP, later called the Democratic Labour Party, or DLP). The party was founded by the same man, Bhadase Sagan Maraj, who had united the two preexisting, rival Hindu associations to create the Maha Sabha. Subsequently, the Maha Sabha and PDP-DLP virtually functioned as one, in that Maraj headed both and many of the executive officers performed roles in each. Also, at religious gatherings, Brahman priests propounded overtly political messages on behalf of the PDP-DLP and against the African-dominated party. In other words, soon after its founding, the party "became widely recognized as the political arm of the orthodox Hindu community" in Trinidad (Ryan 1972: 139). In order to appreciate further the reasons and meanings surrounding this important development—a leap, as it were, into a public space of quite a different kind — we must assess a set of wider structural attributes characterizing Trinidad up to that time.

Until the 1950s, doubtless the most significant and encompassing structural feature affecting Trinidad was colonialism. From the time Trinidad was seized from the Spanish by the British in 1797, it was administered wholly for the purposes of plantation production serving the empire. By the latter half of the nineteenth century, migrations of various kinds gave rise to the presence, in the same small, island-bound society, of French, Spanish,

English, African, Asian Indian, miscegenational descendants of Amerinds, Chinese, Portuguese, Madeirans, European Jews, and a population mixed from all of these strains. Each of these population segments, who were often also geographically concentrated in specific parts of the island, generally came to play special roles and have particular statuses within the colonial plantation society. Thus for much of its history, Trinidad exhibited classic traits of what has been called a colonial "plural society."

In the sense employed here, description of the colonial plural society as a kind of Weberian ideal type was first put forward by J. S. Furnivall (1939, 1948) and later elaborated by M. G. Smith (1965, 1969, 1974; it has also been discussed and criticized by numerous writers, among them Morris 1967; Despres 1968; van den Berghe 1973). Such societies were said to be characterized by several population segments living in "economic symbiosis and mutual avoidance" (M. G. Smith 1965: vii). In these societies comprised of sharply demarcated, institutionally differentiated, and closed social units, Furnivall observed, "each group holds by its own religion, its own culture and language, its own ideas and ways. As individuals they meet, but only in the market place, in buying and selling" (1948: 304). In addition to living separately side-by-side yet with economic interdependence, the segments were said to exist in a single polity where "the union is not voluntary but is imposed by the colonial power and by force of economic circumstance" (ibid.: 307). Further, the segments involved "usually overlapping cleavages of race, culture, class, and authority" (Ley, Peach, and Clarke 1984: 2), as well as "exclusive asymmetrical relationships that such cleavages entail" (M. G. Smith 1974: 210). Together, then, the segments — often coterminous with race, culture, class, geography, and economic activity — formed a highly stratified social structure, with the colonial bureaucracy serving as an instrument of domination by a single segment.

Resistance to colonial domination emerged in many plural society contexts. Within such contexts, Percy Hintzen explains, "In their efforts at mobilization, the aspirations of indigenous political leaders are best served if they are able to exploit patterns of social organization that make sense within the existing context and that relate to the reality of the colonial social structure" (1989: 5).

Initially, an ideology of nationalism directed against the colonizer becomes a powerful mobilizing idiom. Yet when the colonizer eventually becomes committed to the transfer of control of the state to local politicians, the ideology of nationalism can lose much of its mobilizing force.

Leaders, therefore, are forced to look for new organizing idioms. In addressing "the reality of the colonial social structure," the aforementioned coterminous segments become the next focus for political mobilization. Thus, "an appeal by leaders to segmental loyalty can prove dramatically successful since such loyalty is usually reinforced by socio-economic factors. As a result, political ethnicity can become the basis of mass mobilization. The most successful political leaders are typically those who are able to 'define the situation' in communal terms" (ibid.: 6).

   In this way, "political ethnicity becomes particularly important when the issue of colonial control is resolved and when the country is in the tutelary phase prior to independence" (ibid.). All of these features — plural society structures and nationalist to ethnic idioms during a period of decolonization — represent Trinidad up to the 1950s. From the nineteenth century through the 1930s, ethnicity (in this case, again, a combination of race, culture, and class compounded by residential and occupational differentiation) played little part in the public space of state control and its contestation under British colonialism. Indeed, in the late 1930s, inter-ethnic solidarity occupied such incipient political public space that some of the first instances of large-scale mobilization against the reigning power took the form of massive strikes uniting the separate African- and Indian-dominated trade unions (Cross 1978, 1988). Yet in the 1940s, as elsewhere throughout the empire, Britain set processes in motion toward the decolonization of Trinidad. From that time on,

> The democratization of electoral participation and the commitment by Britain to transfer control of the state apparatus to local political leaders led to intense internal political competition. The turning inward of the political campaign brought with it the need for a new mobilizing "idiom" as the issue shifted from colonial domination to competition for state control. (Hintzen 1989: 38–39)

Political ethnicity arose. At first it was not very pronounced, with only minimal ethnic rhetoric and voting patterns evident in the elections of 1946 (LaGuerre 1972). By the early to mid-1950s, however, this came into full force in campaigns pitting the rural, Hindu-dominated PDP-DLP against the urban, African-dominated People's National Movement, or PNM (Ryan 1972). Numerous writers on Trinidad's political history focus on the purely racial conflict this political combat entailed, but the ethnic idioms employed often went beyond this. Though indeed wishing to represent all Indians in Trinidad, especially the working class (Maraj was, not coincidentally, president of the Federation of Unions of Sugar Workers

and Farmers), the PDP-DLP was foremost a *Hindu* party: Brahman dominated, interchangeable with the Maha Sabha in personnel and organization, using a host of religiously evocative symbols to stir its constituency
(such as claims that the sacred status of the *Ramayana* would be threatened
by African political power). The leader of the PNM, Eric Williams, in fact
pointed to this wholly Hindu orientation and Brahmanic domination, and
consequently won many if not most Christian and Muslim Indians to the
PNM (Vasil 1984: 309–12).

In the course of decolonization, through which the dominating social
segment in Trinidad retreated from its bureaucratic control, a new, political
public space opened where the remaining social segments came to compete
for control. Hindus, being a segment that was one of the largest, most
distinct (in culture and religion, geographic concentration, occupation,
and class), and well-organized — with a headstrong and outspoken leader in
Maraj, it must be added — engaged this public space with the intent of
securing a variety of communal interests. In so doing, Hinduism in Trinidad became an ethnic and political ideology.

POSTCOLONIAL COMPETITION
Hindus in Trinidad were generally unsuccessful in their bid for political
power. The African-dominated PNM won the elections of 1956 and maintained practically total control of national politics through independence in
1962 and up until 1986. Many inherent structures of the colonial plural
society remained intact (distinct, coterminous segments living in economic
symbiosis and mutual avoidance, asymmetrical relationships facilitating the
domination of one segment in a single polity). The main aspect that
changed was, of course, the dominating group. The resulting context has
been likened by Malcolm Cross to a kind of internal colonialism which,
"like its external variant, is a condition of structural and entrenched power
differentials. The African groups were inevitably better placed to adopt a
central role. They had the education, the occupational skills and the advantage of cultural proximity to the retreating colonisers" (1978: 49, drawing
upon Hechter 1975). "Subsequently," Cross adds, "heightened ethnic attachment took place at the periphery [that is, among Indians — Hindus in
particular] and, over time, the strength of Creole ethnicity at the core
declined as the 'normal' situation became defined in terms of Creole domination" (ibid.: 56).

The core and periphery to which Cross refers relate directly to the
notions of public space employed in this chapter. With the PNM dominat-

ing national politics, Creole cultural phenomena quickly occupied the public space of media and large-scale events, and assumed life-style and national symbols such that, as suggested earlier, they became Trinidad's "norm."[1] This fourth, and still current, phase in the development of Hinduism in Trinidad, then, is one in which Hindus — having failed in the bid for political power during decolonization — have had to engage a postcolonial public space largely characterized by African-Creole cultural hegemony.

Through the 1960s, riding on the elated wave of independence, the PNM became further entrenched, and Creole culture predominated. In this period, most informants attest, Hindu ethnic sentiments flagged. The DLP gradually became less and less effective as a party of opposition (see Malik 1966), and finally by the beginning of the 1970s, the failures of the party in the face of the PNM's power "virtually finished off East Indians as a political factor in Trinidad, at least for many years" (Tinker 1977: 82). The Maha Sabha, meanwhile, had lost much respect among Hindus because of allegations of corruption and misrepresentation. Further, a deluge of Christian evangelists from the United States came to Trinidad in the mid-1960s, many of whom singled out Hindus (as "heathen idolaters") for criticism and conversion; the fact that many Hindus did actually convert tended to sap further the collective morale of the community. And in 1970, the Black Power movement briefly exploded into the public space, causing a great upheaval in Trinidad (in fact, leading to the declaration of a state of emergency). Though some young Indian intellectuals took up its cause, the general Hindu populace — under the still combative rhetoric of Bhadase Maraj — saw the movement as a serious threat to communal well-being, although by this time there was little they could do about it.

The 1970s, however, brought about a remarkable change in the trajectory of Hindus and Hinduism in Trinidad. At the start of the decade, Hindus were still the population segment with the poorest socioeconomic traits in the country, were excluded from political power, and were culturally pushed to the periphery of public space. Yet during the 1970s, the entire society was transformed by an oil boom initiated on a global scale by price hikes from the Organization of Petroleum Exporting Countries and the ensuing world oil crisis. In the course of a few short years, the small country of Trinidad received a massive financial injection (Vertovec 1990a, 1992a). The PNM used much of the nation's newfound wealth to initiate programs to expand its system of patronage directed at its African working-class clientele, as well as to increase its influence over the middle and upper classes of all segments (Hintzen 1989). This government strategy, which included a conspicuous neglect of the Indian-dominated agricultural sector, infuriated the mostly Hindu rural working class. Yet despite this, through a number of Indian-controlled spin-off industries (especially construction and transport) and contemporary price hikes in the sugar industry, rural Indians, too, suddenly began to receive large paychecks.

By the late 1970s and early 1980s, much of the wealth among Hindus was being poured into newly elaborated forms of religious ritual (Vertovec 1991, 1992a). Domestic, villagewide, and national rituals and religious events proliferated, as did a range of Hindu organizations, many formed by energetic Hindu youths (Vertovec 1990b). A self-proclaimed Hindu renaissance was under way in Trinidad, bankrolled by the oil boom. At first, like the original processes undertaken by the early migrants, this reconstruction of Hinduism took place in the public space of local Hindu communities: homes, settlement clusters, villages. Eventually it came to engage the national, Creole-dominated public space when some of the new youth organizations began to publish newspapers and journals castigating aspects of Creole culture, and to organize rallies calling for "equal time" for Hinduism and Indian culture in the national media (ibid.). By the late 1980s, Hinduism was put forward into the public space as an ethnic communal ideology in bold and conscious contradistinction to the hegemonic Creole norm.

In this way the kind of public space in which Trinidad Hindus exercised their collective identity, as well as the kind of Hinduism with which Trinidad Hindus identified themselves, codeveloped in light of a variety of changing contextual factors. In Britain, too, this general statement pertains, although in light of entirely different spaces, collectivities, identities, and contexts.

Hindus in Britain

The migration of South Asians in the 1950s and early 1960s — essentially to fill a gap in expanding, postwar British industry by providing cheap labor in the least desired jobs — was one almost wholly undertaken by men between twenty and forty years of age. Systems of recruitment and patterns of chain migration led to the establishment of, in various locations throughout Britain, pockets of men largely from the same kinship groups, villages, districts or regions of India. Parts of Gujarat and the Punjab, both regions with long-standing traditions of migration, became the prime source locations for migrants to Britain. The main strategy of most migrants was to work and save money for a few years before returning home to the subcontinent. With increasingly restrictive (and racially politicized) immigration legislation during the 1960s, however, the number of those allowed entry was greatly curtailed, and original intentions of many who had come to Britain changed to a longer-term orientation. By the late 1960s and early 1970s, wives and dependents of the men migrated; contrasting ecological and cultural variables among certain regional and religious groups, however, led to different patterns and periods of South Asian family reunion in Britain (Ballard 1990).

While families from the subcontinent were being reunited in Britain, there was an increasing movement of South Asians from territories in East Africa (Kenya, Uganda, Tanzania, Zambia, Malawi). Though South Asians had conducted trade along the East African coast for centuries, it was only in the nineteenth century that large, settled communities of South Asians were established there. These were comprised largely of entrepreneurs from parts of what is now the state of Gujarat, plus some ex-indentured laborers from Punjab (brought especially to build the Mombasa-Lake Victoria railway) and artisans from both regions of India. As the 1960s progressed, postcolonial East African governments promoted various "africanization" policies calling for the commercial and professional sectors of each state to be exclusively in the hands of indigenous black Africans. For the East African Asians, life became increasingly unpleasant; therefore, holding British passports, great numbers came to Britain in the late 1960s. In 1972, the wholesale expulsion of Asians from Uganda sent tens of thousands en masse to Britain.

It is important to underscore the geographical variance of British Hindu origins, for provenance has played a fundamental role in determining patterns of postmigration settlement, social institutions, religious practices, and identity formation. And with regard to such developments, distinctions of provenance are by no means limited to general regions (such as Punjab, Gujarat, or East Africa), but extend to particular provinces and districts, even towns and villages therein. This is so because each level of provenance can be associated with salient differences of language and dialect, socioeconomic bases, caste composition, kinship and domestic structures, and religious tradition.

On perhaps the most obvious, broad level, distinctions between Punjabis and Gujaratis are marked. In addition to major language differences (the former speaking Panjabi, Hindi, and some Urdu, the latter speaking

Gujarati and Hindi), there are overt and subtle social and cultural differences (linked to unique physical and human geographies, political and economic histories). Most British Punjabis are from the adjacent areas of Jullundur and Ludhiana — thereby sharing much in terms of geographic, economic, sociocultural, and political heritage — yet their composition includes various caste groups (including Jats, Khatris, Brahmans, Chuhras, and Chamars). The overall salience of caste distinctions among Punjabis in Britain, and in India itself, however, is arguably less marked than those associated with other regional social structures (Sharma 1969; Vertovec 1992b).

Among British Gujaratis, in contrast, there are many significant levels or spheres of differentiation. Most generally, distinct regions of origin within the modern state of Gujarat are associated in Britain with distinct cultural characteristics and, thereby, with separate social groups. British Gujaratis hail from parts of Surat and Charottar (Kaira) on the mainland, and from Saurashtra (Kathiawar) and Kutch further west. Linked to a large extent with linguistic traits (given over twenty varieties of Gujarati language), there is often considerable social differentiation among Gujaratis, such as that between Kathiawaris and Surtis and between Kutchis and mainland Gujaratis (see Knott n.d.). Kutchis, for example, purposefully utilize their language "to distinguish themselves as a category apart from other Gujarati groups" (Barot 1981: 124).

Also among British Gujaratis there exist important characteristics and developments with regard to East Africans vis-à-vis Indians. One consequential source of difference arose through the migration process itself. As mentioned, the original Indian migrants came as individual, usually young males, who only at a later stage were joined by their wives and children; the East Africans, who were essentially refugees, arrived as complete multigenerational family units.

With regard to these social identities, too, stereotypes among and between the groups persist. East Africans are usually associated with higher educational and occupational backgrounds than Indians — subsequently equated with greater status and wealth — and their supposed longer and deeper acquaintance with the English language and with urban, middle-class European (albeit colonial) life-styles has connoted a better preparation for successful living in Britain. Recent surveys indicate real differences in educational and occupational levels (Jones 1993), and among British Asians such traits contribute to common stereotypes, which determine much by way of attitudes and social formations.

Gujarat is well known in the subcontinent for the number, complexity, and distinctiveness of caste and subcaste groups, and the same can be said for Gujarati caste phenomena in Britain. Maureen Michaelson (1983) notes the presence of at least thirty distinct Gujarati castes in Britain, each with a specific provenance in India. These prominently include Patidars from Surat and Charottar, Lohanas and Visa Halari Oshwalis from Kathiawar, Bhattias and Leva Kanbi Patels from Kutch. Although in East Africa and in Britain — as throughout the South Asian diaspora (Schwartz 1967) — a caste system could no longer govern social, economic, ritual, or other relationships, caste identities among Gujaratis have continued to be of considerable importance with regard to status, marriage, social networks, and formal institutions (see later).

Disparate religious traditions among British Hindus derive from diverse regional, caste, and sectarian origins. Such diversity is reproduced in several ways within Britain. The presence of specific *sampradayas* (schools of thought and religious practice deriving from the teachings of a specific sage) and other identifiable doctrinal or devotional traditions (again, many of which having regional and caste-based affiliations) further complicates the British Hindu makeup. These include three rival sects of Swaminarayanis, Arya Samajis, Radhasoamis, Pushtimargis (Vallabhacharyas), and people with particular dedication to the Mother Goddess, Sathya Sai Baba, Shirdi Sai Baba, Santoshi Ma, Baba Balak Nath, or Jalaram Bapa. There are also what might be called regional minority communities (especially Bengalis, Tamils and Telugus, Indo-Caribbeans, Indo-Mauritians, and Indo-Fijians) with their own styles and focuses of worship. And even though generally both Punjabi and Gujarati religious cultures at large are steeped in Vaishnavism, one can witness a greater emphasis on Rama and the *Ramayana* in the former, and on Krishna and the *Bhagavata Purana* in the latter.

From all of these divisions or orientations, a complicated pattern is emerging with regard to institutionalization. David Bowen (1987) has outlined three phases of institutional development among British Hindus which, although initially intended to describe the evolution of the Gujarati population in Bradford, may serve to characterize processes on the national scale. "Taken together," he writes, "the phases entail a dialectic between homogeneity and heterogeneity, unity and diversity" (ibid.: 15).

The first phase pertains especially to the period in which the British Asian population was comprised predominantly of young male migrants. Because the number of migrants was relatively few, living and working conditions dire, racism and discrimination unabated, most migrants desired a routinization of mutual networks for moral support and socializing along with some collective "cultural" activity, no matter how artificial or watered down. Hence in the late 1950s and early 1960s, some loosely knit associations or committees were formed locally in various cities around Britain, particularly functioning to organize for all — regardless of area, sect, social group, or caste of origin — modest celebrations of important All-India Hindu holy days (Diwali, Navratri, and so on).

The second phase witnessed the growth of diverse regional-linguistic, sectarian, and caste associations. Toward the end of the 1960s, coinciding with the reunion of husbands with their wives and children, there had been a marked growth in the number of persons from distinct regions, sects, and castes in each locale around Britain. This growth in numbers was also marked by much secondary migration within Britain, leading to geographically self-segregated groups within the British Asian populations, particularly regional ones (see Jackson and Smith 1981; Robinson 1986). The growth of regional, sectarian, and caste communities in given locales combined with individuals' concerns about social, cultural, and religious provisions for their newly established families (who now especially developed views toward their children's future in an alien environment). These factors led directly to the establishment of numerous group-specific associations and institutions. Also, many people arriving from East Africa in the late 1960s and early 1970s had gained considerable experience there in organizing and maintaining caste, sectarian, and other communal organizations (Morris 1968); such experience was quickly utilized to create or expand similar associations after settlement in Britain.

This phase of particularistic institutionalization has continued with momentum to the present day: from but a handful of Hindu associations dotting the map of Britain in the early 1960s, there are currently some 737 Hindu organizations of many kinds, including 303 places of Hindu worship, spread over at least 146 British towns and cities and boroughs of greater London. Although a number of "generalized Hindu" temples and associations exist, the great majority are characterized by regional, caste, and sectarian orientations (Vertovec 1992b).

The third phase characterizing institutional development is that marked by the formation of umbrella organizations. Thus far little actually exists, on either national or local levels, which operates effectively to undertake or to coordinate Hindu activities, or to express and to safeguard common interests across the board of regional, sectarian, and caste groups.

The National Council of Hindu Temples (United Kingdom) is at present the body that comes closest to this ideal. Over thirty temples and societies are directly affiliated with the council, and it publishes a quarterly newsletter and sponsors large-scale weekend Hindu Youth Festivals. Despite its broad network, however, some Punjabis complain that the council appears Gujarati dominated, that it seems to favor Gujarati temples and organizations, and that, therefore, its name should be changed to reflect a regional bias.

We are left, then, with a rather fragmented picture of Hinduism and Hindus in Britain. Although some attempts are being made to organize Hindus and to formulate Hinduism on a national scale, in local quarters it is mainly segmentary forms of religion reflecting traditions specific to provenance, caste, and sect that are practiced and institutionalized. How has this reflected Hindus' engagement with public space in Britain?

From the early years of South Asian immigration through the 1960s, a broadly assimilationist public policy and common view toward migrants held sway: if they want to live here, it was reasoned, they have to drop their alien ways and "become British" because, according to a 1964 Commonwealth Immigrants Advisory Council, "a national system cannot be expected to perpetuate the different values of immigrant groups" (in Rex 1991: 8). It was during this time, when numbers were relatively few and comprised largely only of men, that some of the broadly defined Hindu collective activities were organized. These were undertaken within the limited public space of the local Indian population in any given area, as any engagement with a broader public space was closed to immigrants.

Through the course of the 1970s and 1980s, however, assimilationism gave way to a mainstream discourse surrounding multiculturalism. In its most general formulation, the goal of the latter discourse is to achieve a society characterized by mutual tolerance of sociocultural and religious difference coupled with equality of opportunity free from discrimination. "The ideal of a Multi-Cultural Society," John Rex (ibid.: 13) suggests, "sees British society as involving simply a confrontation between private familial and communal cultures, on the one hand, and the shared political culture of the public domain, on the other." The public domain or space is occupied by political, economic, legal, and educational systems, whereas the private is considered to be that in which particularistic sociocultural and religious institutions are maintained (Rex 1987). The latter set of phenomena are to be tolerated, according to the premises of this discourse of multiculturalism, as long as they do not impinge on the former. But in actual practice, multiculturalism in Britain becomes highly problematic because, Rex points out, "In much public debate the confrontation is seen as being between 'British culture' in the public domain and the culture of immigrants in the private, and this 'British culture' is not thought of in political terms at all. Rather it is thought of as itself a whole way of life which distinguishes the British from other nations" (1991: 13). Talal Asad adds, "The question of traditions and identities—that is, of maintaining and elaborating one's own difference—is assumed to be either already settled or something to be settled outside the sphere of national politics, for that sphere is where something called 'core values' and 'what we have in common' [as 'British'] are said to be located" (1990: 467).

Further, in discussing a document addressing multiculturalism that was published by John Patten, the Home Office minister responsible for race relations, Asad observes that,

> Since "family" and "community" are the only groups mentioned in the document, the implication seems to be that groups have no place in the public sphere. But as this is patently false (the public sphere is occupied by a complex array of business institutions, professional bodies, trades unions, social movements, and opinion groups representing each of these), the formulation here must be read as having the intention of discouraging "cultural minorities" from establishing themselves as corporate political actors. As far as "cultural minority" members are concerned, they must participate in Britishness (the quality that makes them part of the essential culture) as individuals.
>
> This participation, Patten insists, does not mean assimilation, "forgetting one's cultural roots." But that is only because, and to the extent that, "being British" to which he refers presupposes a hierarchy of cultural spaces not mentioned here. (Ibid.: 460)

At the lower end of the hierarchy, cultural variety is tolerated and even facilitated; at the higher end, imagined "Britishness" (which largely equates to "Englishness") must not be assailed. It is precisely because Muslims attempted to engage the national public space, Asad (1990) convincingly argues, that the Salman Rushdie affair assumed the crisis proportions it did throughout British society.

This dominant multicultural discourse has contributed to the maintenance, even proliferation, of segmentary identities, traditions, and institutions among the Hindu population of Britain. Large-scale mobilization as Hindus has not been given cause or opportunity to take place in a society-wide public space. To the extent that engagements with public space have occurred, these have arisen variably and locally in certain cities or parts of cities around Britain (Knott 1986; Burghart 1987; Nye 1993). Here, the construction of Hinduism has been affected by contestations and negotiations in the public space of specific, local Hindu populations (by way of establishing organizations, ritual activities, festivals, temples) and within the local public space overseen by local government (by way of applications for grants and building permission, gaining the participation of politicians in community events, and participating in municipal multicultural festivals). In engaging the latter space, serious controversies have often arisen as city government authorities assume a given definition of "Hinduism" and "Hindu community," whereas these are usually highly contested between segmentary units reflecting differences of provenance, caste, or sect (see Kalka 1991; Werbner 1991).

In addition to significant variance in modes of migration and settlement, the dominant discourse of multiculturalism in Britain has conditioned the construction of Hinduism and other developments among Hindus much in contrast to those among Trinidadian Hindus conditioned by the heritage of the colonial plural society of Trinidad. In Britain a multitude of segmentary traits predominate, loosely linked, at best, by rather vague and generalized formulations of Hinduism. In Trinidad, a generalized formulation arose early on, was enacted in a shared corpus of ritual, became institutionalized in national organizations, manifested as a communal political platform, and now serves as a foundation for challenging Creole cultural hegemony. This is not to say, however, that Trinidad Hindus have, and British Hindus do not have, a strong Hindu identity; indeed, most in both countries will proclaim their "Hinduness" with pride and conviction. That is, in both places, Hinduism has a very strong personal meaning. But given structural and historical variations affecting collectivities of Hindus in each country, "Hinduism" has come to have different ethnic meanings. Central to such developments are differential processes of reification.

On Reification

Drawing largely upon important works by Max Gluckman (1958) and Clyde Mitchell (1956, 1987), Bruce Kapferer (1988, n.d.) focuses on certain key features concerning processes of ethnic group formation. Central to the formation of ethnic groups, he suggests, is the process whereby cultural attributes are reified, or "systematically removed from their embeddedness in the flow of daily life, fashioned into symbolic things, and placed in a stable, dominant, and determinate relation to action" (1988: 210). In this sense, then (*albeit* among others; see Pitkin 1987), reification can refer to the way that cultural traits are consciously selected and called on in order to reformulate social interactions (particularly by way of group mobilization). Kapferer also describes this as a process of "symbolic disarticulation" which "removes ideas embedded in the fabric of social practices and symbolically idealizes them. Joined with the formation of a unified ethnic consciousness these symbols — customs, rites, language — are made emblematic of a unifying ethnic identity. Their idea comes to function in a new way, constituting relations rather than constituted within relationships" (1988: 97).

Through such a "process of the reification of culture, the production of culture as an object in itself," he suggests that "as an object, a thing, culture [becomes] vital in the consciousness and realization of ethnic identity and to an ethnic unity" (ibid.: 97–98). Such processes, one must bear in mind, take place in an ongoing manner within variable, encompassing structural contexts (including patterns of class relations and resource control) and in relation to public spaces comprised of specific discourses (especially, here, with respect to the construction of politically salient cultural categories and the specification of symbolic capital surrounding them). Such political environments strongly influence the selection and use of cultural markers and identities at critical phases in the formation of ethnic groups (Kapferer n.d.).

Conclusion

Context-bound, public space–directed processes of reification differentially characterize the construction of Hinduism in the past and present among Indians in Trinidad and Britain. In Trinidad, during the earliest period of Hindu presence, a single, common set of cultural and religious forms were distilled from the wide range represented among the indentured migrants; Hindus had to discern what was common among them and essential to maintain (with regard to religious elements, this was mainly under the direction of Brahmans). Subsequently, these isolated characteristics were placed in a position such that they were formative of social relationships (including settlement patterns, marriage networks, temple congregations). In the next phase, marked by reaction to Arya Samaji missionaries, certain religious symbols, beliefs, and practices were given special value as orthodox and authentic; collective "Sanatanist" Hindu identity was further reified and, for the first time, nationally organized. The phase of Hindu party politicking culminated the trend: through electioneering rhetoric and emotive symbols, Trinidad Hindu culture was made an object in itself so as to articulate a shared ethnic identity in the face of potentially intensified patterns of ethnic inequality and resource competition. Since then, the revitalization of Hinduism in the 1970s to 1980s and the current activism of certain Hindu youth organizations can be attributed in many ways to continued calls for collective social and economic parity with the politically dominant Afro-Trinidadians (Vertovec 1990b). In each phase — and again, by way of engaging different kinds of public space — there has emerged greater self-conscious reflection, on the part of Trinidad Hindus, as to who they are collectively in relation to others and as to what their most distinguishing traits and values are.

Such processes of self-reflective cultural selection and reification are still under way among Hindus in Britain. There, because of the prevalence of regional, caste, and sectarian groups, Hindus continue to be faced with the dilemma over which aspects of these traditions-within-Hinduism are to be collectively asserted in the new context and which should be set aside as nonessential. David Pocock (1976: 357) has described this conundrum, entailing a self-conscious "rationalization of the distinction religion/culture," among one branch (the Bochasanwasi Shri Akshar Purushottam Sanstha) of the Swaminarayan tradition. The Sanstha members are in the position of having to decide, for future generations in Britain, to what extent exclusively Gujarati cultural elements (such as language, diet, family structure, and women's roles) are to remain in the tradition, as opposed to maintaining the *sampradaya* through ideological tenets only. It is a dilemma found throughout the Hindu diaspora, as Raymond B. Williams has described in America:

> The critical assumption here is that there are some aspects associated with past religious practice that are fundamental and essential to the continuation of the religion and others that are cultural accoutrements that are not so fundamental. Thus, the process of searching for an adaptive strategy becomes the attempt to distinguish what is essential in the religion and what is not. (1988: 191)

In some places in Britain where, due to small numbers, Hindus of differing regional, caste, and sectarian background have had to arrange for ritual practice in shared temples, common forms have had to be negotiated by committee (Knott 1986). Their resulting ideas about what Hinduism is have acted to structure new patterns of relationship and a new, shared identity. It is possible that such negotiated formulations and social patterns may eventually come to characterize Hinduism and Hindus across the broad public space of Britain. But at present, these formulations are only applicable to a few immediate or localized public spaces.

In situations structured by ethnic and religious heterogeneity and conditioned by variable forms of engagement with public space, Indian migrants and their descendants reflect on just what Hinduism is and what makes them Hindu. Such reflection, in turn, is catalyst to processes of "symbolic disarticulation" and reification affecting ethnic identities, social forms, and cultural practices. In Britain, due to a particular dominant discourse surrounding multiculturalism and certain concomitant attempts to exclude minority groups from the public space, such processes affecting Hinduism are largely confined to a localized—private or community—space. In Trinidad, it is a societywide public space, long conditioned by communal competition which was set in course by the legacy of colonial plural society structures, wherein a collective, generalized set of symbols and institutions has been deemed Hindu. These are but two examples indicating how outside of India, as in the subcontinent, Hinduism remains resilient as an organizing conceptual category and highly malleable as a source of social mobilization.

Acknowledgments

Information regarding Hindu organizations is derived from materials of the Multifaith Directory Research Project based at the Religious Resource and Research Centre, University of Derby (in conjunction with the Inter-Faith Network for the United Kingdom). My thanks to Paul Weller and Rachelle Castle of the center; and to Brian Pearce of the Inter-Faith Network, for their kind help and assistance.

Note

1. This was further strengthened by a pan-Caribbean movement as the entire British West Indies underwent decolonization. Creole symbols—carnival, calypso, and other musical forms, local dialects, aesthetics, prominent individuals—became equated with the Caribbean as a whole. The substantial non-Creole segments—

particularly Indians and Chinese, although important actors in the region for over one hundred years — were consequently considered, in the public space, to be non-Caribbean.

References

Asad, T.
  1990   "Multiculturalism and British Identity in the Wake of the Rushdie Affair." *Politics and Society* 18: 455–80.
Ballard, R.
  1990   "Migration and Kinship: The Differential Effect of Marriage Rules on the Processes of Punjabi Migration to Britain." In C. Clarke, C. Peach, and S. Vertovec, eds., *South Asians Overseas: Migration and Ethnicity.* Cambridge: Cambridge University Press, 219–49.
Barot, R.
  1981   "The Social Organisation of a Swaminarayan Sect in Britain." Unpublished Ph.D. thesis, School of Oriental and African Studies, University of London.
Bowen, D.
  1987   "The Evolution of Gujarati Hindu Organizations in Bradford." In Burghart, *Hinduism in Great Britain,* 33–60.
Burghart, R., ed.
  1987   *Hinduism in Great Britain.* London: Tavistock.
Cross, M.
  1978   "Colonialism and Ethnicity: A Theory and Comparative Case Study." *Ethnic and Racial Studies* 1: 37–59.
  1988   "The Political Representation of Organised Labour in Trinidad and Guyana: A Comparative Puzzle." In M. Cross and G. Heuman, eds., *Labour in the Caribbean.* London: Macmillan, 285–308.
Crowley, D.
  1957   "Plural and Differential Acculturation." *American Anthropologist* 59: 817–24.
Despres, L. A.
  1968   "Anthropological Theory, Cultural Pluralism, and the Study of Complex Societies." *Current Anthropology* 9: 3–26.
Forbes, R.
  1984   "Arya Samaj in Trinidad: An Historical Study of Hindu Organizational Process in Acculturative Conditions." Unpublished Ph.D. thesis, University of Miami.
Freitag, S. B.
  1989   *Collective Action and Community: Public Arenas and the Emergence of Communalism in North India.* Berkeley: University of California Press.
Frykenberg, R.
  1989   "The Emergence of Modern 'Hinduism' as a Concept and as an Institu-

tion." In G. D. Sontheimer and H. Kulke, eds., *Hinduism Reconsidered.* New Delhi: Manohar, 29–49.

Furnivall, J. S.

1939   *Netherlands India: A Study of a Plural Economy.* Cambridge: Cambridge University Press.

1948   *Colonial Policy and Practice: A Comparative Study of Burma and Netherlands India.* London: Cambridge University Press.

Gluckmann, M.

1958   "Analysis of a Social Situation in Modern Zululand." *Rhodes-Livingstone Papers* 28. Manchester: University of Manchester Press.

Hardy, F.

1990   "Hinduism." In U. King, ed., *Turning Points in Religious Studies.* Edinburgh: T. & T. Clark, 145–55.

Hechter, M.

1975   *Internal Colonialism: The Celtic Fringe in British National Development, 1536–1966.* London: Routledge and Kegan Paul.

Hintzen, P.

1989   *The Costs of Regime Survival: Racial Mobilization, Elite Domination and Control of the State in Guyana and Trinidad.* Cambridge: Cambridge University Press.

Jackson, P., and S. J. Smith, eds.

1981   *Social Interaction and Ethnic Segregation.* London: Academic Press.

Jayawardena, C.

1971   "The Disintegration of Caste in Fiji Indian Rural Society." In L. R. Hiatt and C. Jayawardena, eds., *Anthropology in Oceania.* Sydney: Angus and Robertson, 89–119.

Jones, T.

1993   *Britain's Ethnic Minorities: An Analysis of the Labour Force Survey.* London: Policy Studies Institute.

Kalka, I.

1991   "Striking a Bargain: Political Radicalism in a Middle-Class London Borough." In P. Werbner and M. Anwar, eds., *Black and Ethnic Leaderships in Britain.* London: Routledge, 203–25.

Kapferer, B.

1988   *Legends of People, Myths of State: Violence, Intolerance and Political Culture in Sri Lanka and Australia.* Washington, D.C.: Smithsonian Institution Press.

n.d.   "The Performance of Categories: Plays of Identity in Africa and Australia." In A. Rogers and S. Vertovec, eds., *The Urban Context: Ethnicity, Social Networks and Situational Analysis.* Oxford: Berg. In press.

Kirpalani, M., et al.

1945   *Indian Centenary Review.* Port of Spain: Indian Centenary Review Committee.

Knott, K.

1986   *Hinduism in Leeds: A Study of Religious Practice in the Indian Hindu Community and in Hindu-Related Groups.* Leeds: Community Religions Project Monograph Series, Department of Theology and Religious Studies, University of Leeds.

n.d.   "From Leather Stockings to Surgical Boots and Beyond: The Gujarati Mochis of Leeds." In R. Ballard, ed., *Desh Pardesh: The South Asian Presence in Britain.* London: C. Hurst. In press.

LaGuerre, J. G.

1972   "The General Elections of 1946 in Trinidad and Tobago." *Social and Economic Studies* 21: 184–203.

Ley, D., C. Peach, and C. Clarke

1984   "Introduction: Pluralism and Human Geography." In D. Ley, C. Peach, and C. Clarke, eds., *Geography and Ethnic Pluralism.* London: Allen and Unwin, 1–22.

Malik, Y. K.

1966   "The Democratic Labour Party of Trinidad: An Attempt at the Formation of a Mass Party in a Multi-Ethnic Society." Unpublished Ph.D. thesis, University of Florida.

Michaelson, M.

1983   "Caste, Kinship and Marriage: A Study of Two Gujarati Trading Castes in England." Unpublished Ph.D. thesis, School of Oriental and African Studies, University of London.

Mitchell, J. C.

1956   "The Kalela Dance." *Rhodes-Livingstone Papers* 26. Manchester: Manchester University Press.

1987   *Cities, Society and Social Perception: A Central African Perspective.* Oxford: Clarendon Press.

Morris, H. S.

1967   "Some Aspects of the Concept Plural Society." *Man* (n.s.). 2: 169–84.

1968   *The Indians of Uganda.* London: Weidenfeld and Nicolson.

Nye, M.

1993   "Temple Congregations and Communities: Hindu Constructions in Edinburgh." *New Community* 19: 201–15.

Pitkin, H. F.

1987   "Rethinking Reification." *Theory and Society* 16: 263–93.

Pocock, D.

1976   "Preservation of the Religious Life: Hindu Immigrants in England." *Contributions to Indian Sociology* 10: 341–65.

Rex, J.

1987   "The Concept of a Multi-Cultural Society." *New Community* 14: 218–29.

1991   "The Political Sociology of a Multi-Cultural Society." *European Journal of Intercultural Studies* 2: 7–19.

Robinson, V.

1986   *Transients, Settlers and Refugees: Asians in Britain.* Oxford: Clarendon Press.

Ryan, S.

1972   *Race and Nationalism in Trinidad and Tobago.* Toronto: University of Toronto Press.

Schwartz, B. M., ed.
  1967   *Caste in Overseas Indian Communities.* San Francisco: Chandler.
Sharma, U. M.
  1969   "Hinduism in a Kangra Village." Unpublished Ph.D. thesis, School of
         Oriental and African Studies, University of London.
Smith, M. G.
  1965   *The Plural Society in the British West Indies.* Berkeley: University of
         California Press.
  1969   "Some Developments in the Analytical Framework of Pluralism." In
         L. Kuper and M. G. Smith, eds., *Pluralism in Africa.* Berkeley: Univer-
         sity of California Press, 415–59.
  1974   *Corporations and Society.* London: Duckworth.
Smith, W. C.
  1964   *The Meaning and End of Religion.* New York: Mentor.
Thapar, R.
  1989   "Imagined Religious Communities? Ancient History and the Modern
         Search for a Hindu Identity." *Modern Asian Studies* 23: 209–31.
Tinker, H.
  1977   *The Banyan Tree: Overseas Emigrants from India, Pakistan and Bangla-
         desh.* Oxford: Oxford University Press.
van den Berghe, P.
  1973   "Pluralism." In J. Honigmann, ed., *Handbook of Social and Cultural
         Anthropology.* Chicago: Rand McNally, 19–29.
van der Veer, P.
  n.d.   "Hindu 'Nationalism' and the Discourse with 'Modernity': The Vishva
         Hindu Parishad." In M. Morty and S. Appleby, eds., *Fundamentalism
         Observed.* Chicago: University of Chicago Press. In press.
van der Veer, P., and S. Vertovec
  1991   "Brahmanism Abroad: On Caribbean Hinduism as an Ethnic Reli-
         gion." *Ethnology* 30: 149–66.
Vasil, R. K.
  1984   *Politics in Bi-Racial Societies.* New Delhi: Vikas.
Vertovec, S.
  1989   "Hinduism in Diaspora: The Transformation of Tradition in Trinidad."
         In G. D. Sontheimer and H. Kulke, eds., *Hinduism Reconsidered.* New
         Delhi: Manohar, 152–79.
  1990a "Oil Boom and Recession in Trinidad Indian Villages." In C. Clarke,
         C. Peach, and S. Vertovec, eds., *South Asians Overseas: Migration and
         Ethnicity.* Cambridge: Cambridge University Press, 89–111.
  1990b "Religion and Ethnic Ideology: The Hindu Youth Movement in Trin-
         idad." *Ethnic and Racial Studies* 13: 225–49.
  1991   "Inventing Religious Tradition: Yagnas and Hindu Renewal in Trin-
         idad." In A. Geertz and J. S. Jensen, eds., *Religion, Tradition and
         Renewal.* Aarhus: Universitats Forlag, 77–95.
  1992a *Hindu Trinidad: Religion, Ethnicity and Socio-Economic Change.* Lon-
         don: Macmillan.

1992b "Community and Congregation in London Hindu Temples: Divergent Trends." *New Community* 18: 251–64.

Werbner, P.

1991   "The Fiction of Unity in Ethnic Politics: Aspects of Representation and the State among British Pakistanis." In P. Werbner and M. Anwar, eds., *Black and Ethnic Leaderships in Britain*. London: Routledge, 113–45.

Williams, R. B.

1988   *Religions of Immigrants from India and Pakistan: New Threads in the American Tapestry*. Cambridge: Cambridge University Press.

6. New York City's Muslim World Day Parade

The fifth annual Muslim World Day Parade of New York City took place on Sunday, September 23, 1990, and the sixth annual parade one year later on Sunday, September 22. The parade route laid claim to the prominent New York City midtown public space of Lexington Avenue from Thirty-third Street to Twenty-third Street, a stretch that has come to be identified with South Asian commercial establishments such as South Asian food stores, travel bureaus, restaurants, and sari stores.

Muslims in New York City are not closely associated with a specific neighborhood (the way African Americans are identified with Harlem, Greeks with Astoria, and Italians with Bensonhurst); rather, they are scattered throughout several urban areas. Although South Asians, regardless of religious affiliation, have concentrated in certain areas of the borough of Queens, notably Jackson Heights, they are more diffusely visible in the urban environment: in the city's scattered newspaper kiosks, in South Asian stores along part of the parade route, and in the row of "Indian" (Bangladeshi) restaurants along East Sixth Street on Manhattan's Lower East Side.

Demographically, it is still difficult to determine the shape of both the immigrant Muslim and the native, largely African American Muslim population. The United States census provides no data on religion. The category of "Asian-Indian" first appeared in the 1980 census and "Arab" only in the 1990 census; the Muslim component of these groups is therefore unknown. Another problem is that the census lists the *legal* Asian-Indian immigrants from countries such as Guyana, Pakistan, India, and Bangladesh — 94,500 in 1990. The New York Bangladeshi and Pakistani communities each claim 50,000 immigrants, making a total of 100,000 Muslims from these countries alone. These communities count both legal and illegal residents and believe that all official figures should be doubled for a realistic representation.

According to Francis P. Vardy, New York City's demographer at the Department of City Planning, the Catholic archdiocese of New York tabulates Catholics, the New York Council of Churches counts Protestants, the organized Jewish community supports a demographer, but no umbrella association exists to count Muslims.[1] As a coauthor of *The Newest New Yorkers* (Salvo et al. 1993), Vardy lists figures provided by the Immigration and Naturalization Service for legal immigrants (green card recipients) by country of origin. There is no information on their religion; for example the approximately 1,000 Israeli citizens who receive green cards every year in New York City include Jews, Arab Christians, and Arab Muslims.

City newspapers routinely estimate the Muslim population at between 500,000 and 850,000 legal and illegal, native and immigrant Muslims. These figures apply only to the population within the boundaries of New York City and disregard the South Asian spillover into adjacent Long Island suburbs and the growing Middle Eastern population across the Hudson River in New Jersey. In short, population figures are scattered, inconsistent, and open to challenge. In addition, the Pakistani organizers of the Muslim World Day Parade resisted my attempts to classify participants by ethnicity, insisting that the only worthy category was adherence to Islam. For these reasons, my account of the Muslim World Day Parade in New York City does not attempt to assess the representation of different ethnic groups in the parade. Instead, I investigate first the relationship between a street drama and the social context in which it is performed. I discuss second the connection between public enactments (a civic parade) and an additional event that transforms the nature of the Muslim World Day Parade, namely the evocation of the more private social life of the mosque. How do Muslim city dwellers in New York use public gatherings and vernacular dramatic techniques to propose ideas about social relations? More specifically, why have South Asian Muslims in New York City, a religious minority within a variety of ethnic minorities, brought together the disparate performative activities of procession and prayer to speak for the larger Muslim community to other New Yorkers? Why have they chosen the form of a parade?[2]

According to Barbara Kirshenblatt-Gimblett and Brooks McNamara, a parade is a subset term of "civic procession," which in turn belongs to the larger category of "processional performance." These authors descriptively characterize the parade as movement from one place to another that is symbolically and ceremonially resonant. The event consists of distinctive elements (costumes, music, floats, and so on) that distinguish it from everyday movement but are presented in ways comprehensible to spectators; it is functional and referential as well as religious, political, and social; and it may combine procession (movement) and station (significant stopping).[3] According to this definition, all parades have a performative character because they are about *spectacle* and how to present an impressive perambulatory event for display and entertainment to the public. Other students of civic parades refer to a Durkheimian paradigm in which parades, like great religious festivals, function as a social unifier. New York City's Puerto Rican Day Parade, for example, presents "a unity that masks internal political differences under a visible leadership" (Kasinitz and Freidenberg-Herbstein 1987: 346) and it does so in order to mark out the place for Puerto Rican ascendancy in New York City's ethnically based political system. Parades can thus be seen as reinforcements of the ideologies that legitimize the inequalities of ethnic participation in the wider society. Other analysts of parades maintain that while presenting an imaginary unified ethnicity to the public, many ethnic parades also insist that Americanness resides in dual identification: to be a member of a specific ethnic subgroup is to be an American (Schneider 1990: 41).

In contrast, Susan Davis stresses the potential of parades for confrontation:

> Parades do more than reflect society. Such public enactments, in their multi-plicitous and varied forms, are not only patterned by social forces — they have been part of the very building and challenging of social relations. As dramatic representations, parades and public ceremonies are political acts: They have pragmatic objectives, and concrete material results. . . . As political acts, parades and ceremonies take place in a context of contest and confrontation. (1986: 5–6)

An extreme instance of contest and confrontation is the parade as a ceremony of subversion. In its annual Greenwich Village Halloween Parade, the lesbian and gay constituency promotes its vision of a Bakhtinian carnival that questions the legitimacy of the heterosexual and homophobic social and cultural order (Kugelmass 1991: 444). In California, Pasadena's century-old New Year's Day Rose Parade is currently mimicked and mocked by a consciously oppositional, "alternative" Doo Dah Parade established in 1977 (Lawrence 1982: 155).

It is likely that the Muslim World Day Parade, the self-assertion of a religious grouping, is nonetheless perceived by New Yorkers as yet another manifestation of ethnic pride. Such an impression may be encouraged by the visible presence of South Asian Muslims among the organizers and participants. There are no Catholic or Jewish parades (a Sikh parade is a recent addition to the New York City calendar), although the Catholic church and archdiocese are given particular prominence during the Saint Patrick's Day Parade and Jewish religious institutions figure prominently in the Israel Day Parade. Though a parade reflects the religious, economic, and social bases of its primary support group, New Yorkers more readily perceive festive behavior as a manifestation of ethnic culture. It is possible to conjecture that Muslims in New York City, in order to gain political and economic power, are reconfiguring religion into ethnicity to take advantage of the discourse of ethnicity. Their parade may be a symbol of this effort. Ethnicity in America means that new immigrants are defined, as were the white ethnics of previous generations, as the latest wave of successful and potentially assimilable citizens. It seems that the parade organizers, as South Asian Muslims, must negotiate the paradoxical task of reconciling their pan-Islamic aspirations, which would lead them to include their African American coreligionists, and the need to distance themselves from the stigmatized race of African Americans. In interviews, parade organizers were not forthcoming about their relations with African American Muslims.

South Asians will undoubtedly succeed in inserting themselves into the New York political arena as white and ethnic new Americans. My own ethnographic fieldwork on urban mosques, for example, documents how a white, middle-class New York section of the Bronx readily accepted immigrant Muslim mosques in their neighborhood but rejected the presence of African American Muslim places of worship (Slyomovics n.d.).

The principal organizer of the Muslim World Day Parade is Naveed Anwar, a Pakistani businessman who is currently director of the Board of Trustees of the Muslim Foundation of America, an organization founded in 1984 as a cultural, nonprofit institution to promote better understanding between Islam and other religions and ethnic communities in the tristate area. Another prime mover is Muhammad Abdul Munim, publisher and journalist of the *Minaret,* and English-language newspaper established in 1974 to serve the Muslim community in New York City.

Why a parade? The organizers told me: "New York City is a city of parades. We saw other parades show their communities' strength, so we thought we have to do this too." The principle evoked is one of ceremonial copying. Participants reproduce parades and civic pageants, thereby offering their interpretation of the history of the city. It is a history constructed by the organizers and participants of each event, and the Muslim World Day Parade moving from Thirty-third Street to Twenty-third Street unfolds in ceremonially and symbolically distinctive ways.[4]

The familiar accoutrements of the New York City ethnic parade are present both in the Muslim World Day Parade and in another allied festive national event, the Pakistan Independence Day Parade, which takes place on the last Sunday in August and moves along approximately the same route down Lexington Avenue from Forty-seventh Street to Twenty-third Street. It is noteworthy that many of the South Asian organizers and participants of the Muslim World Day Parade are also involved in their own Pakistan national day celebration. They also participate in the Ashura Day Parade, another strictly Muslim religious event in Manhattan. Ashura Day was originally organized by the Chicago-based Jafria Association of North America in 1973; the first New York City march was held in 1986. Ashura commemorates the death of Imam Hussein, the grandson of the Prophet Muhammad and the son of the fourth Caliph Ali, who fell in 680 A.D. at the battle of Kerbela. The date is marked as a day of mourning by Shiite Muslims, who regard the (Sunni) caliphs who succeeded Ali as heretical and illegitimate. The Ashura procession moves from East Fiftieth Street through Manhattan's chic Upper East Side to the Pakistani consulate at East Sixty-fifth Street. The constellation of three parades with their overlapping constituencies has provided South Asian Muslims with three ceremonial occasions to advertise their presence in the city's social mosaic.

An important indicator of the power of an ethnic group in the city is the route to which the parade is assigned. In the hierarchy of New York City ethnic parades, Fifth Avenue, the most coveted venue, is reserved by provisions of the City Charter for older and now powerful ethnic groups: the Irish, Jews, Italians, Germans, Poles, Greeks, and Hispanics. Latecomers, such as the Koreans, Pakistanis, Sikhs, Indians, Dominicans, Cubans, and Muslims are relegated to Lexington, Sixth Avenue, Broadway, or, lowest on the urban grid, Battery Park, the southern tip of Manhattan.[5] In contrast, subversive or canivalesque parades take place far from the customary routes of civic pageantry. Their organizers deliberately choose the artistic, bohemian, or urban counterculture neighborhoods, such as Pasadena's Old Town and New York City's Greenwich Village.

New York City is so famous for its numerous and annually proliferating parades that in 1991 the cost to the city—in overtime police fees alone—to oversee about 760 parades (168 in Manhattan, 200 in the Bronx, 142 in Queens, 171 in Brooklyn, and 83 on Staten Island) and 3,000 street events was estimated at nine million dollars by Mayor David Dinkins, who hoped to issue fewer parade permits. A *New York Times* article analyzing the ethnic rivalries that would ensue from such a cost-cutting measure quoted

Capt. William Strizl of the Police Department's parade permits division: "For decades the city has had a policy of issuing street event permits to any group that applied for one, providing that the event could be accommodated. 'We've looked upon it, having a parade, as an exercise in people's rights'" (Sims 1992b: B3). Provisionally, a limit of sixty parades per year was imposed for the city's major artery, Fifth Avenue.

The 1990 Muslim World Day Parade

New York City civic and ethnic parades are paradigmatically patterned on the oldest and most famous one, namely the 230-year-old Saint Patrick's Day Parade, which belongs to all Americans and has become an American national holiday (Kelton 1985: 104). Much parade grammar has already been established by the Irish example: forward movement in solemn military march formation, groups or institutions marching together with identifying signs, floats, accompanying marching bands, ethnic costumes, high school and student organizations, and a civic and military presence. The Muslim World Day Parade, like other ethnic parades, represents both continuity with the archetypal New York City parade and innovative departures from that mold. The Saint Patrick's Day Parade might, for example, partially account for why the Pakistan Independence Day Parade included a marching band, in fact the Irish-American Shamrock Marching Band playing "Yankee Doodle." A Pakistani bystander pointed out to me, perhaps facetiously, that the Irish-American band musicians were also wearing the Islamic color green, thereby underscoring not only the polysemic nature of symbols but also that cooptation is a two-way street.

Two bands figured in the Muslim World Day Parade. The first lead group was the Edgewater Park Fife and Drum Corps, an Irish marching band from the Bronx dressed in American Revolutionary War costumes. They too played "Yankee Doodle." They marched alongside the Sufi Tariqa of the Shazliyya-Burhaniyya confraternity, a Sufi brotherhood whose leadership is based in Sudan. The Sufi followers provided an expressive musical and performative counterpoint as they repetitively and rhythmically chanted, "La-illaha-illa-llah" (There is no God but Allah). This particular Sufi group holds its *zikr* (a Sufi form of prayer) every Saturday night in the Bronx, and each year they are the only group to provide song and movement somewhat rooted in the culture of the marchers. There was also a New Orleans–style African American jazz band that played "When the

Saints Go Marching In" throughout the march. The desire to incorporate some of the elements that define a New York City civic parade, but with distinctive touches, accounts for the simultaneous presence of Irish bands and Sufi adepts. It was the Sufis, however, who were continuously reproached by various parade marshals for breaching decorum with their overly ecstatic dances. They also tended to march sideways, backwards, or in circles, in contrast to the Irish marching band, whose forward movements in solemn military formation were deemed entirely appropriate.

The choice of bands was negotiated between the organizers of the parade and the major band broker for New York City, Joe Heineman. In an interview, Heineman described his duties during the Muslim World Day Parade: he coordinates the parade, deals with setup and takedown, and acts as a liaison with the various municipal offices. Heineman takes credit for advising the Muslim Day Parade committee to hire bands from different Irish-American and African American backgrounds, "to give it a little flair," he said, "a little showmanship for the people on the street." The Sufi musicians were not an official band but a recognized group of marchers in the community represented by the parade. Their ecstatic style challenged not only the canons of presenting a religious identity in a civic parade but also the nature of orthodox Islam as it may have been understood by the parade organizers.

The Muslim World Day Parade began at 2:00 P.M. First, the marchers transformed the intersection of Lexington Avenue and Thirty-third Street into a communal praying space or outdoor mosque. Transparent plastic strips placed on a diagonal axis oriented the worshippers to the true east, thereby imposing geographical as well as religious correctness on what appears to be the true north-south and east-west axes of the Manhattan street grid (which in fact are false axes). For the non-Muslim spectator there is a clash of perceptions when an everyday locale of Lexington Avenue is inscribed by a new group with its own interpretation of the city as a transient sacred location. On one Sunday in each year, Muslim ritual space and time invest a civic location with alternative, albeit ephemeral, meanings. An area of Lexington Avenue, prosaically commercial during the weekday, is remapped first into Muslim praying space and then into a trajectory of processional movement. The creation of an ephemeral mosque praying space on the ground competes with the surrounding built environment of skyscrapers and secular advertising. As Yi-Fu Tuan notes, it is clear that the city is a place of highly visible symbols, but that "the city itself is a symbol . . . achieving power and eminence through the scale and solemnity of its rites and festivals" (1977: 173). It is not merely a stage on which to enact inherited cultural repertoires; urban life is an "urban frontier," an arena in which to invent festival sites and behavior (Kirshenblatt-Gimblett 1983: 180).

Worshippers bowing to the true geographical east must turn toward a northeast Manhattan street corner. A mass of diagonal axes is created as hundreds of worshippers line up to pray in unison (see Figures 6.1 and 6.2). The result is that parade leaders and worshippers performing their religious duties directly face marchers and floats prepared to perform their civic duties, as well as groups gathered at the northeast corner. Each year the parade is significantly delayed as it reorients participants from the direction toward Mecca (due northeast) to the customary parade route southward down Lexington Avenue. The clash between two modes of gathering creates distinctive rhythms and a dramatic structure that segregates the majority of participant-believers from a minority of secular onlookers. The parade begins be realigning categories of participation and viewing: Muslim prayer segregates Muslim believers from non-Muslims but at the same time intermingles Muslim onlookers and parade participants. Mounted New York City police facing southward in a single row of four to six set the tempo and direction for any ethnic parade. If the ethnic group is politically powerful, they are followed by a limousine carrying the current mayor of New York. The police establish norms necessary to conduct a parade: forward directional movement, an ordering of participants, and obedience to the urban street grid. In the case of the Muslim World Day Parade, the police reestablish these norms after the period of prayer. The parade announces its start with a prominent symbol of national authority, the line of all-male mounted police followed by a phalanx of all-male parade flagbearers displaying flags of countries with Muslim populations. Each year the head of the Afghan community, an unusually tall, imposing figure, leads the lines of dignitaries and parade organizers (see Figure 6.3). It is an ecumenical day, uniting three religions with representatives from the Catholic archdiocese and the New York Board of Rabbis. A rare female presence in the line of dignitaries was Manhattan Borough President Ruth Messinger.

Despite the presence of non-Muslim politicians and Irish and New Orleans–style bands, what we are seeing is the temporary creation of Muslim space on a New York City avenue. This is achieved, I claim, by combining two seemingly disparate forms: on the one hand, there is the evanescent format of a civic procession, resembling that of an ethnic or

Figures 6.1 and 6.2. The Muslim World Day Parade: Lexington Avenue and Thirty-third Street transformed into an outdoor mosque. (Photo: Susan Slyomovics)

Figure 6.3. The Muslim World Day Parade: Opening parade of flags headed by the Afghan community leader. (Photo: Susan Slyomovics)

national day parade; and on the other hand, there are representations of mosques, those solid architectural structures that usually signify permanently occupied places. The mosques are cardboard and papier-mâché representations of Jerusalem's Dome of the Rock and the Black Stone, or Kaaba, of Mecca; they float down Lexington Avenue as emblems of the New York City Muslim community. I recall that the floating Kaaba provoked an exclamation of wonder from a bystander who was unknown to me. He exclaimed, "Only in America," and then said there is an Islamic tradition that only at the end of days would the Kaaba become unmoored from Mecca and float freely.

In the next section, I elaborate on the significance of mosque floats as spectacle and the relationship of parade participants to sacred writing.

Writing and Signs

What characterizes the Muslim World Day Parade and sets it apart from other parades is not so much the fact that it is a civic procession organized by a religious group, but the singularly important role of signs, which frame the event. Parading banners or carrying the word becomes the main feature if not the point of the parade. This emphasis is underlined by the paucity or absence of other classic parade attractions, such as scantily clad females — in fact, the general lack of women on display on floats is noteworthy. The only exception to this rule is a single float in the Pakistan Independence Day Parade. Because there is a significant overlap between executive committees of that event and the Muslim World Day Parade, however, it is worth mentioning the presence of a possibly idolatrous representation of the human female form that appeared on one of the parade floats. It was the iconic figure of the woman who guards New York harbor and welcomes new immigrants, the Statue of Liberty. Here, she was backed by a map of Pakistan. The Pakistan Independence Day Parade organizers thus expressed their idea of the parade as a day to educate the younger generation born in the United States about the history of their parents' immigration to a nation of immigrants and to inculcate pride in their two countries. America's most recognizable icon superimposed on a map of the old country was the symbol of pride in a dual national and cultural heritage.

In the Muslim World Day Parade there is no Statue of Liberty, no costumed dancing troupes, parade queens, beauty pageant princesses, performers, acrobats, stilt-walkers, or giant balloons. The unifying characteristic of the marchers is Islamic dress, defined to me as clothing that covers the body. According to the New York City police captain in charge, the Muslim parade never has an alcohol problem, unlike many parades, including the infamous Saint Patrick's Day Parade, which has in recent years been forced to institute stringent alcohol consumption regulation. In the 1989 Saint Patrick's Day Parade, 3,237 police were called out to maintain order at a cost to the city of $473,000 in overtime pay, and the Sanitation Department estimated an extra $30,000 per event to clean up (Sims 1992a: 6).

For the pleasure and education of the viewers, Muslim marchers were colorful ethnic dress and, most significant, carry signs. They do so for two main purposes, one of which is to identify themselves as members of a specific Islamic organization. Identification by means of signs contributes to the spectators' gaining knowledge through the presentation of an unfolding, written narrative about the breadth of Islam in the world or about its presence on the local scene. Banners proclaim the existence of the Islamic Society of Staten Island, the Chinese Muslim organization, and PIEDAD, the acronym for the emerging Hispanic Muslim community (see Figure 6.4). In the last case, the juxtaposition of Islam with New York's Hispanic

Figures 6.4 and 6.5. The Muslim World Day Parade: Texts and organizations. (Photo: Susan Slyomovics)

community is only made manifest by the message of the banner, which is legible and knowable in immediate, informative ways not evidenced by the banner's carriers: the marchers' distinctive combination of Hispanic ethnicity and Muslim religious identification were remarked upon by the spectators only after they read the sign — without the scorecard you cannot identify the players.

A second way Muslim marchers carry their message is by means of signs quoting sayings or Koranic verses explaining Islam. To help the onlookers, signs are mainly in English so that we can read the ambulating sacred texts. There are parallels here to the language of cinema, in which overtitles are used to identify speakers to the viewers, or the very words of the speakers are translated in subtitles. In some ways, signs enable participants to identify themselves and to bring forth complex utterances about religious faith. For example, the Muslim credo, "There is no God but Allah the One, the Absolute, the Almighty, One Creator, One Humanity," appears on a large white banner followed in marching succession by the names of Jewish and Christian prophets recognized by Islam and ending with Muhammad, the last seal of prophecy: Noah, Abraham, Moses, Jesus, and Muhammad (see Figure 6.5). Many signs emphasize Islam's inclusive embrace of figures identified with Judeo-Christian religions, all of whom are honored by Islam.

A sign is an act of reading and writing on a two-dimensional surface. With their banners, marchers are mapping onto three-dimensional real space analogues of a two-dimensional text. A different kind of literacy is being learned, one in which sacred Muslim texts are aligned with images of parading South Asian men and women. Islamic religious meanings are nonuniversal for New Yorkers and must be made explicit. The result is that the Koranic texts and sayings cannot be unmediated copies of the actual book. The information that is conveyed is the outcome of a culturally determined relationship in which Muslim New Yorkers choose appropriate messages to translate. They are embedded in a complex political argument about the influx of new immigrants, their shared but dissimilar heritage, and what their place is in the city. To convey these ideas, Muslims represent their community through image making and calligraphy, spectacle and artifice.

A float that appeared at the fifth (but not the sixth) annual Muslim World Day Parade layered yet another level of representation by means of architectural three-dimensionality. This float was an immense, magnified Koran, in the shape of an open book awaiting readers on its stand. It too

Figure 6.6. The Muslim World Day Parade: The Kaaba of Mecca as a float. (Photo: Susan Slyomovics)

rested on a large platform, around which could be read a caption quoting a verse that serendipitously described both the religious path of scripture and the secular pathway that is Lexington Avenue: "Verily this Koran guides unto that path which is the straightest." Sacred writing achieved a transcendent three-dimensional power enhanced by its slow and stately motion through space. The image of the floating Koran became a more complex statement than its well-known words inscribed along the sides of the float: the image subsumed the words. This particular image functioned as a metaphorical representation of creative communal responses to the demands of New York City parades and the strictures within Islam against figurative representation.

Other parade floats represented a more familiar three-dimensionality. For these floats, the organizers chose three additional cultural symbols for their educational and religious value. The first float was the Kaaba, the Black Stone of Mecca and the holiest shrine in Islam, a tradition going back to the time of Abraham (see Figure 6.6). The Kaaba was a center to which all the Arab tribes returned for trade, poetic contests, and worship. It is still sacred territory, an inviolable sanctuary of refuge. Between the fifth and

Figure 6.7. The Muslim World Day Parade: The Masjid al-Haram of Medina as a float. (Photo: Susan Slyomovics)

sixth annual parade, an explanatory title, "Mecca," was added to the floating Kaaba to give the reader-spectator a location marker. Similarly, the second float, a replica of the Dome of the Rock in Jerusalem, exhibited increased signs from one year to the next. The third float, the Masjid al-Haram of Medina, was the third of the three sacred sites of Islam (see Figure 6.7).

According to Robert DeVito, who owns the Bond Parade Float Company and who designs and builds most of New York City's parade floats (with the exception of the Macy's Thanksgiving Day Parade), it costs approximately twenty-five hundred dollars to construct a float such as the Dome of the Rock mosque of Jerusalem. (Compare this to the replica of Columbus's boat, the *Santa Maria*, which was built for the Italian-American Columbus Day Parade at a cost of twenty-five thousand dollars). Floats are owned by the various ethnic parade committees but stored and refurbished at the Bond Company premises in Clifton, New Jersey. This system means that among groups with shared cultural symbols—such as the Greeks and the Turks, who both present a float of Saint Sofia of Constantinople or Istanbul—each group must own and pay for its own replica, because both the American system of individually duplicated ownership of product and the political enmity between Greeks and Turks ensure that neither group would ever agree to split the high costs of their shared symbol.

A fourth mosque float in the Muslim World Day Parade represented a local construction project, the new Muslim Center of Queens, which exists, as of the sixth annual parade (1991), only as a float. When the reality it represents, an architecturally purposeful mosque and Muslim center in Queens, is completed in 1995, it will house a library, a mosque, a gymnasium, a school, and a meeting center for the growing community of South Asian Muslims in the borough of Queens.

As the floats and participants turned westward from Madison Avenue toward the parade's end and entered the square at Broadway and Twenty-third Street, they passed a reviewing stand. Local dignitaries, representatives of the mayor's office, and heads of New York City mosques made speeches about brotherhood, community, and the "gorgeous mosaic" that is New York. Beginning at the viewing section and stretching southward for a few blocks were food stands, book stalls, and tables with literature from the various Muslim organizations. The parade marchers melted into the crowd, picnicking and browsing, or gathered at the far end of the square where a large platform had been erected for speakers and musicians. The procession ended by 4:30 P.M. and the speakers and stands disappeared at sunset.

Meaning and Community

Theoreticians of parades claim that in this particular civic pageant Muslims produce parallel versions of ceremonies and events to reassure the larger society that even Muslims accept and join in American pluralism. New immigrants may alter details of civic festive behavior but the result still recognizably replicates the host population's institutions, now common to the immigrants. I would emphasize, however, that at the same time Muslims are actors in a history that differs from that of their onlookers.

In the context of the opening prayer held on the street, the attempt to represent oneself to an outside world is much less marked than the obvious self-representation of the march which then culminates in the Muslim organizers' hospitably hosting a food fair. The parade is framed by, and must be seen in relation to, both the activity of communal prayer that precedes it and the communal feast that ends it. For example, the parade's beginning with a mass prayer shows that Islamic ritual practice is portable, it can be established anywhere, and it secures meaning and community for participants.

The organizers also believed that the event would be an all-day affair for most of the participants. Surely, they told me when I asked about the food fair, with people marching and moving from morning to evening, you must give them a chance to rest, to freshen up, to meet each other, to eat, and to pray. They maintained that the Muslim World Day Parade was not solely a parade, a matter of showing who they were to themselves and to non-Muslim New Yorkers; rather, the parade was an American setting for an exchange, for everybody to spend time together. Therefore what was needed was prayer, food, and a stationary gathering (not a moving procession) in which participants eat at the same time as they listen to speeches or music.

The day is temporally segmented, but the segments are not necessarily differentiated in terms of Durkheim's classic formulation of the segregation of the sacred from the profane. Instead two spheres of life are marked: one in which Islamic ritual is clearly practiced as the opening prayer sequence, and a second one, in which a composite construction is forged from acquired practices, inherited traditions, and new solutions to the urban experience.

For example, Abdul Munim, one of the parade's organizers, shares the views of Edward Said. They both believe that to speak of Islam in America today is to mean only unpleasant things: "Americans have only the opportunity to view the Islamic world reductively, coercively, and oppositionally" (Said 1981: 9, 51). According to Abdul Munim, Americans judge Islam by television images showing mobs burning Salman Rushdie's book *The Satanic Verses* or chanting, "Death to America." To illustrate the concerns of the Muslim World Day Parade organizers, Munim told me of the opinions of a Catholic priest who participated in the parade. The priest objected to the constant loud call and response of the *takbir*: any marcher can cry out "takbir" (say God is great), which is inevitably followed by the shouted mass response, "Allahu akbar" (God is great). The priest counseled that for Americans the *takbir* formula acoustically resonates with memories of anti-American demonstrations in Teheran that were shown daily on television newscasts during the years of the Iran hostage crisis. In order to avoid offending American sensibilities, he felt, they should eliminate this feature of ritual behavior. The organizers debated at length among themselves whether to eliminate the identifying cry; they were concerned with the image of Muslims in a Christian (albeit secularized) American culture. They intuitively recognized that crowds of Muslims may spell danger to the American public.[6] Nonetheless, they concluded that the *takbir* must be kept in the parade but that the parade participants must take care to act in such a manner as to ensure that the phrase *Allahu akbar* could never be perceived by New Yorkers as an expression of Islamic anger.

By retaining a traditional practice, open to misunderstanding, and by contextualizing it in the familiar, the parade could glide over the meanings of social acts and words derived solely from religion: Muslim rituals could operate simultaneously with secular parade rituals.[7] The result was that the parade does not always keep events apart. Sometimes the two worlds of foreign religion and urban secular American culture clashed, confusing not only Catholic priests but also Sufi musicians who, for varying reasons, resist mixing the two domains. An ethnic parade should exclude frightening religious practices, but a Muslim procession should include Sufi ecstatic dance.

One way the domains mix is through the use of space. Although time may be a way to differentiate the separate moments of prayer, procession, and food fair, the shared space in which these events take place effectively counterbalances any attempt at sustaining mutually exclusive spheres. It is the city and its streets that give prominence to the events and encourage attendance at all three. In temporal terms, the Muslim moment in New York City is ephemeral; spatially the city's linear street grid works to blend together the disparate elements of competing symbolic realms. For one day each year, a religious collectivity within a larger society is recognized by outsiders as an ethnic group. For the occasion, its architectural symbol is the mosque, which has also become a social center for the Muslim immigrant community in the city.

New York City is a center for cultural production and it plays a prominent part in a process Hobsbawm has called "the invention of tradition" (Hobsbawn and Ranger 1983). In Europe, modern nation-states making their transition from monarchy to republic consolidate their power by constructing modes of communication and edification, ceremonies and rituals that are designed to help citizens understand relationships between government and the people and history. In the United States this process has been somewhat different from that in Europe because the creation of traditions such as the ethnic parade has been more laissez-faire, a recourse for those who want to use spectacles and performances for their own purposes.

One purpose of the parade is to introduce non-Muslims to pan-Islamic visual symbols. Arabic writing is generally considered to be a uniquely coherent and consistent vehicle with a wide range of meanings.[8] Perhaps the Muslim World Day Parade is part of a development in which calligraphy — the embellishment of writing, a basic element of Islamic art — is used in new ways that are adapted to the American setting. For Muslims, writing remains a culturally constant, discrete, and clearly identifiable form. Nonetheless, radical changes in its language, alphabet, dimensionality, function, and context have taken place in response to the particularity of a New York City civic pageant and the aesthetic demands of such an occasion.

Parades are public and publicly dramatize social relations. Participants define who can be a social actor and what subjects and ideas should be accommodated and presented. When the parade organizers imagined and proposed new images for Islam, they not only defined images of Muslim identity but were in turn shaped by their actions. Their images of mosques riding on floats, of the Koran itself as a parade float, and calligraphic enhancement of writing by motion through space point to the dynamic processes by which immigrants invent a new vocabulary for putting on public celebrations.

A Muslim civic parade highlights issues with its innovative use of signs, the claims on secular space for prayer and the call to prayer, the creation of images, the orientation to the traditional east, and the presentation of the Muslim self to the American public. In regard to the issue of the *takbir,* the call and response of "God is great," however, it should be noted that Muslims occupying public space in New York City must for the time being lower the volume. They must modulate the passion of the *takbir* and Sufi brotherhoods; likewise, they must obey city noise codes that prohibit the amplified call to prayer five times a day. What Muslims in America articulate ritually about Islam in public should be heard as friendly, accommodating, and familiar, it should not be overheard, and at best it should still be heard only among their own.

Notes

1. The American Muslim Council, a nonprofit organization established in 1990 in Washington, D.C., to serve the interests of the Muslim community in the United States, lists as one of its goals to prepare the first-ever comprehensive demographic study of United States Muslims. The group claims five to six million resident Muslims.

2. For an overview of urban folklore and its historical and methodological concerns with the city, see Kirshenblatt-Gimblett 1983.

3. See the special issue on processional performance in *The Drama Review* (1985), and the introduction by Brooks McNamara and Barbara Kirshenblatt-Gimblett.

4. The principle of ceremonial copying also applies to another venerable New York City institution: suspension of alternate-side-of-the-street parking for religious feast days. Muslim leaders lobbying City Hall for *Id al-Fitr* at the end of Ramadan and *Id al-Adha* were quoted: "It would mean when we look at the overall picture of America itself, we would see equity with Christianity and Judaism in terms of being honored and respected" (Liff 1992: 8).

5. In some cases—for example, the Greenwich Village Halloween Parade—parades take place on home territory; the West Indian Carnival procession on Labor Day marches down Eastern Parkway, a largely West Indian area of Brooklyn. In contrast, the Lesbian and Gay Parade, a more public and civic declaration, marches south from Central Park down Broadway.

6. See also Dorman and Farhang 1987, Ghareeb 1983, and Shaheen 1984.

7. See Bodnar 1991, which emphasizes not only the contested nature of commemoration but that public memory will always alter the past to fit the politics of the present.

8. See, for example, the writings of historians and art historians such as Oleg Grabar, Annemarie Schimmel, and Franz Rosenthal.

References

Bodnar, John.
　　1991　*Remaking America: Public Memory, Commemoration, and Patriotism in the Twentieth Century*. Princeton: Princeton University Press.
Davis, Susan G.
　　1986　*Parades and Power: Street Theatre in Nineteenth-Century Philadelphia*. Philadelphia: Temple University Press.
Dorman, W. A., and M. Farhang
　　1987　*The U.S. Press and Iran*. Berkeley: University of California Press.
Ghareeb, Edmund
　　1983　*Split Vision: The Portrayal of Arabs in the American Media*. Washington, D.C.: The American-Arab Affairs Council.
Hobsbawm, Eric, and Terence Ranger, eds.
　　1983　*The Invention of Tradition*. New York: Cambridge University Press.
Kasinitz, Philip, and Judith Freidenberg-Herbstein
　　1987　"The Puerto Rican Parade and West Indian Carnival." In Constance R. Sutton and Elsa M. Chaney, eds., *Caribbean Life in New York City: Sociocultural Dimensions*. New York: Center for Migration Studies, 327–50.
Kelton, Jane Gladden
　　1985　"The New York City St. Patrick's Day Parade: Invention of Contention and Consensus." *The Drama Review* 29: 93–105.

Kirshenblatt-Gimblett, Barbara
    1983   "The Future of Folklore Studies in America: The Urban Frontier." *Folklore Forum* 16: 175–234.
Kugelmass, Jack
    1991   "Wishes Come True: Designing the Greenwich Village Halloween Parade." *Journal of American Folklore* 104: 443–65.
Lawrence, Denise
    1982   "Parades, Politics, and Competing Urban Images: Doo Dah and Roses." *Urban Anthropology* 11: 155–76.
Liff, Bob
    1992   "Parking Prayers: Muslims Want Special Days." *Newsday,* March 13, p. 8.
McNamara, Brooks, and Barbara Kirshenblatt-Gimblett
    1985   "Introduction" Special issue, "Processional Performance." *The Drama Review* 29: 2–5.
Said, Edward
    1981   *Covering Islam: How the Media and the Experts Determine How We See the Rest of the World.* New York: Pantheon.
Salvo, Joseph J., and Ronald J. Ortiz, with substantial contributions by Francis Vardy
    1993   *The Newest New Yorkers.* New York: New York City Department of City Planning.
Schneider, Jo Anne
    1990   "Defining Boundaries, Creating Contacts: Puerto Rican and Polish Representations of Group Identity through Ethnic Parades." *Journal of Ethnic Studies* 18: 33–57.
Shaheen, Jack
    1984   *TV Arabs.* Bowling Green, Ohio: Popular Culture Press.
Sims, Calvin
    1992a "New York City Rethinks Parades." *New York Times,* April 12, p. 6.
    1992b "To Save Money, City Hall Considers Cutting Parades: A Route to Budget Cuts Fraught with Perils." *New York Times,* April 7, p. B3.
Slyomovics, Susan
    n.d.   "Storefront Mosques of New York City." In Barbara Metcalf, ed., *Muslim Space in the West.* Berkeley: University of California Press. In press.
Tuan, Yi-Fu
    1977   *Space and Place: The Perspective of Experience.* Minneapolis: University of Minnesota Press.

Madhulika S. Khandelwal

7. Indian Immigrants in Queens, New York City: Patterns of Spatial Concentration and Distribution, 1965–1990

This chapter discusses patterns of population distribution of Indians in New York City during a period of constant numerical growth. The rapid expansion of the Indian population in the late 1960s coincided with a shift in concentration from the borough of Manhattan to the borough of Queens. The continuous immigration and changes in the economic and social profile of Indians in the subsequent years have influenced their spatial patterns and conceptions of space. Certain areas of Queens have become receiving areas for newly arrived immigrants, whereas other areas are inhabited by more established Indians. A number of cultural activities and businesses have established themselves in the receiving areas, making them important resource points for the ethnic communities. The idea of space — of using it and claiming it — is perceived differently in different parts of the city. Particular areas have emerged as ethnic spaces where many claims intersect, raising issues about various strata within Indian populations, and about intercultural relations between Indians and other New Yorkers.

Nature of Growth and Changing Concentrations

The present discussion focuses on the recent decades when Indian immigration increased rather dramatically after the 1965 Immigration and Naturalization Act. There is a longer history of anti-Indian discrimination in the United States and political movements by Indians in the pre-1965 period — suggestive of important continuities and differences with the recent Indian immigration — which I do not discuss here (Daniels 1990; Jensen 1988). Whereas in the 1960s, before the 1965 act was implemented, a few hundred

Indians would immigrate every year, annual immigration from India averaged between fifteen and twenty thousand in the 1970s and between twenty and thirty thousand in the 1980s. Thus the rapid increase in the size of the Indian population should be kept in mind as an underlying process of the patterns discussed here.

The post-1965 Indian immigration has been perceived as comprised of professional and highly educated Indians — in both popular and scholarly opinion. Certainly the data from the late 1960s and early 1970s support this image. In the early 1970s, the Immigration and Naturalization Service was recording an astonishing and almost unprecedented rate of about 80 to 90 percent of working Indians as professionals. Articles and books were addressing this phenomenon of the "brain drain" of doctors, scientists, and engineers from developing countries such as India (Khandelwal 1991). From the mid-1970s onward, however, a trend toward greater occupational and economic diversity began to emerge among Indian immigrants which has continued unabated in the following years.

The post-1965 Indians who settled in the United States could sponsor their relatives for immigration and thus started a process of family reunification. Though professionally and technically skilled immigrants predominated among the sponsored family members, such sponsorships implied that Indians were no longer migrating *on the basis* of their qualifications. A second pattern emerged in the changing American economy of the 1970s, which was less expansive than that during the 1960s — the period of "Great Society" programs instituted by President Lyndon Johnson and of major investment in medical and research and development divisions. Evidence of the shift away from the 1960s open-arms welcome to foreign professionals can be seen in the 1976 Health Professions Educational Assistance Act, which, in response to intense lobbying in Congress, amended the previous 1965 act to restrict immigration of medical professionals (*India Abroad,* October 29, 1976).

Such trends resulted in the occupational diversity of Indian immigrants. Attracted by the growing size of the ethnic Indian market, many professionals turned to businesses in insurance and travel agencies, ethnic clothing, and groceries. Increasingly, not only would the qualifications of Indian immigrants diversify, but professionally trained immigrants would undertake new — and often lesser-paying — occupations.

Although the process of economic and occupational diversity exists to some degree in Indian populations in other parts of the United States, it is more pronounced in large cities, such as New York, than in smaller urban centers and their suburbs. For both family reunification and diversity of occupations, New York, with its substantial number of earlier settlers and relatively wider range of careers, was the natural choice for many new arrivals. In the early 1990s, after many years of this process of diversification, Indians in New York are employed not only in professional occupations but also at newsstands, tollbooths, auto shops, and candy stores, and work as taxi drivers, clerks, and salespersons. This occupational variety is only one aspect of the larger diversity, which is also expressed in the social organization of the Indian population through mushrooming religious, regional, caste, and other associations, and their expression in different cultural standards.

Most Indian organizations of the late 1960s and the early 1970s, unaffected by the expansion in size of the population and shift in concentration from Manhattan to Queens, brought together Indians of different regional and religious persuasions under one organization. Parallel to this organizational activity, the first half of the 1970s saw a spate of new organizations based on the regional affiliations of Indians: Maharashtra Mandal in 1970, Tamil Sangam in 1970, the Cultural Association of Bengal in 1971, Kerala Samajam of New York in 1971, Telugu Literary and Cultural Society in 1971, Kannada Koota in 1973, the Gujarati Samaj in 1973, and so on (Fisher 1980). The diverse religious activities — usually practiced in rented spaces or members' houses — began to be established in their own buildings. The Richmond Hill Gurdwara opened in 1972 and the Hindu Temple of Flushing in 1976. Also in 1976 the first Indian television program, "Vision of Asia," was inaugurated.

I am aware that the patterns among New York's Indian immigrants cannot be applied to the rest of the Indian populations living in the United States, each group no doubt having its particular features. Nevertheless, this discussion about New York is relevant to Indian immigrants at large, because economic heterogeneity is a growing nationwide trend for Indians in the United States; though distinct, New York is not unique in this respect. Signs of smaller or bigger doses of social and economic diversity have made their appearances in different parts of the country (Gardner et al. 1985). Among the urban centers in the United States, New York has the largest concentration of Indians (about 10 percent of total 1990 Indian population in the country), and this calls for a careful look at its dynamics.

Within New York City, the shift in locale of Indian concentration was more than evident in the late 1960s. In this discussion of spatial patterns of Indians in New York City, I focus on the features in one borough of the city, that is, Queens. By 1980, of the total New York City Indian population of 40,945, only 6,037 (15 percent) lived in Manhattan, as opposed to 21,736 (53 percent) in Queens. According to 1990 Census, of the total New York City Indian population of 94,590, 7,395 (8 percent) lived in Manhattan in comparison with 56,601 (60 percent) in Queens (U.S. Census 1980, 1990).

The Queens neighborhoods where Indians concentrate, such as Flushing, Jackson Heights, Elmhurst, Corona, Rego Park, Forest Hills, and Richmond Hill, have received large doses of recent immigration from countries in Asia, Latin America, and the Caribbean, giving these areas some of the most diverse populations in the world. Roger Sanjek writes about the population of two Queens neighborhoods:

> Elmhurst-Corona today is a complex mix of long-established Italian, Irish, German and Jewish white Americans; more recently arrived white young professionals; Black Americans who have moved in since desegregation of the Lefrak City apartment complex in the late 1970s; and immigrant and second generation Koreans, Chinese, Indians, Filipinos, Colombians, Ecuadorians, Dominicans, Cubans, Puerto Ricans, and other Asians, Latin Americans, Caribbeans, and Africans. There is no majority ethnic group. Elmhurst-Corona today is a "majority minority" neighborhood where Hispanics, Asians and blacks together outnumber white Americans. (Sanjek 1989)

Whereas some ethnic groups concentrate more heavily in certain areas and some business clusters have emerged, the populations are ethnically and culturally mixed and no exclusive ethnic neighborhoods have developed. This implies that Indians have to conceive their spaces — residential, business, and cultural — within the complex intercultural relations emerging in Queens.

Clear stratification in spatial arrangements and use of territory is seen within Indian immigrant groups. Whereas the upper-class immigrants have looked to more pan-Indian activities, and classical culture and sophisticated life-styles, lower middle-class Indians have created more popular standards of ethnic life. Large Indian events continue to prosper in Manhattan, such as the Diwali celebration at South Street Seaport and the India Day Parade for India's Independence Day in August of every year (Mukhi 1994). Parallel to these developments, regional subcultures and religious activities have thrived in Queens' receiving areas. This separation of spatial patterns is also reflected in Indian organizations and leadership roles. The two worlds of Indian immigrants are growing quite separately from each other, with few Indian organizations addressing the needs of the poorer classes. That task is left to a handful of progressive and service-oriented organizations which turn to the receiving areas as the places of people whom they wish to serve.

Numbers, Location, and Integration

Until the late 1960s, when the volume of Indian immigration increased manifold rather suddenly, most Indians in New York lived in Manhattan. They were largely students and a small number of merchants and professionals. I consider them as early waves of New Immigrants of the post-1965 period, who, on the basis of their educational qualifications and other backgrounds, may be distinguished from the traditional image of the United States immigrant. Their group characteristics and activities suggest distinct patterns of spatial arrangements.

Though relatively new in the United States, this population had already had considerable exposure to Western ways. They had received their schooling in the British education system in India (or some part of their education internationally, mainly in European countries), and so their familiarity with the English language and their high technical and educational qualifications made them easy candidates for participation in American education or mainstream professional life. Such characteristics brought them in close contact with white Americans of similar economic and educational levels. The level of integration of the early waves of Indians in the American educational and occupational sectors was remarkable.

These achievements, however, were accomplished parallel to their maintenance of Indian traditions and cultural traits in more private and social aspects of life. These Indians were actively involved in organizing concerts of classical Indian music and dance, arranging movie shows, and pursuing Indian cooking, and the women continued to wear traditional Indian dresses. Indian student groups at Columbia University were known for organizing cultural activities, film shows, and conferences that would foster ethnic networks. There was no evidence of religious conversion among these immigrants, who established ways of pursuing their religious faiths in the new land. Limited numbers, high education levels, and a strong nationalist Indian sentiment contributed to their pan-Indian activities. Perceiving themselves as able representatives of sophisticated Indian culture and champions of Indian nationalism, they presented these causes with marked confidence to white Americans, particularly those who formed friendships and showed interest in Indian culture and society.

The activities of Indians of this period suggest that they tried hard to establish Indian practices in the United States, but that these efforts were restricted to social and cultural life. Indian religions were practiced but only in households or rented spaces. Similarly, movies and concerts were conspicuous as ethnic activities but could not be frequent. A small number of Indian restaurants and businesses existed in Manhattan — of considerable importance as ethnic symbols to the small number of city's Indians — but they shared their clientele between Indians and non-Indians. Of the stores that sold Indian dresses or groceries, few were owned by Indians themselves. The celebration of ethnic life in New York City, influenced by the class and educational level of the immigrants, was marked by crossing racial and ethnic boundaries. The small size of the Indian population and its integration in certain sectors of American society could not create permanent spaces in New York City that were distinctly Indian.

In this scenario, the clash for Indian spaces was not fully experienced. Establishing separate Indian spaces was not the goal of the early Indians and, given their numbers and orientation, not even feasible. They were perceived by their fellow Americans as a different kind of immigrant group, different at least from the traditional image of American immigrants. Quite a few Indians were perceived as able representatives of the ancient land and culture they came from. In a 1951 issue of *The New Yorker*, an article described Jagjit Singh, an Indian leader and an import merchant:

> Sirdar Jagjit Singh, the president of the India League of America, a privately sponsored nonprofit organization that seeks to interpret India to, and to further Indian causes in, this country, is, at fifty-three, a handsome, six-foot Sikh who by means of persistent salesmanship, urbane manners, and undeviating enthusiasm, has established himself as the principal link between numberless Americans and the vast mysterious Eastern subcontinent where he was born. (Daniels 1990)

Obviously, all Indians in the United States, regardless of their economic and occupational status, have not received such acclaim. Negative statements about Indian immigrants engaged in farm labor and other such occupations abound in documents from the early decades of the twentieth century. The positive image of New York's limited, highly educated, affluent, and integrative Indian population changed with the arrival of new waves of Indian immigration in the late 1960s.

Indians have continued to live in Manhattan but with no sharp changes in their life-styles from those described for the 1960s. In terms of socioeconomic profile and interaction with American society, little has changed. Ethnic Indian businesses have multiplied in Manhattan and more Indian restaurants have appeared. But the clientele of such businesses is mixed and different from the Indian customers of Queens. When the primary locale of Indians shifted in the late 1960s, the patterns of the new concentration in Queens were qualitatively different from those of previous concentration in Manhattan.

New Concentrations and Patterns

One of the first Indian concentrations in Queens developed in the late 1960s in the neighborhood of Flushing where some Indian professionals arrived with their families. They became pioneers whose selection of Flushing attracted more newcomers from India to the neighborhood. In a few years, Flushing had a few thousand Indians, mainly professional men and their families who had decided to settle permanently in the United States. Members of this population did not establish an exclusive residential area for Indians. Instead, they lived interspersed with people of different ethnicities, though concentrated in certain apartment buildings. Around 1970, some businesses opened on Main Street (near Queens Botanical Gardens) to cater to this new and growing Indian population.

This Indian presence emerged before Chinese businesses flourished dramatically in Flushing around the mid-1970s. Indians were perceived as primarily a residential group whose occupational activities and economic pursuits were conducted in other parts of the city, still mainly in Manhattan. Though the few local Indian businesses expanded into a cluster in the following years, Flushing did not become the economic center for Indians in the same way that it developed for Chinese, and later, for Koreans as well (Chen and Tchen 1989; Chen 1992). Most Indians still shopped for major purchases in Manhattan. Though Queens had experienced a population shift of Indians, it was not to be their business center until after 1976, when the Indian shopping district began to grow on Seventy-fourth Street in Jackson Heights.

Between 1965 and 1990, Indians spread out to different parts of Queens. By 1980 and 1990, virtually all of the areas in Queens had Indian residents, although certain neighborhoods developed as their residential and business centers. Many businesses interspersed with residential areas shared by immigrants and established Americans of other ethnic groups;

thus there is no sharp distinction between residential and business areas. In such intense ethnically diverse areas, Indians at best share spatial concentrations. To carve out exclusive Indian spaces and designate them as such is not a simple process.

Most recent arrivals in Queens would begin their immigrant experience in neighborhoods such as Flushing and Elmhurst. These areas have rental apartments within easy proximity to public transport—a necessity for new immigrants. As Indians have been arriving in these areas for many years now, these neighborhoods are perceived as suitable areas for new Indian arrivals, thus fostering a pattern of ethnic chain migration. After initial years in these neighborhoods, the immigrants tend to move to "better" residential areas in suburban settings. This step coincides with their process of "settling down" in a new land and their climb in upward economic mobility. The move indicates that these households are ready to mortgage single-family homes, to afford automobile transportation, and to choose "better" school districts for their children.

Most of the Indian immigrants ready to move out of receiving areas select middle-class, upper middle-class, or affluent residential areas within or around Queens. Within the borough of Queens such neighborhoods are Bayside, Forest Hills, Whitestone, Douglaston, and Jamaica Estates. In the same pursuit, many Indians move out of Queens to areas in nearby counties such as Nassau (Long Island), Westchester, and Rockland. These areas, whether within the city limits or beyond them, have a predominantly white American population (*U.S. Census* 1980, 1990).

The Indians dwelling in suburbia primarily form well-to-do professional households. Some may own reasonably successful businesses. On the basis of their economic strength and their educational qualifications, these Indians seek to find a place amid their counterpart economic class in white American populations. They have continued ethnic Indian activities, but those circles are limited to affluent Indians. Such Indians participate in organizations such as Rotary and golf clubs. Almost reminiscent of the earlier Indian immigrants of Manhattan, they have achieved a striking, though partial, level of integration in American society.

As older waves of Indians have engaged in the process of making the transition to suburban life, newer immigrants have continued to arrive in the receiving areas. This ongoing process of moving into and out of certain neighborhoods—which is now over two decades old—has converted receiving areas into centers of ethnic Indian life. They house many places of worship, businesses, and other activities that serve a variety of Indians.

Indians residing in these areas, generally more recent arrivals, walk up to these services. Families strolling in the areas of ethnic Indian business areas, elderly individuals walking to and from the temples, and young people gathering in small groups are all common sights in such areas. Indians living in outlying areas return to these places to do their shopping for Indian goods, practice their religions, and visit their relatives who arrived later and are as yet still living in the receiving areas.

In keeping with the increasing socioeconomic diversity of Indian immigration of the past two decades, the receiving areas of Queens have also been fueled by a constant stream of new arrivals of mixed economic and educational profiles. As a result, a popular cultural life has emerged in these areas that is distinct from integrative patterns practiced in Manhattan and suburbs, where the Indian population is more homogeneous in its economic status and thinly scattered in its geographical spread. These Queens neighborhoods serve as such important resource centers for Indian immigrants that I consider them *core areas* of ethnic life.

I have selected two spheres of activity to highlight ethnic Indian life in the Queens core areas: first, cultural and religious activities, and second, ethnic Indian businesses.

Cultural and Religious Activities in Core Areas

The landscape of Queens is characterized by many houses of worship. Sikh gurdwaras exist in Richmond Hill and Flushing, and Islam is practiced in different mosques in Corona, Jamaica, and Flushing. Several Christian services are also conducted in Indian languages for Indians of Christian faith.

Efforts to transplant religious traditions in one's new land is quite visible in the case of Hindu Indians (Khandelwal 1989). Among the many Hindu temples in New York area, most are located in Queens. The two more prominent ones are the Hindu Temple of Flushing and the Geeta Temple of Elmhurst. Both these temples replicate temple systems of India. The Hindu Temple of Flushing was founded along the lines of Tirupati Devasthanam, a large Hindu temple in South India. The temple architecture and the interior are very much South Indian in style and appear striking in a primarily middle-class residential New York neighborhood. In terms of its ceremonies, atmosphere, and appeal, the temple attracts more South Indians than North Indians. No one is excluded, however, and an increasing participation is felt from North Indians living in the vicinity of the temple, for whom it is convenient to use this place of worship.

The Geeta Temple is a North Indian temple, and the deities in it have a distinct North Indian appeal. Quite different from the Hindu Temple of Flushing, the Geeta Temple's all-embracing Hinduism incorporates among its deities images of Mahavira, the founder of Jainism (a religion practiced more in northern and western India than in the south), and some modern Indian saints. The participants here are almost exclusively North Indian.

Besides these two temples, other Hindu religious places operate in Queens. In Flushing, a block away from the Hindu Temple, is the Swaminarayan Temple, which serves as the national headquarters of this flourishing sect of the Gujarati Indian community. The fact that this sect can found a full-fledged temple of its own indicates the resources and organized efforts of this religious community. The Swaminarayan Bochasanvasi Sanstha that supports these religious activities has also been very active in other Indian cultural representations; in 1991, it organized a large event called "Festival of India" in New Jersey.

Other essentially Hindu religious activities are carried out from offices of organizations such as Chinmoy Mission, Brahmakumaris, and Arunachal Ashram, all located in Queens. These organizations have a distinct philosophy and path, usually set by a religious order or leader, and have sister organizations in India and other parts of the world. Many of them have a spiritual appeal that transcends ethnicity. Thus it is common to find non-Indians among followers of such sects, and often their recent conversion makes them ardent participants. Many other Hindu religious activities take place in temporary or rented spaces. This is specially true of smaller groups or sects that do not as yet have resources for permanent spaces.

These places of worship in Queens core areas are visited by Indian residents of nearby receiving areas. Those who live in the suburbs travel to them to partake in these activities. Particularly on weekends these spaces attract a large number of suburban Indians who travel to ethnic spaces from their mixed but essentially white neighborhoods. The same is true of other cultural activities. Queens features a range of concerts and cultural festivals which attract Indians from different parts of the tristate area.

An important landmark in creating ethnic Indian spaces in core areas was the creation of a community center by Gujarati Samaj in Flushing in 1990. This community center includes a large space for holding festivals, religious events, film showings, parties, and lectures. Though this space has been arranged by leaders of a Gujarati organization, it is used by a variety of

Indian organizations for different purposes. In its life of just a few years, it has housed functions as varied as a religious ceremony by a local Bengali group, a dance party attended by young Indian Americans, a large *garba* (a folk dance popular among the Gujarati communities in India, but joined in by other Indian groups in the United States) dance event, and a talk by scholars of India.

From one point of view, these spaces can be seen as adding to the rich cultural diversity of Queens. From a different angle, as representations of the continuation of religious traditions that seek to reestablish themselves in a new land, these places of worship stand as symbols of nonassimilable cultures. Individuals wearing traditional Indian dress and pursuing distinct ethnic activities are perceived by many Queens residents as aliens. The Indian temples and mosques in the core areas have often been vandalized. Many Indian visitors to these places, especially those who stand apart from others because of their dress and other features, have been harassed. Cases of anti-Indian violence are not entirely absent in the suburbs, nor are cases of resisting the growth of Indian religious and cultural activities. In core areas, however, the creation of and contests for cultural spaces are constructed differently.

Business Spaces

During this period of growth and establishment of the Indian population in the New York area along distinct spatial patterns, a few blocks in Jackson Heights, Queens, have developed as the primary business area for Indians. Discussion of this business concentration reveals many salient features of the Indian experience in New York City.

Indian businesses existed in the New York area before the Jackson Heights shopping area developed in the mid-1970s. A few stores on Lexington Avenue in downtown Manhattan (Twenty-eighth and Twenty-ninth Streets), as a continuation of the pre-1965 patterns, grew into a cluster in the following decades. Though often known as "Little India" to many Manhattanites, these businesses stood distinct and separate from the largest concentration of Indian population that had emerged in Queens. Small clusters and individual Indian businesses have continued to exist in various parts of New York City, but the emergence, within fifteen years, of Jackson Heights as the leading national and international stop for the Indian diaspora calls for a detailed analysis of its success and issues.

In 1976, the first Indian store, by the name of Sam & Raj, opened on Seventy-fourth Street. A little detail about it is relevant to this discussion. Two Indian engineer friends, who could not quench their spirit of entrepreneurship in the American firm where they worked, decided to start an electronics and appliance business in Manhattan in 1973. After losing their lease in 1976, they searched for another place to reopen and thus moved to Seventy-fourth Street in Jackson Heights.

A quick succession of businesses opened, which, the owners of Sam & Raj explained to me, was unplanned. We do see, however, many interrelated patterns in the mid-1970s which made the Jackson Heights business concentration such a success. In 1976 itself, when Seventy-fourth Street had but a few Indian stores, Parmatma Saran, a scholar of Indian immigration to the United States, observed that something new was happening—a permanent Indian residential community was being established in the city, with the "major part of it living in Queens" (*India Abroad,* May 14, 1976). The growth of the Indian shopping area in Jackson Heights from one store to a prime business concentration of about one hundred stores in 1990 coincided with the continuous growth of the Indian population in the United States. In the 1980s, every year twenty to thirty thousand Indians were arriving in the United States. Between 1982 and 1987 Indian businesses in the United States grew by 120 percent, from 23,770 to 52,266 (*Little India,* October 1991). In New York City, which has the largest number of Indian businesses in the entire country, Indians were found not only dealing in items for an Indian clientele, but also serving mixed populations. Besides creating niches for themselves in businesses of garments, diamonds, and motels, Indians also started operating candy stores, newsstands, auto shops, and gas stations. A business survey in the Queens neighborhoods of Elmhurst and Corona (adjoining Jackson Heights) conducted by Queens College New Immigrants and Old Americans Project in 1986 recorded 51 Indian businesses interspersed among the total 912 businesses surveyed. Of the 39 who provided information, most had opened in the 1980s; only three stores existed before 1976 (Sanjek 1989). Many Indian businesses—some in clusters and others scattered—have sprung up in New York City in the last two decades, but the Jackson Heights concentration is central among them.

Indians are employed in Jackson Heights businesses in many capacities. First, are the business owners, many of whom are professionals turned proprietors. As Jackson Heights became well known as the prime Indian shopping area, it also attracted traditional business families. Many of the store owners have other businesses in different parts of the United States, and some even in different centers of overseas Indian communities. They are part of the business families that run a chain of transnational enterprises. Although many have migrated directly from India, others are twice migrants or sometimes even thrice migrants from Indian concentrations in East Africa, Australia, Canada, or Britain. These owners are not residents of Jackson Heights. They conduct their business in this neighborhood primarily because of its image as an ethnic business concentration. They have also become employers of a number of Indians working as assistants, sales clerks, waiters, and flyer distributors. Every day, unemployed Indians find their way to these businesses in search of jobs. Many are undocumented and/or seeking permanent residency in this country.

Customers visiting Seventy-fourth Street are as varied as the economic profile of those employed there. Although some visitors are local Indians from adjoining Queens neighborhoods, many travel from the suburbs for an "Indian" shopping spree, or from various short or long distances. According to the merchants, a significant proportion of their customers are traveling either from or to India, making purchases for their families and friends living there. This is particularly true of those shopping for saris, electronics, appliances, and sometimes, according to fluctuating prices, gold jewelry. Obviously, most of the customers are South Asians. Occasionally a person of different nationality may visit looking for good bargains or Indian cuisine. According to some estimates, every week about ten thousand people visit these few blocks. The general ambiance is of an Indian bazaar, and visitors treat their time like an outing, traveling with families and stopping to eat at a neighborhood Indian restaurant.

This atmosphere is qualitatively different from that of Indian businesses in Manhattan, where the clientele is largely either affluent and professional Indians or white Americans. Indian restaurants in Manhattan attract significantly large proportions of non-Indian customers. In distinct contrast, Queens represents more of popular culture, particularly in areas such as Jackson Heights, which are surrounded by the receiving areas of Indian immigrant arrivals. During the last two decades, both kinds of Indian spaces exist parallel to each other — the first, in Manhattan, a continuation of the intellectual, upper middle-class and elite Indians of the pre-1965 patterns, and the second, in Queens, representing increased diversity and population expansion.

The ethnic identity of business spaces in Queens has created other new identities among Indians. On one hand, "ethnic Indianness" as opposed to integration in American cultural life-styles is evident through the emphasis on saris, Indian jewelry, and Indian foods. On the other hand, transcendence of regional and national boundaries is attempted in the creation of a new South Asian identity. "Indo-Pak-Bangla" is a phrase commonly used on store signs. Hardly any Pakistani businesses declare exclusive appeal to their nationals and are known to have special sales on the essentially Indian festivals of Diwali and Holi. Some customers of other ethnic origins, such as Afghanistan and the Middle East, shop for Indian rice and spices. Almost everything in these stores is made to attract *all* customers of South Asian origin. Grocery stores sell ingredients of different South Asian cuisines. Shelves in one store may carry sambhar masala for South Indian food next to Panjabi pickles and Afghani bread. Video rentals feature recorded movies in different languages — Malayalam, Telugu, Tamil, and Panjabi — the majority being from Hindi movies produced by the Bombay film industry. No doubt, the motivation is primarily business promotion. Abraham Mamin, one of the Indian merchants, owns two restaurants in this area: Udupi Palace, specializing in South Indian cuisine, and Delhi Palace, serving North Indian food.

Seventy-fourth Street in Jackson Heights has forged important links with the Indian market beyond Queens. In addition to the customers who visit this area, a substantial business is conducted with other states through mail orders. Many merchants have shifted from retail only to wholesale business as well. Some have stores outside of Jackson Heights, in different parts of the United States and the world. Business names in Jackson Heights such as Raj Jewels of London and Singapore Emporium are but a few signs of the growing network of Indian overseas businesses. Visitors traveling from other parts of the United States and other countries see Jackson Heights as reminiscent of Southall in London and, to some extent, of smaller clusters of Indian businesses in Chicago and Houston. Most Indians observe that it reminds them of an Indian bazaar. In fact, many say, half-seriously, that instead of Jackson Heights it should be named Jai Kishan (a popular Hindu God and a common first name for Indian men) Heights!

Although Indian immigrants have enjoyed the emergence of their business concentration, the reaction from other groups has not been always positive. Surrounding this business district is a primarily residential area where white Americans of Irish, Jewish, and Italian ancestry have lived for many decades. Growing Indian businesses signify rapid changes in their neighborhood that arouse feelings of displacement. The arrival of large waves of post-1965 immigrants into Queens neighborhoods such as Jackson Heights and "white flight" from them have been interconnected phenomena. In other parts of Queens, as well, the white American population has declined. The entire borough of Queens has witnessed significant increases in populations of Chinese, Koreans, and Indians, particularly in the neighborhoods of Flushing, Elmhurst, Corona, and Jackson Heights.

Most of the white Americans living in Jackson Heights now constitute the established and older resident population of the area. They themselves came into Jackson Heights in the 1940s and 1950s and were agents of change in the neighborhood during those years. A considerable number of them are the elderly, whose friends and neighbors have either died or moved to less crowded areas. They are alarmed by what they perceive as inroads of "foreign" cultures into essentially white American neighborhoods.

In Jackson Heights the tension expresses itself most around "quality of life" issues — increasing litter and growing traffic, crowded streets due to the large number of business customers. The local residents contend that the Indian merchants who do not live in the neighborhood should participate and share more in these civic concerns. Several interviews with merchants and Indian leaders made it clear that all this time Indians had been thinking that by maintaining a nonconfrontational approach to other groups, by tolerating and even respecting them, by paying taxes regularly, they had been acting as "good citizens" of the United States. A gap between perceptions of civic responsibilities in a local neighborhood was evident.

During 1989–90, such issues became the subject of a series of meetings and seminars organized by neighborhood resident groups. Indian merchants or their representatives were invited to present their perspectives. In these sessions of intercultural dialogue, it became clear that merchants had their own problems as well. Besides parking and traffic issues, this area has witnessed a spate of burglaries and muggings in the past few years. Cars are often vandalized — perhaps owing to the common perception that Indians shopping in this area travel with large amounts of cash and valuables. To deal with such problems, business owners had formed their own organization, the Jackson Heights Merchants' Association. On the one hand, it represented Indian interests to neighborhood associations and government authorities, and on the other hand, it sought to remedy problems through tightened security and cleaner blocks.

The intergroup tensions reached a highpoint in November 1990 when a local residents' organization, the Jackson Heights Beautification Group, planned a rally against increasing Indian businesses. Though the idea was to emphasize cleanliness and other civic issues, the messages were clearly anti-Indian. Even before the rally could be held, the New York City Human Rights Division's Crisis Prevention Unit intervened to tone down "biased" slogans. Several Human Rights officials said that though they saw no problem with the basic motive of the rally, the organizers should seek cooperation and participation from Indian merchants in this task.

Such events have resulted in both sides — local residents and Indian merchants — seeking more communication with each other and trying to deal with problems through dialogue and negotiation. In one such attempt, Abraham Mamin, the owner of Udupi Palace and Delhi Palace, was given a position in the Jackson Heights Beautification Group. Since then, leaders from among both the Indian merchants and the older residents have gotten together to address mutual concerns. Resident members of groups such as the Jackson Heights Awareness Council have continued to hold discussions with other immigrant groups besides Indians, such as Koreans and Chinese.

Through this process the Jackson Heights Merchants' Association has emerged as a viable body which seeks to represent Indian immigrants in official forums. As such, they present Jackson Heights as a symbol of ethnic Indian life in the United States. In 1992, on the festival of Diwali, this association invited Mayor David Dinkins to join the celebration. The mayor referred to the plan of renaming the Seventy-fourth Street area "Little India." On that occasion, a white American carried a placard of protest. It read, "Mayor Dinkins: Wrong. I live here. This is my American home. Not 'Little India'" (*India Abroad,* October 30, 1992).

Increasing intercultural tensions around businesses and other places of Asian presence have flared in Queens, in other parts of New York City, and all over the country in the past few years. In Brooklyn, the neighbor borough of Queens, the boycott of a Korean business by African Americans has brought issues of racial hatred and anti-Asian violence to the surface.

Conclusion

This chapter contextualizes the case of Jackson Heights and the issues of space in the tension between the transnational identities and networks of the Indian diaspora and those of local situations, which feature different ethnic groups with concerns pertaining to their immediate neighborhood.

An impressive and growing body of literature exists on Indian and other South Asian communities spread in different parts of the world (Clarke, Peach, and Vertovec 1990). Though these works bring out the distinct characteristics of each situation, they are based on the ethnic and cultural commonality of South Asians. Few focus on interactions of South Asians with other groups in a particular situation. Different from this tradition of studies of overseas Indian populations is Asian American studies, a field that has tried to see Asian groups in the United States within this nation's boundaries. In a critique of the influence of Robert E. Park's assimilationist model on Asian American studies, Sucheta Mazumdar reminds us that

> the implicit acceptance of this [Park's model] has meant that Asian American studies has been located within the context of American Studies and stripped of its international links. . . . To isolate Asian American history from its international underpinnings, to abstract it from the global context of capital and labor migration, is to distort this history. (Mazumdar 1991)

I would like to present a third perspective — complementing the two just mentioned — for the study of New York Indians. Any study of Indians must not isolate its subjects from the groups with whom they interact in ethnically and racially diverse situations. In the United States, Indians are only one among several large groups of Asians — such as the Chinese, Filipinos, Japanese, Koreans, and Southeast Asians — with whom other ethnic groups and races share neighborhoods and cities. This is particularly true of places such as Queens, where new immigration has intensified diversity. As such they are part of the larger United States politics of contesting space and power.

For Indians of various pursuits — business people, workers, customers, and community activists — Jackson Heights has become the symbol of ethnic Indian life in the United States. In business concentrations and cultural activities in core areas of Queens, Indians celebrate the creation of their own ethnic spaces as another addition to the diaspora tradition of their overseas communities. Strong affinities and networks exist among these diasporic homes beyond national boundaries. This transnationalism and seeking home in diasporic space clashes with the local situation in New York's multicultural population, where claims are made on immediate neighborhoods.

Acknowledgments

I owe special thanks to Roger Sanjek for his comments on this paper.

References

Chen, Hsiang-shui
    1992   *Chinatown No More: Taiwan Immigrants in Contemporary New York.*
        Ithaca, N.Y.: Cornell University Press.
Chen, Hsiang-shui, and John Kuo Wei Tchen
    1989   "Towards a History of Chinese in Queens." *Asian/American Center*
        Working Papers. Flushing, N.Y.: Asian/American Center, Queens Col-
        lege.
Clarke, Colin, Ceri Peach, and Steven Vertovec, eds.
    1990   *South Asians Overseas: Migration and Ethnicity.* New York: Cambridge
        University Press.
Daniels, Roger
    1990   *History of Indian Immigration in the United States: An Interpretive Essay.*
        New York: The Asia Society.
Fisher, Maxine P.
    1980   *The Indians of New York City: A Study of Immigrants from India.* New
        Delhi: Heritage Publishers.
Gardner, Robert W., Bryant Robey, and Peter C. Smith
    1985   *Asian Americans: Growth, Change, and Diversity.* Washington, D.C.:
        Population Reference Bureau.
India Abroad.
    1976a   May 14, p. 4. New York.
    1976b   October 29, 1976, p. 1. New York.
    1992   October 30, p. 40. New York.
Jensen, Joan M.
    1988   *Passage from India: Asian Indian Immigrants in North America.* New
        Haven, Conn.: Yale University Press.
Khandelwal, Madhulika S.
    1989   "Hindu Religious Activities of Indians in Queens." In Roger Sanjek,
        ed., *Worship and Community: Christianity and Hinduism in Contempo-*
        rary Queens. Flushing, N.Y.: Asian/American Center, Queens College.
    1991   *Indians of New York City: Patterns of Growth and Diversification, 1965–*
        1990. Doctor of Arts dissertation, Department of History, Carnegie
        Mellon University.
Little India.
    1991   October, Reading, Pa.
Mazumdar, Sucheta
    1991   "Asian American and Asian Studies: Rethinking Roots." In Shirley
        Hune, Hyung-chan Kim, Stephen S. Fugita, and Amy Ling, eds. *Asian*
        Americans: Comparative and Global Perspectives. Pullman: Washington
        State University Press.
Mukhi, Sunita Sunder
    1994   "Indian Identity at the South Street Seaport Deepavali Festival." Un-
        published paper.

Sanjek, Roger
   1988   "The People of Queens from Now to Then." *Asian/American Center Working Papers*. Flushing, N.Y.: Asian/American Center, Queens College.
   1989   *Worship and Community: Christianity and Hinduism in Contemporary Queens*. Flushing, N.Y.: Asian/American Center, Queens College.
U.S. Census
   1980   "General Population Characteristics, U.S. and New York Sections." Washington, D.C.: U.S. Department of Commerce, Bureau of the Census.
   1990   "Population Change by Race and Hispanic Origin, New York City, Boroughs and Community Districts." Washington, D.C.: U.S. Department of Commerce, Bureau of the Census.

Sallie Westwood

8. Gendering Diaspora: Space, Politics, and South Asian Masculinities in Britain

Preamble: Lost in Translation

Insofar as this chapter focuses attention on the contexts and politics of an understanding of "diasporic masculinities," I am faced with an immediate problem — the translation of terms between the United States and the United Kingdom. Thus, I start with an important digression.

During the 1980s, the struggles against racism and for the civil, political, and economic rights of African Caribbean and South Asian peoples in Britain were articulated through the attempted construction of a black political identity which, though it acknowledged difference, sought to unite the diasporic South Asian and African Caribbean populations. The language of "blackness" and Black Power from the United States meant that the construction of a black political identity was hegemonic within antiracist and radical left discourse. This distinction did not go uncontested, however, especially by sections of the South Asian population, but also by those involved in Palestinian, Chinese, Jewish, or Irish struggles, who felt marginalized by the insistence on a black identity as *the* oppositional identity. Consequently, there has been a growing disengagement from a politically unifying identity and connection, instead, with a politics of difference in which not only ethnic but also religious identities are preeminent. These disengagements and rearticulations have been underpinned both by the increasing class differences found among African Caribbean and South Asian populations and by the post–*Satanic Verses* period of Muslim identities. The disengagements are not part of an even, unilinear process however, and though the re-visioned political identity of Muslims in Britain is now important, the discourse on black identities still survives for some activists and radicals of both South Asian and African Caribbean descent. But the trajectory is undoubtedly more toward diasporic identities — such as British Asian, British Muslim, and black British — as reappropriations of Britishness and toward the use of the term *African Caribbean,* stressing the African diaspora rather than Fritz Fanon's phrase "the fact of Blackness." On both sides of the Atlantic there is now a growing emphasis on the social and ideological construction of "whiteness" rather than "blackness." Similarly, the term *Asian* has also been reappropriated in Britain by people of South Asian descent because it was, initially, a term generated within colonial discourse. Reclaimed and given the prefix *British,* it speaks for the complex histories of the South Asian diaspora and the settlement of those in Britain with origins in Pakistan, Sri Lanka, Bangladesh, and India. This usage contrasts with the expression "people of color" used in the United States, which is more difficult in Britain because of the colonial and racial connotations of "colored."

Diasporic lives generate hybridization, however, and South Asian populations have entered cities in Britain that have accommodated hundreds of years of African, Caribbean, and South Asian settlement and in which there has been a black urban culture throughout this century. In contemporary Britain this black urban culture has an enormous impact on South Asian and white young people, generating a diasporic urban culture via food, dress, and music. It is a creative reappropriation of the cityscape, the spaces of the urban world. Thus, although rap music is everywhere a specific form, Patel Rap is popular at discos and clubs among young British Asians who are also listening to revised Bhangra music known as Bhangra Beat, which is being exported from Britain to India. And, to add to this, Apache Indian is now an international star.

This preamble goes some way toward explaining the uses in this chapter of the terms *black, Asian,* and *South Asian* in relation to an analysis of masculinities and the politics of space in Britain. It is necessary to maintain throughout the juxtaposition of difference and similarity. The chapter returns to the concerns elaborated by Peter van der Veer in the Introduction to this volume: nationalism, belonging, and identities, here in relation to elements of an ethnography of the lives of a group of South Asian men in a provincial British city. I seek to illuminate the local and current conditions of diaspora in relation to current theories on diasporic identities, but also in relation to a gendered account framed by the Foucauldian understanding of space or "sites." In no way do I seek to represent the South Asian population in Britain on the basis of some pseudoscientific understanding of the work of social research. This is, rather, an ongoing discussion begun in 1989 and continuing into the 1990s.

"I Could Not Fall in Love in a Strange Land"

Thus sang Alaur Rahman in a 1992 television program about the Bangladeshi community of East London. His songs speak not only to the loss of a sense of belonging but also to the material conditions that underpin his life in Britain. He cannot fall in love, he cannot marry because his earnings from the long, grueling days and nights at the restaurant are sent "home" to Bangladesh to repay family debts. It is one story of migration — painful, lonely, and filled with loss — but it is not the only story: the Bangladeshi singer Bina sings instead of finding love in a strange land. Still, the land remains strange, and this sensation fuels the desire to transplant religious and cultural institutions from India, Pakistan, and Bangladesh and place them at the center of life in the metropolitan core, by so doing to reconstitute life as it is known. These reconstructions have often received more attention in the literature and the popular imagination than the recreations that have marked diasporic lives. The importance of mosques and temples in terms of the politics of space and the ways in which, symbolically and materially, the buildings and organization around them mark the South Asian presence cannot be underestimated. Equally, these are important sites for the growing nationalisms of the subcontinent, located both, as van der Veer makes clear, with ethnos and with place, or *desh* (land). The contradictions of the national story in relation to the modern nation-state, the imperial past, and decolonization, plus the crucial insistence on a privileged and essentialist account of ethnicity, demand that the story be constantly reinvented and reiterated as part of the diasporic experience. This chapter, like other contributions in this volume, is concerned with the major themes of diaspora — nationalism, belonging, and identities — but it focuses attention less on migration and reconstructions and more on the creative appropriation of social and political space in urban Britain. It also suggests that a gendered account of diasporic dynamics is crucial to our understanding of the processes in play.

Attempts by writers like Nira Yuval-Davis and Floya Anthias (1989) to provide a gendered account of state and nation suggest that nationalisms offer specific positions to women and men. Women are placed centrally as "mothers of the nation," whereas men are "defenders of the nation." Similarly, it is clear from the work of Sonia Alvarez (1991) that the discourses within which the state articulates nationalism and specific forms of populism employ "genderic" modes, making specific appeals to women and men as gendered subjects and offering different forms of protection under the law. Thus family and national responsibilities and loyalties are often fused. These are complex articulations which cannot be pursued here. I wish, instead, to focus attention on a variant of nationalism that is tied to locality. This "nationalism of the neighbourhood" suggested by Philip Cohen (1988) has a long history, which more recent arrivals in the metropolitan core have entered and reappropriated. This idea of the defense of locale has, of course, marked the lives of young men (as defenders of the nation) for generations in the urban landscape, and it had often been organized in relation to ethnic differences. It is at one level about territory or geography, yet as a politics of space it is fundamental to a sense of belonging and to the creation and sustenance of diasporic identities, which are not ethnicities only. The politics of space and the nationalism of the neighborhood are articulated with and played out in relation to masculinities, but also in relation to time. The processes bring together gender and generation in a specific historical moment. I explore here the articulations between gender, generation, and ethnicities in relation to the politics of space, initially as they pertain to a predominantly South Asian youth project that became a cause célèbre in the local politics of Leicester, a provincial city north of London with a large South Asian population.

The Red Star Story

The South Asian youth project known as Red Star has been part of the political scene in Leicester since 1980. As I write in the summer of 1993, Red Star is back in the headlines and once again in conflict with the local state over the building in which it conducts its activities. The story of Red Star has been told in greater detail elsewhere (Westwood 1991). Red Star is a black inner-city youth project that began life in 1980 as a soccer team of the same name. In the subsequent struggle to secure resources for inner-city youth, the project became politicized and thereby joined the long history of organized black struggle in Britain. The voices of South Asian protest were heard throughout the cities of Britain in the late 1970s and early 1980s from Southall and Bradford to Newham and Leicester. The politics forged through these urban protests was a new antiracist politics called into being by a new generation of young South Asian women and men who, though they drew on extant political discourses, produced new collective subjects and forms of expression. This was, and is, an oppositional politics forged against racism and class exploitation but also against the power of the older generation. As Harwant Bains (1988) points out, however, this new approach did not necessarily challenge patriarchal power in relation to women. It was a politics redolent with masculinity and the power of young men, during a period when young black men in particular were racialized and criminalized in response to a moral panic that reached its height with the urban riots of the early 1980s (Hall et al. 1978; Gilroy 1987; Benyon and Solomos 1987). It was against this background that young South Asian men who had initially come together as a soccer team sought ways to secure funding for leisure activities and a location for a youth club. After the urban riots of 1981, government grants were directed toward projects for South Asian and African Caribbean youth, and Red Star secured funding and, more important, a base for their operations. This base was and remains highly significant, because the building itself had housed the boys' school that most Red Star members had attended; after a reorganization of the schools in inner-city Leicester, it had been left vacant. Struggles over who has access and control within this building are ongoing. The school is contested terrain in every sense.

Once Red Star was constituted as a youth project with state funding, it then became accountable to the local state. In 1984 the failure of the project to return audited accounts met with a swift response — funds were stopped, and worse, the project was asked to move out of the school building while it was being renovated for further community use. Red Star asked for an alternative site in the area, and a prolonged period of negotiation began which, as far as Red Star's management was concerned, produced nothing. Red Star members decided to occupy the building and did so; this produced a court order for the project to leave, which the Red Star leader contested in the courts. In court, Red Star secured limited rights to the building, while the local council secured a possession order that was never invoked. Then the project shifted into a more overtly political strategy by taking on the local Labour party through the local ward in which the project was (and is) situated. Despite lack of funds and an ambiguous tenancy, Red Star has not gone away and has, instead, involved a new generation of South Asian and African Caribbean young people in the project.

The Politics of Red Star

The politics of Red Star is part of a precious history retold by members of Red Star with great pride. I am conscious of my responsibilities toward these memories and these individuals as I reorganize this "thick description" into an analysis that concentrates initially on the development of political identities as part of the diasporic condition and subsequently on issues surrounding state, nation, and citizenship. For the members of Red Star, politics is not an external, institutionalized reality into which they are inserted as political subjects. On the contrary, it is part and parcel of inner-city lives and everyday experiences, which include hostility and racial discrimination encountered in school, the job market, and via racial violence on the streets. But experience does not have a linear relationship to politicization, which requires interventions that reorganize experience into politics and subjects into political subjects. This is a complex process and, in relation to Red Star, one that required crucial intervention from the leadership of the project who reorganized commonsense understandings into collective memories, out of which could be born the collective political subject, Red Star. It is Red Star as a collective political subject that has mounted and sustained political campaigns and inserted its presence into the public imagination and political arena.

In order to engage in political campaigning, the leader of Red Star sought ways to galvanize a collective identity among a diverse group of young South Asian and African Caribbean men. They shared their inner-city locality, their schooling, and their masculinity, but ethnically they were highly diverse. The project brought together South Asians and African Caribbeans who used joking banter to manage the complexities of South Asians who were Sikhs (both Jat and Ramgarhia), Hindus, and Muslims (both Sunni and Shia). Similarly, there were Gujaratis both Muslim and Hindu with their roots in India or East Africa, Punjabis, Pakistanis, and Bangladeshis who stood alongside African Caribbeans with origins in the different islands of the Caribbean—Antigua, Saint Kitts, Barbados, and Jamaica. This national, regional, ethnic, and linguistic diversity born out of diaspora could have exploded in an antagonistic politics of difference, but pitted against this possibility was the commonality invoked and reiterated by the leader of Red Star, who brought specific discourses from his own political history to revision diversity and emphasize the strengths of diaspora. The leader of Red Star was a young Sikh with a background in socialist politics, student activism, and shop and trade union work who had grown up in the area and had been to the same school as the members. He was, in the Gramscian sense, an organic intellectual who reorganized the commonsense of the membership in ways that still allowed them to feel that they owned the rhetoric with which he worked. He recognized clearly the marginalization of young black people within political discourses, including the socialist discourse of class struggle, but he used this and the Gramscian understanding of relations between civil society and the state to position Red Star and claim a voice for the project.

In forging a sense of political identity, the leadership drew on the shared experiences of locality — the same streets and schools that made the men friends and neighbors. And although family background contributed to the specific cultural, ethnic, and religious identities of Red Star members, the discourse of class positioned them in relation to the economic and social commonalities of their lives in Britain. Thus place and space were crucial in defining a collective identity. These elements were combined with their sense of themselves in time, as a generation that had known the defeats of the classroom and police harassment, and which had engendered a specific view of white authority and institutions. To be a specific generation of young men is to be constituted as *youth*, a term that in this case is most significantly about gender and masculinity. Until recently the Red Star project was not considered an appropriate place for young women and girls, but in 1993 the voices of young African Caribbean women could be heard. Historically, the project has been marked by a collectivism that invoked a particular machismo style of politics, in which South Asian and African Caribbean masculinities were predominant. It is hardly surprising that a call to shared masculinities via the collectivity of youth should be invoked; it was, and is, a powerful unifying force. As Paul Gilroy (1987) notes, the appeal is tied to the ways in which the body is used as an important site for street style. The visibility of the body in relation to the disciplinary modes of police and other authorities is reclaimed as a site for expressions of individuality and collectivity. Red Star members made themselves self-consciously visible by packing Labour party meetings and behaving in a noisy, exuberant manner that was described by some white people as intimidating. Their collective presence was further invoked in relation to the sit-ins staged to defend their building. They used their physical presence as a political weapon and by so doing invoked a defense of locale and signaled a "nationalism of the neighborhood" that was to mark Red Star politics consistently. It was a creative reappropriation of the city neighborhood where they had grown up and lived their lives. It is significant that this defense of space and struggle for resources against racism was positioned within discourses that stressed honor, *izzat*, which in itself emphasizes masculinity.

The emphasis on honor and dignity was a powerful call to young

South Asian and African Caribbean men who, living in 1980s Britain, sought to force their own political identity within the discourse of the "black struggle." The political identity being forged was a black political identity in combination with popular street culture expressed in language, dress, and, most of all, soccer. Red Star brought masculinity, physical prowess, and political identities together in their soccer team, which refused an ethnic identification and presented itself as a "black" team composed of both South Asian and African Caribbean players. The first team soon showed the power of this concentration of prowess in the game by moving up in the league and carrying off trophies after knockout competitions. Red Star members enjoyed their power and success, especially their ability to beat white teams, and they traveled locally with a large group of supporters whose enthusiasm earned Red Star members the designation of "the mob." Red Star members enjoyed this too, and reappropriated the label by referring to themselves as the "Red Star mob." Soccer (of which more later in the chapter) was a powerful unifying element in the Red Star story, bringing together honor, loyalty, and locale organized around a "black" identity. This appeal to a black identity was well understood by Red Star members. Aziz, for example, commented, "We come from all kinds of families, but when it comes to our rights we are black." "Black" was clearly perceived as a political category in relation to the state and racism in Britain, not as simple description. This point of view also allowed for a difference in which ethnic, religious, and linguistic identities were not negated but understood to exist simultaneously with a commonality among Red Star members that was organized around the identity of "black youth." This was the terrain marked out by Red Star into which it would insert its political presence, make strategic engagements, and struggle for resources and recognition.

The Red Star project was both celebrated and vilified and, once it stepped into the political arena, it encountered organized opposition. The city Labour party drew on the complexity of the political identities of Red Star members and sought ways in which to exploit the contradictions. Within the Muslim community, for example, there were older men who never accepted their sons' identification with the project. The young men, however, used the project to point out the complexities of South Asian identities in Britain and to protest a unitary identity as Muslims. (This tack has shifted again with the revisioned Muslim identity since the Salman Rushdie affair, in which young Muslim men have been key players.) At this juncture young Muslims are contending with multiplicity, playing soccer but not drinking, attending the mosque but also participating in the Red Star activities.

By the mid-1980s Red Star was a political force to be reckoned with, but a project with no funding and a threat to their base in the school building. The response to this situation was the first occupation of the buildings, which politicized the membership, confirmed the leadership, and gave Red Star members a taste of power. Mehboob recalled, "There we were in this huge building with the run of the place, talking all night, playing pool, eating, and living it up and the police never came, they never dared because they thought they would have a riot on their hands. We had real power then, nobody could touch us." The occupation was a strategic response to the threat of dispossession in the wake of the riots in British cities—a time when Red Star members felt their collective power. The occupation produced a sense of political agency for Red Star members, formed by direct action against the local state and the city Labour party. These events occurred inside walls of the school that, for so many of them, had been their major encounter with white society and authority and in which they had felt marginalized and humiliated. It was a sweet victory to be in control of this space and to claim it as their own.

Diasporic Politics: Nation, State, and Citizenship

The politics of diaspora raise crucial issues of nation, state, and citizenship, and it was onto this terrain that the political identities of Red Star members moved. By making this shift Red Star extended its political struggle beyond the streets and into first the Labour party and then the legal system, two arenas in which Red Star members invoked their rights as citizens and their place in the nation. That is, their engagement in Labour party politics and their fight in the courts against possession orders for the building were not simply strategic engagements over resources, but a symbolic challenge to the extant notions of the nation and citizenship which sought to recon-struct the language of both.

The current politics of Europe make clear that conceptions of nation are contested, in contrast to the commonly assumed geographical inertia of state boundaries. On the contrary, nations are "imagined communities" (Anderson 1983) that are "not a bit less real because they are symbolic" (Hall 1987: 45). The ideological construction of the nation is organized around specific ethnicities and creates "fictive ethnicities" and national identities as part of the national story. In part, there also exists an elision between "the people" and "the nation" that brings these two fictions together so powerfully that the coincidence is naturalized. Thus the British national story is one in which Englishness is hegemonic, thereby rendering invisible the Scottish, Welsh, and Irish stories — but though they may be subordinated they have not disappeared. Similarly, the long history of African, Caribbean, Jewish, Chinese, Irish, and South Asian settlement in Britain is silenced but has been recently recovered in works such as Peter Fryer's (1984) history of the black British presence. By making claims on the nation as citizens, Red Star members fractured the consensus and the ideological construction of "black youth" as marginal in favor of a different story which challenged the invisibility of British people of African Caribbean and South Asian descent. At the same time, they brought into sharp relief the hegemonic account of Britishness constructed around white Englishness — that fictive ethnicity which is also highly gendered.

The Red Star project did not "take on the nation" in any simple sense. Initially, the power of street style and the importance of control within a specific locale were the primary motivators, but this politics was itself a form of the "nationalism of the neighbourhood," in which a specific urban space was defended as territory and as part of the discourse of possession and ownership. But, as Frank Reeves (1986: 108) writes: "As Winston Churchill recognised, a continuum exists between the lofty defence of the abstraction of the nation and the mundane defence of the neighbourhood street." The context of Churchill's appeal was World War II, and he had specific aims in terms of rousing nationalistic sentiments for the defense of Britain. But in diasporic politics these resonances between the local and the national were recast when the South Asian and African Caribbean populations in Britain laid claim to a part in the nation from which they had been excluded. The connection was as central to the Red Star agenda in the 1980s as it is for the Muslim presence in Britain. To engage with the national story is to consider national identities and hybridity as central to citizenship rights and interaction with the state.

Although the occupations and defense of "their" building had politicized and empowered Red Star members, it was also clear to them that decisions about resources and the future of the project were being made within the corridors of the town hall. Red Star decided to move its field of action beyond the neighborhood and into the halls of power in a bid to confront the local state and the power brokers within the Labour party. In a show of force, Red Star members went collectively to demand a meeting with the leader of the local council. When they were denied access, they invoked street style, set off a fire alarm that cleared the building, and were as noisy and witty as they could be. For them it was the margin come to the center, to make politicians and bureaucrats accountable to the citizens of the city — in this case, Red Star members.

Direct action in the form of lobbying local politicians was one strategy to lay claim to citizenship and a part in the nation, but it was matched by Red Star's recourse to legal remedies through the courts. Faced with an eviction and possession order, Red Star, or more precisely the leader of Red Star, countered to defend the group's tenancy through the High Court. This case has gone on for years and currently gives Red Star an ambiguous tenancy, in that the local authority's right to a possession order was upheld but not invoked. For Red Star it was a victory and one within a realm central to the conception of Britishness and the individual rights of citizens when faced with the state. The victory would not have been politicized but for the earlier sit-ins and the acumen with which Red Star used the law. Strategically it altered the view of Red Star within the politics of the local state and among Red Star members themselves. Most important, it confirmed the power of the leader of Red Star and welded together the project with the leader, forging an identity that continues in the current local politics. Red Star was not simply on the streets or occupying a building but was in court, its arguments marshalled and sustained. The legal battle was one element of Red Star's politics, but in addition the group had to try to shift the agenda within the Labour party, the local ruling party, which was so crucial for resources and recognition.

The move into the Labour party by Red Star members could be understood strategically as a move into the space where decisions on resources were exercised. Yet although this explanation is clearly part of the story, it omits the power of the symbolic in the politics of the new social movements of which Red Star was a part. The shift into the Labour party needs to be understood as an another attempt by the margin to come to the center. In this case it is the politics of the streets and of youth repositioned within the terrain of representative democracy. What Red Star members discovered was a politics of the rule book, the constitution, and alliances and political machinations. Members of the project joined the Labour party in an organized campaign within their local ward, the ward that housed the project and that elected the leader of the council and the powerful head of the Manpower Committee. Red Star members used their collective strength at meetings as well as their strategic sense by constantly presenting motions on Red Star and its future. Not only did they join the party in large numbers, but some of the leaders became officers of the ward and sought ways to keep the debate on Red Star alive and public. The ward became the liveliest in the city, rocked by debate and by Red Star's attempts to shame the Labour party into replacing the leader of the council with their own leader, by nominating him at the time of the local elections. The leader of Red Star invoked Shakespearean tragedy with references to Macbeth as a precursor to the machinations of the leaders of the Labour group. Both in speeches and in leaflets, Red Star accused the Labour party of racism and of the disenfranchisement of its members. Thus the leader of Red Star not only invoked the racism of the Labour party but also used an icon of British culture in the service of black youth.

The politics of Red Star did considerable damage to the cohesion of the Labour group in the city and was an embarrassment to the leadership of a city where over a quarter of the population were South Asian and African Caribbean[1] and in a time of high youth unemployment. But the Labour party also marshalled its forces within the ward and the city more widely through a vilification campaign directed most specifically at the leader of Red Star. More significant for the fortunes of Red Star, the city councillors sought an alliance with Muslim members in a politics of difference to thwart the political aspirations of the Red Star leader. The Labour party also knew how to pack meetings and did so at the time of the nominations, securing an alternative candidate on a Muslim vote (a candidate who was later discredited). Furthermore, Labour party members held meetings in secret, away from the ward, thereby marginalizing Red Star. The Labour party closed ranks against Red Star, but it refused to go away, although it is no longer active in the ward.

Red Star survives today even though, despite its energy and political acumen, resources for the project were never forthcoming. Now it is again in the news over its occupancy of the community building and attempts by the local authorities to evict the project. Alongside the attempts to remove Red Star are the familiar tactics which seek to discredit the members and their actions. Red Star has continued to pose a problem for the local authorities and the Labour party in the city. During their most active phase, in the middle to late 1980s, the politics of Red Star disrupted the political agenda in the city and in the Labour party. The accommodation that the Labour party had secured with sections of the city population did not include black youth, and Red Star sought to, and succeeded in, exposing the racism of laborism and the marginalization of a key sector. But the politics of diaspora are not confined to making visible those normally excluded within representative democracy. Red Star demanded not simply a voice but a speaking position and a place on the agenda of British politics. These demands have been reiterated throughout the cities of Britain, most especially by young South Asian and African Caribbean people. Alongside the calls for resources and the strategic engagements are the more fundamental calls for recognition as citizens within a nation of which South Asian and African Caribbean peoples are a part. Alberto Melucci, writing in 1988, sums up the situation in relation to Red Star:

> Concrete concepts such as efficacy of success should be considered unimportant. This is because conflict takes place principally on symbolic ground, by means of challenging and upsetting dominant codes upon which social relationships are founded. . . . The mere existence of a symbolic challenge is in itself a method of unmasking the dominant codes, a different way of perceiving and naming the world. (1988: 248)

The Red Star story shows clearly the impact of diasporic populations within liberal democratic states. It is a story of arrival, of the politics of belonging, of identities and nationalisms recast for postcolonial cityscapes, in which gender and generations are highlighted. It is a story for 1980s Britain in which a "black" political identity assisted antiracist struggles throughout the country. But the mood of the 1990s has shifted the ground and fractured the unitary black subject, emphasizing ethnicities and religious identities in new and profound ways.

Streets, Soccer, and South Asian Masculinities

The unitary black subject fractured by ethnicities and religious identities captures only one part of the complexity, because the unitary black subject was never really unitary but always fractured by gender and generation. The Red Star story is a story of diasporic politics in Britain, but, as I have suggested, it emphasizes gender and generation, and most especially the social construction of South Asian and African Caribbean, or "black," masculinities. These are specific masculinities understood not as finished products but as gender identities in process, a part of cultural configurations that are the products of resistances, appropriations, and accommodations within specific histories. It is this complexity that I wish to pursue further in the latter part of this chapter.

Red Star drew on a public masculinity as a way of forging a collective political identity among a diverse membership. The success of Red Star was bound to the way in which it was able to forge a political identity, and crucial to this formation was the gendered subject and the social constructions of masculinity. In generating this identity the project emphasized street style and soccer which are, in my theorization of masculinities, specific "sites" where a contextual masculinity is produced. This by no means presents the totality of South Asian masculinities nor exhausts the varieties of masculinities, most especially those produced within the family and work, where men are also workers, trade union officials, husbands, sons, fathers, and lovers. Here, in conjunction with the Red Star story, I wish to concentrate on the public world of masculinities in which gender identities are developed and played out in relation to the validation of men. Thus masculinities, like identities more generally, are not finished products — as the old socialization model would have us believe — but instead are constantly in the process of production. Although gendered identities are constantly in process, they are not free-floating, because, as the Red Star story shows, the shifting terrain of identities is positioned in histories, cultures, languages, classes, localities, communities, and politics. Clearly, no one understands this better than the men who are the subjects of this chapter. They are conscious of the multiplicity of their lives and live with this multiplicity against definitions that would fix them in one identity or one place. The men were clear that as South Asians in Britain, they were legally British but that cultural Britishness was founded on an Englishness from which they were separated by culture but also by color. As Desh commented, "British means white." Showing some of the hurt of racism, Kuldip said with feeling, "Black people will never be allowed to be British." Again, the politics of Red Star was one answer to this strong sense of exclusion and one attempt to shift the meaning of British and the constituent culture of the nation.

My understanding of masculinities emphasizes the contextual and the contingent in the production of gendered identities that are not fixed. Instead, I concur with the view expressed by John Dollimore: "Identity is a construction and, as such, involves a process of exclusion, negation and repression. And this is a process which even if successful, results in an identity intrinsically unstable. This is bad news for masculinity, one of whose self-conceptions is stability, and whose function is to maintain it socially and psychically" (1986: 6–7).

The understanding that masculinities are not fixed qualities is not simply theoretical — it is also political, because emphasizing a deconstructionist theorization of masculinities is in direct opposition to the stereotypes of South Asian and African Caribbean men, both historically and currently, and their construction as the Other. Yet these stereotypes themselves have not been a simple unity. For black men of African descent the stereotypes are associated with the body, the "natural attributes" of physicality, and strength as a site for European fantasies about black male sexuality. Within orientalism the stereotypes are twofold: the colonial designation of the "martial races" of northern India generated an account of fighting men, of men of vigor and strength, which exists almost in opposition to the second construction, the "wily oriental" who, by being placed within a nexus of manipulation, was actually feminized under the colonial gaze. The problem with stereotypes is that in their fixity they seek to naturalize "races," genders, actions, and motivations in ways that describe complex realities through a vision of simplicity. Politically, there was a moment when it was seen as useful to replace negative stereotypes of black people and women with "positive images," but such a view remains welded to naturalization and simplicity. What is required is a more complex view rooted in the understanding that identities are not fixed and are not therefore amenable to stereotypical designations.

The South Asian men with whom I developed the analysis contained in this chapter were also those who had been involved in the politics of Red Star in the 1980s. My research on masculinities grew out of the original project on Red Star and has been ongoing since 1990. By 1990 the core group of South Asian men involved were between twenty and thirty years old; a third were married or had long-standing partners. For those who were employed, their labor was predominantly manual. The commitment to locale demonstrated so clearly in the Red Star story was, not surprisingly, reproduced within the social and public lives of these men. They were intensely local in their loyalties: they drank in the same inner-city pubs, lived in the area, and generally reproduced their younger years. Forays outside the locality were related to soccer, weddings, and the occasional visit to clubs in nearby cities. Usually, however, they lived the "nationalism of the neighborhood" that is so crucial to politics, identities, and the sense of belonging that was expressed in their relations to street life.

The Streets

The life of the streets has a long history in official discourses on masculinities in Britain, but lately has become specifically racialized. Young black men are stereotyped in commentary ranging from the moral panics surrounding mugging and criminality, explored by Stuart Hall et al. (1978) and Paul Gilroy (1987), to the more recent accounts of the riots in Britain. These later accounts, both from the media and within official discourse, articulate a moral panic about the current crises in British society and the state (Benyon and Solomos 1987; Solomos 1988). Black men are highly visible elements of street life, which is expressed in the media through visual representations and in discourses on law and order. What it means for these men's lives is that they are subject to "the Empire of the gaze," or as Michel Foucault elaborates: "It is the fact of being constantly seen that maintains the disciplined individual in this subjection" (1979: 187). As we have seen, however, the "disciplined individual" has multiple ways of resisting "the Empire of the gaze" and becoming a disobedient subject. Life on the streets generates a series of discourses from the men about the importance of being streetwise but, insofar as these are common sense, they are not easily articulated. Being streetwise is the ability to handle the dangers of street life, and this links masculinity, defense, and manly behavior. Contrary to a popular view that being streetwise privileges physical prowess and fighting ability, it is instead a cerebral attitude positioned by an intimate knowledge of locality. Thus the links between territoriality and working-class masculinity for white men, presented in the work of Andrew Tolson (1977) and Philip Cohen (1988), are equally powerful in the lives of African Caribbean and South Asian men.

The inner-city area where the Red Star men live and socialize is contested terrain in the material sense of struggles with white gangs or the National Front[2] who, until routed in the late 1970s, sought preeminence and intimidated the local population. Lately, it is the police who provide both routine and special operations surveillance within the new model of inner-city policing. Encounters with the police are viewed as harassment and have included physical duress and abusive, racist name-calling. The men emphasized that, in the face of the power of the police, it was "vital to know how to handle yourself." As Dev commented "You have to stay cool and let them heat up." Staying cool is essentially about maintaining dignity and control in a situation that usually offers little of either. Using a quiet and reasonable voice denotes calm, which is the outward sign of staying mentally alert and agile. In addition, the men were highly conscious of their knowledge of the locale and the consequent protection this secured for them by making the area "safe" in contrast to other city areas that were dangerous, especially the center of town at night, which they avoided. The language of safety also applied to people who could be trusted, and it offered the sense of "home" and belonging that they felt in their locality. An intimate knowledge of the streets allowed them to disappear and reappear if there was trouble on the streets. Speed was essential and was symbolically and practically signaled by the tracksuits and trainers that the men wore. Tracksuits and trainers are not just about the whims of fashion; they express something about street life and the importance of physical fitness.

Street politics as a clash between young men and men in blue uniforms has a long history as part of the urban landscape, but the documented racism of the police (Broadwater Farm Inquiry 1986; Institute of Race Relations 1987) is a crucial element in the lives of black people generally and South Asian and African Caribbean men in particular. Changes in police strategies in the 1980s have brought a new armory of weapons onto the streets. The men were acutely aware of this technology and the changes in tactics. "They try to wind up so they can show off their hardware," said Amrit, who continued: "But we're not stupid. We know their games." Wiliness, not confrontation, was seen to be the best way to resist. "You've got to use your brain and act fast," said Mark with a grin. "The coppers don't have much brain or pace."

Life on the streets, therefore, requires courage, wit, and knowledge. But even with their acknowledged abilities to "handle themselves," the men still had uncomfortable encounters with the police and with white men in other parts of the city. One evening Kuldip was beaten up by two white men while waiting for Chinese takeout food. When he recounted the incident to his friends, they were halfway to the door as the first move in finding the attackers and administering some rough justice, but he dissuaded them. When they discussed the incident it was understood not as an isolated event but part of the pattern of racial attacks in Britain. It was politicized by the understandings brought to it, and the men kept a close watch on the Chinese restaurant and sought ways to fight back. This incident, and others like it in pubs and the city center, added a powerful dimension to my understanding of the men's intense localism. It was quite clear that the city was not "safe" and that the decision to claim a space and defend it was essential.

Being streetwise incorporated other dimensions apart from negotiating the city, including the ability to satisfy needs and demands through a local network. For example, the men would organize vans and drivers to take them to see local soccer matches or acquire the latest fashion gear cheaply. Similarly, they could exchange advice on welfare benefits or legal matters and borrow money. They could have a house painted or building and electrical jobs done through a complex network of reciprocal relations, which allowed them to earn some money, acquire the things they needed, and have some fun. Being able to summon up resources in this way is a mark of power and status and an acknowledgment of male control over the immediate environment. It therefore has a direct bearing on masculinity and the power a man could exercise in the group. Favors are traded and power is demonstrated in relation to the favors owed to any one man. Thus there was a micropolitical aspect to the reciprocal relations within the economic system of the inner city.

Football (Soccer)

Football, known in the United States as soccer, was a passion for this group of men. During 1989–90 their football team excelled, carrying off trophies in the local league and competitions. Although their interest in football was a general one, fired by international competitions, their passion and loyalty were reserved for the local team that had emanated from Red Star and which played in the local league. It was a thrill to see South Asian and African Caribbean men beat their white counterparts and carry off the cups, and these moments of triumph were constantly relived as part of a shared and precious history, which was enthusiastically told and told again in the pub. This racial competition is not in any way surprising; English soccer is well known for its racism and racist chants, despite the numbers of African Caribbean players on all the major teams. The racism and masculinity of white working-class men are welded into one by the articulations between white working-class masculinity socially and ideologically constructed out of the postimperial chauvinism of British society. Modern soccer, growing up as it did in the Victorian and Edwardian eras, is redolent with the politics of race. But the growing number of black players has forced the Football Association to launch the slogan "Kick Racism Out of Football" for the 1993 season.

South Asian men play soccer because they love the game, but their entry into this arena means that they are immediately involved in the cultural politics of race. But this politics cannot be understood without reference to local amateur and semiprofessional leagues. The men did not offer their loyalty to the city team largely because the city team did not support local South Asian and African Caribbean players. They were acutely aware that in a city where over 25 percent of the population was South Asian and African Caribbean there were no city players from this pool of talent that went for trials at the club. Manjit's view expressed a general sentiment: "A city with so many black people and no black footballers. Ask the manager why is that? We know why, it's racism, that's why." The absence of South Asian men from the national soccer scene is discussed by Rajan Datar. Writing in the *Guardian* (June 18, 1989), he points out the passion for football among Bengali boys and comments: "Frustrated by the lack of opportunities to play organised football, many young Asians are now involved in their own leagues. From Huddersfield to Hayes in west London new competitions are sprouting up to accommodate the demand."

The response from black footballers and supporters is a collective one, generated and sustained at the local level in the amateur Football Association leagues. Like other towns and cities, Leicester has a thriving amateur section with a growing number of leagues and competitions. There are separate South Asian and African Caribbean teams and also those, like the Red Star team, that bring both groups together. Some teams have been generated from gurdwaras (Sikh temples) and some of the most fiercely contested tournaments are those organized around the Sikh festival of Vaisakhi. In this way ethnicity, masculinity, and popular culture are brought together within the South Asian diaspora.

Soccer games between "black" and white teams take place on a fiercely contested terrain, in which old rivalries are replayed and new ones instigated. For the black teams a win is a collective statement about the prowess of black players in a realm where white men consider themselves superior. A win over a white team is a source of celebration and pride for black men because, as the supporters and players say; "White teams don't like being beat by a black team."

The game of soccer, like all organized sports is a formal, rule-bound game, a set of discursive practices in a discursive space. All men play the game but they are constructed as players in difference, in the image of the Other. Thus African Caribbean players are characterized as loud and aggressive, whereas the South Asian player mirrors the orientalist view by being seen as the fellow who jabbers a lot. The half-mad Indian is set against the stoical, disciplined white footballer. White teams and referees complain about the lack of discipline of black teams and judge them differently. For the black players and supporters, this difference is one of the ways in which their progress through the leagues is impeded and one way to suppress the obvious skills that South Asian and African Caribbean players exhibit.

The disappointments and unfair decisions do nothing to quell the enthusiasm for the game, however, because the black players' romance with football invokes loyalty and camaraderie while allowing the men to perform and earn status and acclaim. Football allows a space in which the nuances of masculinity can be elaborated and publicly expressed: loyalty, collective responsibilities, brotherhood, and status, all relived repeatedly through the history of the team, the disastrous starts and eventual triumphs, the matches stolen by bad decisions on the part of biased referees, the trials and tribulations born and resolved. This history expresses in part the commonality and shared experience of masculinity among South Asian men but also speaks to what Ashis Nandy (1989), writing on cricket, has called "the structure of fate" — knowing how to work with and against fate at the same time.

Soccer offers status through performance validated by other men and the chance to be celebrated in an important area of life. It is part of the cultural politics of race in Britain today and it is a politics deeply rooted in masculinity. The discourses on soccer developed through the discussion of the game and its history are also displayed when the men appear in the pub on crutches with a variety of knee and leg injuries, shown off like battle wounds with considerable pride. Injuries separate the player from the spectator and signal deeds of daring and flair that can be displayed and celebrated.

The discourses on physical dexterity and tactical process are, for South Asian and African Caribbean players, about manliness and vigor, but are also linked to loyalty and support. Supporters are important especially when a player feels that the referees are not with him. "It makes you feel good to have a big crowd with you." Loyalty demands that errors are discussed in the semipublic space of the pub with other supporters as part of the analysis of the game. Similarly, although white teams try to steal the best of the black players, to change teams is an act of treachery even though there may be financial incentives. Instead, the players want a clear structure of opportunities for the team, for the collective.

Although loyalty requires a collective sense, this does not mean that individual performance is not celebrated. There are stars of the team, known and applauded for their speed, skill, and tactical verve. In discussing this the men were swift to point out that football "is an easy game, the ball does the work for you *but* . . . not without vision. A good player has to think, to read the game." It is important to all the men to be good football players, but as the responses to my questions on what makes a good player showed, success, like being streetwise, derives from a cerebral attribute as much as physical skill and dexterity. Thus soccer is tied to the body as a vehicle for the creative deployment of strategic acumen displayed in the ability to "read" the game. The importance of the game is expressed by Dev: "I can't explain football, deep satisfaction when I know I've played well, and when we lose I am so miserable I keep going over it. There are bad losers and bad losers! But you've got to accept the losses, it's part of the game. You can't win every time."

Consistent with the politics of Red Star, the teams that I watched had a deep commitment to bringing together African Caribbean and South Asian players. It was, in part, the nationalism of the neighborhood symbolized by the soccer team. The men were proud of their multiethnic teams, contrasting them with the specifically South Asian or African Caribbean teams that played locally. Stars on the team were both South Asian, previous players who bore the burdens of organizing the fixtures list, attending disciplinary hearings, and washing the team kit (shorts and jerseys). In fact, the multiethnic nature of the team led to problems for the team, which was barred from a Sikh tournament in a nearby city because the event was declared an "Indian" event. The team appealed to the Football Association (FA), was given FA support, and has continued to play as a team of South Asian and African Caribbean players. As I have suggested, however, a politics of difference has disrupted the forging of a "black" identity between South Asians and African Caribbeans.

Soccer managers may be in charge of the kit, a crucial responsibility, but that is nothing compared to the responsibility they carry for the performance of the team. In this they exercise a ruthless power over the playing lives of the men, who are their friends. Poor performance is met with sharp disapproval and the player will be dropped from the team. A manager also has to have "vision" and an especially good tactical sense with which he can motivate the players. The power of the manager is demonstrated by the performance of the team and by his ability to attract and keep star players. As one manager put it: "Football is all about politics." This is not a power, however, that is unaccountable; team members and friends are in constant contact with the manager and he treads a fine line between maintaining his authority and listening to the counsel of his "mates." It is a difficult balancing act, especially when unpopular decisions are made, players are upset, and their loyalties to each other are invoked.

The belief that "football is all about politics" returns us to the cultural politics of race so clearly understood by C. L. R. James and expressed in his work on cricket, *Beyond a Boundary*. There is a collective mobilization through soccer that relates to both locale and the wider political terrain. A crucial element in this politics is the way South Asian and African Caribbean masculinities are evoked as part of the resistance that black men generate in response to the racism of British society and by which they validate each other. It is a male space; women are not involved, but the men bring babies and toddlers to the matches, caring for them and demonstrating that even within the male world of football men, too, can display very different masculinities from those associated with the machismo world of the soccer pitch. The juxtaposition is an important visual reminder of the varieties of South Asian and African Caribbean masculinities and our understanding of them as shifting terrain.

Gendering Diaspora: Politics, Identities

The foregoing glimpse into the lives of some South Asian men in a British city during the 1990s tells a story that emphasizes the importance of gender and generation in relation to diaspora. Further, it highlights the creative reappropriation of the urban landscape and the ways members of the South Asian diaspora seek to render their experience intelligible and meaningful. I cannot stress too strongly that this is a story of arrival and settlement rather than one constructed within the realm of migration and looking backward. The defense of space and the relationship between ethnicity and place so crucial to nationalism are recast in the Red Star story as a tale of locality and neighborhood — the nationalism of the neighborhood — within the postcolonial state that is Britain and all that this implies for racism in its institutional and commonsense variants. The defense of a building involves resource-based politics in the arena of collective consumption and the politics of the local state but, more significant, it is a symbolic politics in which the terrain of British identity, the British nation, and belonging is being recast. As Gilroy (1987) suggests, it is a direct confrontation with the notion, "There ain't no black in the union jack" (which began as a football chant and was reappropriated as an expression of the feelings of the black population on Britain). This is a politics of youth, in which calls to loyalty, courage, and a collective identity are highlighted. A crucial aspect of this call — through which political identities are forged within a group of ethnically diverse young men — is the call to masculinity, allied to the discourses on physicality, power, loyalty, and courage.

Red Star's leadership used the common sense of the streets to act politically and sustain a campaign. The streets are a masculine space and this was reinforced by the importance of football in the lives of the young men. It is clear that masculinity is fractured, however; it is not settled but is a contested domain with multiplicities that require gender-identity work. My suggestion here is that masculinities are given context by specific "sites" and that the setting is crucial to the understanding of the variants of masculinity. My account of South Asian masculinities concentrates on the public arenas of the streets and football, but this in no way diminishes the importance of family life and economic activities. The decentered view of masculinity contributes to the dismantling of stereotypes of South Asian and African Caribbean men and of the simplistic understanding of masculinity as fixed and essential. Masculinities are constantly being remade through the inter- actions of men's lives and the discourses that are brought to bear on them. But this is not an outside view of interpellations via discourses external to subjects. The men who are the subjects of this chapter are "knowing subjects" and discourse producers, as the politics of Red Star shows so clearly. These are the voices of diaspora revising the assumptions of metro- politan lives as they claim a place and forge a sense of belonging in un- promising circumstances. It is a creative response in everyday life and it is not easily characterized within social science discourse, which is why we have shifted our attention to the poetics of belonging and identity.

Acknowledgments

This chapter would not have been possible without the warm and generous support of Red Star members, the leader of Red Star, and the men who are the subjects of this chapter. I owe them all heartfelt thanks, but most especially warmest thanks to: Rashpal, Scratch, Ajit, Daljit, Hari, Burgess, Stuart, Trevor, Nitin, Yogi, Archie, and Raj. Thanks also to Ali Rattansi for his insightful comments on earlier drafts of the chapter and to Stephanie Kneller for word processing.

Notes

1. The 1990 census recorded a population of 270,493 for Leicester. The South Asian and African Caribbean population is recorded as 76,991, of whom 60,297 are of Indian descent.

2. The National Front (NF), a neofascist organization, was active in Leicester in the late 1970s. The current version is called the British National Party.

References

Alvarez, S.
  1991 *Engendering Democracy in Brazil.* Princeton: Princeton University Press.
Anderson, B.
  1983 *Imagined Communities: Reflections on the Origin and Spread of Nationalism.* London: Verso.
Bains, H.
  1988 "Southall Youth: An old-fashioned story." In P. Cohen and H. Bains, eds., *Multi-Racist Britain.* London: Macmillan, pp. 226–43.
Benyon, J., and J. Solomos, eds.
  1987 *The Roots of Urban Unrest.* London: Pergamon Press.
Broadwater Farm Inquiry
  1986 *Report of the Independent Inquiry into Disturbances of October 1985 at the Broadwater Farm Estate, Tottenham.* Chaired by Lord Gifford Q.C. London: Karia.
Cohen, P.
  1988 "The Perversions of Inheritance: Studies in the Making of Multi-Racist Britain." In P. Cohen and H. Bains, eds., *Multi-Racist Britain.* London: Macmillan, pp. 9–118.
Dollimore, J.
  1986 "Homophobia and Sexual Difference." *Oxford Literary Review* 8: 5–12.
Fanon, F.
  1986 *Black Skin, White Mask* [1952]. London: Pluto Press.
Foucault, M.
  1977 *Discipline and Punish: The Birth of the Prison.* London: Allen Lane.
Fryer, P.
  1984 *Staying Power: The History of Black People in Britain.* London: Pluto Press.
Gilroy, P.
  1987 *There Ain't No Black in the Union Jack: The Cultural Politics of Race and Nation.* London: Hutchinson.
Hall, S.
  1987 "Minimal Selves." In ICA document, *Identity.* London: Institute of Contemporary Arts.
Hall, S., C. Critcher, T. Jefferson, J. Clarke, and B. Roberts
  1978 *Policing the Crisis: Mugging, the State, and Law and Order.* London: Macmillan.
Institute of Race Relations
  1987 *Policing against Black People.* London: Institute of Race Relations.

James, C. L. R.
    1963   *Beyond a Boundary.* London: Stanley Paul.
Melucci, A.
    1988   "Social Movements and the Democratisation of Everyday Life." In J. Keane, ed., *Civil Society and the State.* London: Verso, pp. 245–60.
Nandy, A.
    1989   *The Tao of Cricket.* London: Penguin.
Reeves, F.
    1986   *British Racial Discourses: A Study of British Political Discourse about Race and Race-related Matters.* Cambridge: Cambridge University Press.
Solomos, J.
    1988   *Black Youth, Racism and the State: The Politics of Ideology and Policy.* Cambridge: Cambridge University Press.
Tolson, A.
    1977   *The Limits of Masculinity.* London: Tavistock.
Westwood, S.
    1991   "Red Star over Leicester: Racism, the Politics of Identity and Black Youth in Britain." In P. Werbner and M. Anwar, eds., *Black and Ethnic Leadership in Britain.* London: Routledge, 146–67.
Yuval-Davis, N., and F. Anthias, eds.
    1989   *Woman-Nation-State.* London: Macmillan.

Parminder Bhachu

9. New Cultural Forms and Transnational South Asian Women: Culture, Class, and Consumption among British South Asian Women in the Diaspora

This chapter has two main themes. First, I discuss the complex nature of migration and settlement. I point to variations in migration and settlement trajectories, which produce a range of diasporic cultures in which South Asian women are situated internationally.[1] The vast majority of literature available on the subject treats migration as the single first movement of direct migrants to their destination economies. Yet there are direct, twice, and thrice migrant women, many of whom are further involved in fourth movements, especially in the 1990s. These multiple migrations are important to the ways different migrants and settlers view themselves, to their orientations to a homeland, and to the impact of these movements on cultural reproduction in local, regional, and transnational settings.

I focus on South Asian women of Punjabi Sikh descent from the Indian subcontinent and its diaspora, especially in Britain. These migrant women have varied histories of migration and settlement in Britain and the United States. I propose a more complex conceptualization of their economic and cultural locations than is conveyed in the literature and by media images, where Asian women are frequently represented as "working-class victims" forced to struggle with what are constructed as their "oppressive cultural systems." Yet Asian women actively engage with the British and American economies and occupy a range of class niches, which is further reflected in their cultural systems and consumption styles.

The second point I make concerns the transformative role of diasporic Asian women, who, by engaging with their "ethnic" cultural base in the context of their local, regional, and national cultures and class codes, transform these to generate new cultural forms. By examining their consumption patterns and cultural styles through an analysis of the wedding economy, in particular the dowry system, I emphasize their role as cultural entrepreneurs who choose their cultural forms and create new ones. Migrant women's agency and their self-defining roles are largely ignored in the literature and in mainstream portrayals, which describe them as passive recipients of their cultures. I also explore the construction and reconstruction of their ethnicity and diasporic identities to show that these are contextualized products of time and space occupied by these women in the migration process. Their marriage and dowry patterns are elastic, like their identities: not only continuously negotiated and determined by their migration histories but powerfully shaped by the codes of their local and national cultures and by their class positions. Equally important are international forces, which have a strong impact on the women's engagement with global economies and on their cultural patterns that are negotiated in these contexts.

Direct, Twice, and Thrice Migrants: Transnational Asian Women

Direct, twice, and thrice migrant women represent different histories of migration and settlement in the diaspora. In previous work (Bhachu 1985, 1992; Gibson and Bhachu 1988) on the twice migrant British Asians who migrated from the Indian subcontinent to East Africa, and thence to Britain in the late 1960s, I demonstrated that migrants and settlers have differential skills and experiences of migration and settlement. This diversity is further reflected in their destination economies in cultural reproduction, in economic participation rates, and in the varying speeds with which the infrastructures of their communities are established. I explored the dynamics of migration through an analysis of the migrants' cultural base as it is reproduced through the axis of race, caste, and class in Britain. Experienced settlers, twice (that is, in the British context) and thrice (in the United States context) migrant women possess considerable expertise in the management of their minority status, in the reconstruction of their ethnicities, and in the negotiation of their cultural systems. Their communities migrated from rural India in the late nineteenth century to East Africa, where they urbanized and established defined East African Asian identities. From Africa, they migrated to metropolitan Britain in the late 1960s, after their jobs were africanized in postindependence East Africa. Many of them further migrated to the United States, Australia, and other European countries in the 1980s and 1990s. As relatively prosperous twice migrants in Britain with great command of mainstream skills (in comparison to the less experienced direct migrants who are not as skilled at the "game of migration"), they also occupy separate class as well as caste positions and maintain exclusive marriage and community circuits. These are precisely some of the people who constitute the thrice migrants in the United States. As expert migrants, they were able to enhance their already considerable migration skills initiated and developed in Africa, established and refined in Britain, and further reproduced efficiently in the United States and in other tertiary destination economies in the diaspora.

Twice, thrice, and quadruple migrants possess powerful communication networks, which are facilitated by the ease of global communications. Their command of Western bureaucratic skills and the English language has given them considerable expertise at reproducing their cultural bases and community infrastructures in a range of countries. Such a scenario is in complete contrast to that of the less "culturally and ethnically skilled" direct migrants, who are often characterized by home orientation and a "myth of return." An important consequence of the latter characteristic is that the resources they generate in their destination economies are frequently remitted to a country of origin, where their positive (or for that matter negative) reference groups and status hierarchies remain. For direct migrants, migration, especially in the initial stages, is frequently a temporary, economically goal-oriented move. For twice and thrice migrants, however, migration is not a sojourn but a more permanent move to settle. They lack home orientation and are geared toward staying in their destination economies from the point of entry and retaining their capital and resources. The phases of settlement that apply to direct migrants, from preliminary bachelor households to the later reconstitution of their communities and then family unification many years later, are highly condensed in the case of multiple migrants. Twice and thrice migrants often migrate with three-generation family units or are united with their families within a year or two of settlement. Their communities possess a balanced age profile, unlike the direct migrants who often have a much younger age profile and only two-generation nuclear families.

This pattern of migration involving a series of moves is applicable to a wide range of groups in the United States: for example, the Vietnamese, Armenians, Iranians, and so on. It also applies to migrants in other countries, especially Canada, Australia, New Zealand, and prosperous European and Asian countries such as Germany and Japan. Situated as these experienced migrants are in an international milieu, migration in the 1980s and 1990s is for them no longer a first move, but a second, third, or even fourth movement; thus they constitute a transnational people with established international, national, and local connections. These features are critical to the reproduction of their cultural bases and ethnicities and to their engagement with the economies and polities of their countries of settlement. In all these processes of the construction and reconstruction of their identities and the reproduction of diasporic cultures, migrant women are the key actors.

Female Economic Activity and New Cultural Forms

The new cultural patterns and identities generated by these diasporic women are evident in their consumption patterns, which are analyzed here through the wedding economy. Migrant women play a much more significant economic and cultural role in shaping this event as a result of migration. The wedding gift exchange system has become more elaborate since migration, especially as a result of women's entry into the waged labor market in Britain. The translation of their earnings, especially by the brides into specific parts of dowries, has transformed and reinterpreted a "traditional" cultural arena that has existed for centuries. One reason for this development is more control over cash by young Asians than ever before, due to their more active engagement with the British economy as wage earners. This is obvious from some of the recent labor market statistics.

Asian women have always occupied and still currently occupy a cross-section of the class hierarchy, and this is reflected in their cultural and consumption styles. The class locations and the cultural systems that Asian women occupy are much more complex than is obvious from the literature, which focuses on particular sectors of the class groups — for example, working-class women and their struggles and oppression. The complexity of their class locations is not a new phenomenon. It has existed for as long as the Indian presence in Britain, and ranges from aristocrats like Princess Victoria Gouramma of the Coorgs and Maharanee Jinda Kaur (see Login 1904) to Indian wives of British men in the eighteenth and nineteenth centuries (Ballhatchet 1980), the Ayahs who were housed in the East End, and women servants (e.g., slave girls employed as ladies' maids) in the service of East India Company employees in Britain from the mid-seventeenth century onward (Visram 1986).

In addition to the Indian women situated at the top, middle, and bottom of the class hierarchy, there were also a number of Indian women students. The most well-known in the nineteenth century was Cornelia Sorabji, who was one of the earliest practicing women barristers; she later became a renowned social reformer and prolific writer.[2] In the 1930s, more than a hundred Indian women studied for professions such as medicine, law, and education at British universities (Visram 1986) and some stayed on in Britain. Similarly, during World War II, Noor Inayat Khan was among the first forty Women's Auxiliary Air Force members to be trained for intelligence work in occupied France. She was a secret agent based in Paris as a wireless operator and also involved in more dangerous missions in other parts of France. She was awarded the Croix de Guerre with a Gold Star and the George Cross posthumously, after being captured by the Gestapo and executed in Dachau in 1944 (Fuller 1952). Although her story has appeared in popular war soap operas on television (based around her code name, Madeleine), she has always been portrayed as a white woman of English and French parentage, thereby negating her Asianness. In the 1930s, the famous Hollywood actress Merle Oberon, whose career initially took off in Britain, was at her peak, winning the most prestigious acting roles. She was the illegitimate child of a Eurasian plantation owner in India and a poor Indian woman who brought her up in Calcutta before sending her to Britain as an adult (Higham and Moseley 1983). Thus the presence of Asian women both outside and within working-class sectors is not new in Britain: it is rooted in the past.

My purpose in referring to these distinguished women is not so much to counter the hegemonic construction of them as passive, docile, conflicted, and dominated by oppressive traditions and men — models that have so much currency in representations of Asian women — but to point to the historical roots of the heterogeneity of their experiences and positions, which is further manifested in Britain in the 1990s in a whole range of economic and cultural spheres. I do not want to deflect attention away from the predominantly working-class locations of Asian women to focus on prominent and successful Indian women, because I think this is patronizing. There is a tendency among minority-indigenous-ethnic scholars to refer endlessly to the economic and educational success stories and to famous individuals of the communities to which they belong, in defensive protest at the deficient models, and to present a positive alternative picture.[3] I do want to emphasize, however, the variety of Asian women's experiences and the complexity of the different niches they occupy both now and in the past. This diversity is reflected in their labor market profile and their engagement with the economy, which has further implications for the reproduction of facets of their cultural systems and a strong impact on their cultural reproduction.

Recent Labor Market Profile of British Asian Women

Asian women actively engage in the British economy, contrary to the stereotype of them. In certain cases they have higher economic activity rates than indigenous white women. The consequences for ethnic entrepreneurship of this active engagement of migrant women with the British waged economy are explored elsewhere (Westwood and Bhachu 1988), though they are also critical to the elaboration of the wedding economy.

For example, during the middle to the late 1980s, a higher proportion of Afro-Caribbean and non-Muslim women, including Sikh women, were in the British labor market in full-time employment than white indigenous women who were economically active. Of women between twenty-five and forty-four years old, 66 percent of white indigenous origin are economically active, as were 77 percent of West Indian origin, 62 percent of Indian origin, and only 17 percent of Pakistani and Bangladeshi origin. These latter categories are comprised of mostly directly migrant women from the subcontinent. This officially recorded figure should be higher for Pakistani and Bangladeshi women; the latter rather low figure does not include the paid homework, such as home sewing, done by Muslim women, who are more economically active than recorded figures show (Brah 1987: 41). The reasons for the considerably lower rates of entry into waged labor by Pakistani and Bangladeshi women are not clear and need further research. Bangladeshi women are certainly among the last group of South Asians to reconstitute their families by joining their husbands in Britain in the 1970s, a number of whom had migrated in the relatively early days of the 1940s and 1950s. These Bangladeshi women come mostly from rural areas and occupy a different class position from that of the experienced and highly metropolitan East African Asian women. The class position of Pakistani Muslim women is much more complex. Many women are from metropolitan Pakistan and occupy a range of class groups. It is possible that they have labor histories of much less involvement in the waged market sectors than the twice and thrice migrant women. In addition, Islamic religious ideologies, especially during the 1980s, must have a considerable impact on the construction of "masculine" and "feminine" roles. Such factors are important in determining Pakistani and Bangladeshi women's labor market histories and their current engagement with the waged economy.

Twice migrant East African Asian women have slightly higher rates of employment (at 69 percent) than either indigenous white women or the directly migrant Indian and Pakistani women (*Employment Gazette* 1987). The higher rate of economic activity among East African Asian women in Britain is a product of their urban experiences in formal employment sectors in Africa, in contrast to the mainly rural background of the majority of the directly migrant women from the subcontinent. This higher rate of engagement with the British wage labor market was also a consequence of the continuation of the employment trends established prior to migration from metropolitan Africa to metropolitan Britain. For example, the number of Asian female employees in Kenya had risen from 600 in 1948 to 3,750 in 1962, which was 10 percent of the total Asian labor force there (Ghai 1965: 95). By 1967, this statistic had risen to 18 percent (Ghai 1970). This period coincided with the most intense amount of Asian migration to Britain from Africa after the full impact of the Africanization policies became clear in the mid-1960s. This history was different from that of the directly migrant women, most of whom came either from rural areas or from places where there were fewer opportunities for female waged employment, or from traditions in which waged employment for women was discouraged.

The interesting development in the late 1980s' officially recorded figures for Bangladeshi and Pakistani women, especially the younger women of this group, is that there is a much higher rate of entry into the labor market of women between sixteen and twenty-four years of age (23 percent). These younger women, presumably, have been benefiting from a longer stay in Britain or have been locally born or raised. In years to come, this shift will have particular cultural and social implications for this group, which is economically the worst off of the directly migrant groups. Pakistanis and Bangladeshis at this time and in this age group are at least twice as likely to suffer unemployment than their white counterparts. The unemployment during a time of intense recession in 1990s Britain is, of course, affecting all British Asians and blacks severely. Current labor market figures are not available as yet, but they are sure to have had a major impact on consumption patterns.

In the late 1980s, however, the Pakistani and Bangladeshi migrant group also included "young Indian women most likely to be students . . . at

27% in comparison to the general figure of 13% of all women in this age group" (*Employment Gazette* 1987: 22). This interest in education among migrant Asian women is also evident in the Inner London Education Authority 1987 report on examination results and performance, which showed that Asian girls are not only entering examinations in considerable numbers but also outperforming the boys. This report states: "The average performance score obtained by girls was 17.7 compared with 13.7 for boys. In all ethnic groups, girls did better than boys" (ibid: 7). I will not elaborate the implications of this trend here, because I have discussed educational choices and changes, both current and potential, elsewhere (Bhachu 1986, 1989; Gibson and Bhachu 1988).

The high interest in female education is demonstrated by women's labor market positions. The differences between white and Asian women in managerial and professional groups are slight, in fact proportionately the same in the case of the twice and thrice migrant East African Asian women: 7 percent for white women, 7 percent for African Asian women, and 1 percent for West Indian women (Brown 1984: 198). As Sheila Allen points out,

> The difference in types of jobs and earnings found among black and white women are much less than those found among men. There are proportionately almost as many Asian women in professional, employer or management sectors (6%) as white women (7%) and the percentage of white women in unskilled jobs at 11% is higher than either west Indian (7%) or Asian women (2%). (1987: 182)

The implications of this greater overlap between women's earnings and jobs is that their expenditure and consumption patterns are also more likely to share a common ground — regardless of ethnicity and class — than is the case for men, who are much more unequally distributed in managerial positions.

There are significant regional differences in the economic participation rates of Asian women, depending on opportunity structures. Until the recent recession, which has hit the southeastern section of Britain particularly badly, the southeast was characterized by high rates of economic activity and lower unemployment rates, a situation applicable to whites and blacks alike. This is an important region for Asians, since over half the Indian population (54 percent) and three-fifths of the East African Asian population in Britain is based in the southeast of Britain (especially in London), in comparison with 31 percent for whites. There is a considerable difference in the number of economically active women in the southeast who were in full-time employment from that of like groups of women anywhere else in the country (*Employment Gazette* 1988). In addition, in the southeast many more Asian women are in white-collar/clerical and managerial/professional jobs than anywhere else. The increasing amount of waged employment for Indian women in the Midlands in the late 1980s filled the jobs created by the rapid growth of the "anorak industry," the clothing manufacturing sectors. Thus there are significant regional differences in the economic niches and employment opportunities of British Asian women.

It should by now be clear that the labor market profile of Asian women is much more complex than presented in most literature. In fact, Asian women are more widely distributed in a range of economic niches and employment structures than I have outlined here. Their occupational profile is, therefore, determined by local economies and the opportunity structures in them; however, I want to reiterate that this should not detract from their predominantly working-class locations. It should equally be emphasized that they also occupy a number of nonworking-class sectors and that they have had different histories of participation in the labor market prior to settlement in Britain and also since settlement in different regional economies in Britain. These varied economic histories influence the reinterpretation and reproduction of the wedding gift exchange system in the diaspora.

Migration and Dowries in the Diaspora

I examine the important cultural reproduction by British Punjabi Sikh women by analyzing one facet of their culture that reflects their British consumption styles and class locations.

Dowries represent the legitimate and recognized property rights of women and have become more elaborate since migration to Britain, as a result of women's entry into the waged labor market. Young Sikh women play a central role in manufacturing dowries, and the arena of dowry in the 1980s and 1990s in Britain has become, among other dimensions, a more important realm of creative consumption and reinterpretation than ever before (Bhachu 1985, 1986, 1988). It is a cultural idiom that has always been relevant and has seen significant inflation. Its commoditization is determined by the specificities of women's class positions and subcultural consumption styles, especially during the 1980s and 1990s, when most brides and younger Punjabi Sikh women are either locally born or have arrived as youngsters, and are therefore educated and socialized to regional and local British cultures. First, some brief background (detailed in Bhachu 1985, 1986) on the development of dowries as related to the migration process and settlement is required.

There is a close similarity between Punjabi Sikh notions of dowries (*daajs*) and those of high-status North Indians. The high-caste North Indian ideology of *kanyadaan,* the pure gift of a maiden for which no return is expected, and the accompanying *stridhanam* — exclusive female property — in the form of movable goods presented as premortem inheritance from the patrimony (Goody 1975: 1), also applies to Punjabi Sikhs regardless of their place within the migration chain and diaspora. Even though the same complex of beliefs as that of the high-caste Brahmans is widely accepted, these Sanskritic terms are rarely used by the Punjabi Sikhs. The four components of the *daaj* are clothes; gold for the bride; household goods including utensils, furniture, linen, quilts, kitchen gadgets, crockery, and consumer items; and affinal gifts. Money payments such as bridegroom price are nonexistent, though the groom and his mother and father receive substantial wedding gifts.

These four major components, constituting the external framework of *daajs,* have remained stable with migration and diasporic cultural reproduction, although there have been content changes in the specific gifts presented. The designated recipient of wedding gifts has also shifted according to the various phases of migration and in response to structural changes in the household and power relations within families. For example, the *daajs* of the 1920s through 1940s presented in India and Africa were designated for the mother-in-law, the most powerful and senior female decision maker regarding consumption choices within the domestic domain. She could redistribute the *daaj,* often using it for further gift giving. The bride of this period had direct control only of her *muklawa* (a presentation of a smaller volume of gifts similar to those presented in the *daaj*), which was received from her parents at the consummation of the marriage, often anywhere from three to seven years after the wedding ceremony and the presentation of the original *daaj.* It was after this rite de passage that the bride took up permanent residence in her affinal home.

The *daajs* of the 1950s and 1960s in Africa — and the 1970s through 1990s in Britain in the case of the twice migrant women — have acquired a different meaning. Affinal gifts were separated so that the mother-in-law had little control over bridal clothing and gold, though household goods in the 1950s and 1960s were often absorbed into extended family households, which were then quite prevalent. Bridal control over her sectors of the *daaj* increased, undermining the mother-in-law's redistributive authority over them. This development coincided with the *daajs* presented in Africa during the late 1940s and 1950s. The previous *daajs* belonged to brides whose marriages had taken place in India, where the joint family system was stronger and when families were less fragmented by migration. None of these Indian-married brides had their own separate households, though an increasing number were establishing nuclear residences in urban Africa, a trend reproduced by the vast majority of twice and thrice migrant brides in the 1970s through 1990s in Britain and the United States.

By the 1970s, the British *daajs* — unlike the African Punjabi and Indian Punjabi ones — contained fewer heavy household goods (such as bedroom, dining room, and sitting room furniture), which had been increasingly replaced by expensive, easily movable consumer items. Also around this time, affinal goods were separated totally from those reserved for the bride. This trend of earmarking affinal gifts began in 1950s Africa and was the norm by the 1970s among twice migrant brides in Britain. This separation of affinal and bridal gifts partly reflected household changes but was also a consequence of shifting residential patterns, which facilitated the establishment of a separate home immediately after marriage. The dramatic increase in the earning powers of the brides in Britain catalyzed this process; wives became contributors to house mortgage payments and sometimes initiators of house purchases. Also, because they helped to make the *daaj,* they expected to control it. None of the pre-1970s brides could exercise such options; as their command over economic resources, if any, was considerably lower.

Thus changes in the structure and control of the *daaj* are a product of the migration process. Some of these trends are obvious among urban households in India, as well, and are a consequence of changing female employment patterns and residential patterns. In East Africa, these processes had already begun (although they have become more firmly established in Britain) as families separated into nuclear units and as women became cash contributors to family incomes. Furthermore, the erosion of control by the affines over the redistribution of bridal gifts and over the residential choices of couples is a result of increased couple-orientation, as opposed to the kinship group-orientation characteristic of the previous phases of migration. Spouse-selection criteria have also shifted to take more account of couple suitability and personal demands rather than extended family expectations (Bhachu 1985).

The size of a *daaj* presented in India during the 1930s and 1940s ranged from five to eleven clothing items. The twenty-one-item *daajs* presented in the 1940s were all connected to East Africa, either through marriages that had taken place in Africa or through brides who were married in India but whose fathers were resident in Africa. By the 1950s, it was rare for East African Punjabi Sikh women to marry non–East African grooms, though some of the men still returned to India to marry Indian brides. Marriages were endogamously arranged only with other East African Punjabis by this time, in observance of the caste and regional endogamy rules; and a *daaj* of fewer than eleven items was never presented. It had increased in size to between fifteen and twenty-one items. By the 1960s, the custom of giving *daajs* of twenty-one clothing sets, generated entirely from parental and bridal kinship group wealth, was firmly established.

By the 1970s, a *daaj* of twenty-one clothing items was almost obligatory for first marriages within the British community that were "correctly" arranged. In fact, it has been common in the past fifteen years to find *daajs* of thirty-one items or more. There has been an increase not only in the amount of clothing items but also in the quality of *daaj* gifts. The pre-1950s *daajs* contained inferior gifts to be used for further gift giving. The *muklawa* was of higher quality because it contained fewer gifts for exclusive bridal use. In addition, the expensive consumer household items, which have become an important part of post-1970s *daajs,* were not commonly given in the 1950s and 1960s East African *daajs,* which contained furniture instead, a category that is present in only a few of the British ones. The 1930s and 1940s premigration Indian *daajs* included neither furniture nor the consumer items, since brass, silver, and steel utensils and bedding sets (including all the bed linen and quilts) were more commonly presented. In contrast, the post-Africa migration to Britain has seen an increase in consumer items, which are easily separable from extended family property when a separate household is established. This type of postmarital residence, the most common in the diaspora since the 1970s, has given the *daaj* a completely different dimension from any prior to this phase of settlement overseas. Neolocal residence further increases the bride's command over her dowry, which also makes it possible for her to be more creative in its interpretation and its elaboration with her own earnings.

To summarize: Dowries that consisted of minimal items both for the bride and for her affinal kin in the late 1950s and 1960s have escalated in size in the 1970s and 1980s. The three components of the *daaj* — the elaborate traditional garments and some Western clothes, household goods including luxury consumer items, and gold ornaments in the form of "sets" — designated specifically for the bride herself, and the fourth component of affinal gifts for the groom and his close affines, are always adhered to rigidly for caste-endogamous East African Asian marriages. The structure of the *daaj* has not changed over time, even though there have been internal changes in the items presented, reflecting the move to urban Britain. The designation of certain components of the *daaj* has also shifted, reflecting structural changes in the organization of the household and the various power relations within it. Migration, changing residential patterns, and increased female economic activity in the diaspora from the late 1960s onward have favored the brides.

Class- and Region-Coded Commoditized British Dowries

The varied economic profile of British Asian women is reflected in their different positions in the class hierarchy and their various cultural and regional locations in Britain, especially during the late 1980s, a period that has the highest number of British-born or British-raised Asian women. This regionality is reflected in the consumption and cultural styles that they adopt, even though patterns that emerge from London are the most influential because they are products of the dominant minority community.[4] The wealth generated through women's relationship with the wage labor market is expended in accordance with their subclass styles and related consumption values. These specificities are reflected in their marriages and dowries.

I present here only a brief summary of the escalation of the dowry system among Punjabi Sikhs since migration to Britain not so much to detail the process of elaboration within it (Bhachu 1985, 1986, 1988), but to point to the significant inflation within it of those spheres that directly concern the brides themselves. This elaboration of the dowry system is just one facet of the cultural and religious effervescence that has taken place among the Sikhs in the settled phases of the 1970s and 1980s in Britain. I have discussed these processes elsewhere (Bhachu 1988, 1989, 1991), in relation to the various phases of settlement in Britain, to highlight women's important role as agents and catalyzers of cultural reproduction and as generators of symbolic capital (Andizian 1986: 265) for their communities.

The spheres within the wedding economy that have been most significantly inflated in Britain, especially since the late 1970s, concern the brides
themselves. The wedding economy has been greatly elaborated since the
1970s, as the twice migrants became increasingly settled. This inflation
applies both to the rituals of the wedding procedure and to the dowry
system, to which young brides are significant contributors. For example, as
mentioned earlier, the clothing included in the dowries has become more
extravagant in quantity and quality. Dowries have increased from eleven to
twenty-one clothing items in the 1950s and 1960s in Africa, to twenty-one
items in Africa and Britain, to anything from twenty-one to fifty-one items
in the 1970s, 1980s, and 1990s in Britain and the United States. Some of the
clothes are high-quality silk saris and prestigious designer clothes, which
are designed by leading European and Bombay-based Indian designers, and
which are accompanied by expensive Gucci and Bally shoes and bags,
especially in the case of high-earning professional brides. The "standard"
East African Punjabi Sikh dowry of twenty-one clothing items and a whole
range accompanying accessories and exclusive consumer items for the bride
are always presented in Britain. This norm persists regardless of the standing of the families involved and has been further reproduced in the United
States. Twenty-one clothing items are also commonly presented in the
Indian subcontinent and Pakistan.

Although a twenty-one-item *daaj* constitutes the British-American-
East African Sikh pattern, there are major qualitative differences in its
content, according to the earning powers of the brides themselves. A bride
who has not earned wages in her own right before marriage invariably has
the basic twenty-one pieces, but the wage-earning brides' *daajs* are much
more elaborate and voluminous. Even though the latter *daajs* may include
twenty-one clothing items, they are characterized by the inclusion not only
of higher quality garments and personal accessories but also of a vaster
range of consumer durables—china sets, silver cutlery, electronic music
equipment, and exclusive linen—which the brides have purchased from
their own earnings and which they themselves are likely to utilize and also
control.

Much more than the 1970s dowries in Britain or the earlier ones in
Africa, the late 1980s and 1990s dowries of the Asian women born and
raised in Britain are particularly reflective of the British subcultural and
regional styles, especially in the interpretation of their traditional ethnic
garments. Now there are dowries that are "very London" emerging from
the various areas and subcultures of the capital and according to the class

positions occupied by the brides and their kinship groups. Similarly, there are dowries that reflect the various regional styles and cultures and accord with dominant consumption choices of the areas in which the brides have been raised and the local cultures to which they have been socialized. These variations also apply to the identities and ethnicities negotiated and generated by these diasporan Asian women according to their situation in specific localities. London Asian women identify themselves differently from those in Northern Ireland and Scotland and according to the class positions and local subcultures they occupy.

British subcultural and regional styles are influential in the interpretation of not only the traditional garments, goods, and gifts but also their class-encoded consumption patterns. Thus, there are *daajs* that are Sloane Rangerish[5] in their interpretation — reflecting the London-Knightsbridge-Sloane Square consumption patterns of some of the high-earning and professional brides — just as there are prestigious designer-ethnic-European *daajs,* the middle- and lower middle-class Oxford Street, Marks and Spencerish, mass-produced department store types, working-class East Ender types, provincial Liverpudlian Sikh and Mancunian types, and so on. Different regional styles are clearly discernable. For example, a Midlands *daaj* is interpreted differently from that of a London bride of an equivalent class group, despite the similarity in the content of the *daajs* and the persistence of the external framework — its three main spheres for the bride and fourth component for the affines. These regional patterns are also obvious from the marriage circuit — an informal metropolitan hypergamy — which operates in Britain. London girls tend not to marry outside London and the southeast. If they are married out, in a majority of cases they move back to London to set up a nuclear residence within a couple of years of marriage. This is not a new phenomenon. In East Africa, Nairobi Sikh girls tended not to marry men living outside the capital, who were considered to be more orthodox and less socially skilled — *paindoos* — in comparison to the Nairobiwallahs. In India, a number of women from the larger cities, such as Delhi and Bombay, prefer not to marry into the small-town provincial families.

I have considerably simplified a complex procedure mainly to point out the elaborations in the bridal spheres that have seen the most significant inflation. Punjabi Sikh women's increased command over productive resources and the translation of their wages into a cultural idiom that has existed for centuries and survived two migrations, from India to Africa and thence to Britain, can also be discerned from the elaborations within the marriage procedure itself and the accompanying gift exchanges which principally concern the groom's family and his immediate kin. It must be emphasized, however, that traditional structures have been not only reproduced but also enhanced in the changed circumstances since the entry of Asian women into the British labor market as wage earners.

The dowry processes are further aided by liberation within the religious ideology. This is especially true in the case of the Sikhs, whose religion accords Sikh women equal status to that of their men and gives them considerable leverage in asserting their roles and in choosing their identities and educational and occupational careers (Bhachu 1989). It is precisely this religious background that is also reflected in their labor market profile and in their active engagement with the British economy, which has allowed them to consume in their own interests and reestablish and actively engage with their cultural framework and female property systems.

By focusing on a cultural trait, I have tried to show that the *daajs* presented to and manufactured by young South Asian women are influenced by and responsive to class and regional trends, being products of particular consumption patterns which encode facets of their experiences and locations and reflect life-styles that shift continuously. All this applies as well to the identities negotiated and generated by Asian women. These too have their specificities, which are multifaceted and activated differently according to the various contexts. They are products of particular periods and of symbolic and material economies. Just as the dowries of these women are ethnically assertive, so also are they assertive of regional and class trends and subcultural consumption styles.

Negotiated Identities: Reconceptualizing Asian Women in the Diaspora

Now that there is a rapidly growing population of British-raised and British-born Asians, some of the commonly used concepts need to be revised. The presence of Asian women in different class and regional cultures and economic niches in Britain produces a variation in their experiences, and the way they define themselves is a product of these experiences. London Asian women are as much Londoners — products of the various subcultures in the capital — as they are Jat or Ramgarhia Sikhs, East African, Malay, or Japanese Asian depending on their migration and diasporic histories. The professional and occupational niches they occupy bring into focus other identities that are representative of their different economic locations. Thus Asian women in Birmingham are highly Brummite in their expenditure choices and in the construction of their identities, just as London Asian women in Camden and Hampstead (the literati- and media-dominated areas and subcultures) are Camdenian and Hampsteadian in their modes of operation and in their interpretation of their wealth, their clothes, and the symbols important to the definition of their identities and styles. In all these areas, the now passe 1980s Yuppie/Buppie Asians shared the symbolic and material culture of that erstwhile subclass. These regionally specific textures and traits are absorbed and also transformed as they filter through Asian women's continuously negotiated class and ethnic codes. Their patterns of consumption and cultural styles grow out of the specificities of their regional and class locations and from particular niches within the large metropolis. This is not because there is no common "ethnic" cultural base, but because younger Asian women emerge from the particular localities in which they have been raised, and from particular class cultures to which they have been socialized (Mac an Ghaill 1988: 110, 138). Whole facets of the existence of Asian women are subject to and determined by common economic, class, and regionally specific forces, which have as much impact on the lives of white British women as they do on Asian women, regardless of their various ethnicities.

My purpose in referring to Asian women's translation of their earnings into a cultural trait — thus commoditizing "traditional" patterns, which are as controlled by their locations within the "ethnic" social structures as by their British class niches and regional locations — is to show that their identities are produced and governed by the same range of forces and are activated differentially in varying contexts. They do not remain static and unchanging, but are negotiated according to the conditions in which they are situated, and in direct relationship to the powers of negotiation that the women can muster in shifting economic and political conditions.

Furthermore, cultural traits frequently portrayed as oppressive for Asian women may be viewed quite differently by the women themselves. My objection is to the prevalence and uniform application of these simplistically conceived models in the analysis of female Asian and black diasporic experiences; models that do not heed mitigating circumstances or the women's different aspirations, perceptions, and cultural ideologies. For example, the liberating ideology of Sikhism accords women equal status and has consequences for their economic activity rates and their general assertiveness in cultural reproduction (Bhachu 1988). Thus the impact of these "oppressive tendencies" is differential depending on their cultural apparatus and the skills that Asian women can muster to negotiate their territories both within the domestic domain and outside it. There are shifts in power according to the changing command Asian women have over both economic and mainstream cultural capital, which in some cases actually leads them to be even more forceful in asserting their "ethnic symbols" — for example, turban-wearing professional Sikh women and Westernized and Western-born Muslim women wearing *burkhas* (dark tent-like garments worn by women over their clothes, covering them almost from head to toe). The acceptability of arranged marriages is another example of this acceptance of "ethnic" cultural values by some of the most highly educated and independent Asian women, in common with other women in their communities. Yet, these behaviors are portrayed by some white feminists as oppressive and reactionary (Parmar 1984: 15). Other examples are the acceptance of purdah by Western-educated Arab women (Altorki 1988) and in recent times the adoption by Sikh women of what are sometimes considered fundamentalist Sikh symbols (Saghal 1989) — the donning of turbans and rejection of the Hinduized sari, in favor of a Sikh Punjabi suit as a dress form. This is not to deny the real threats posed by the intimidating powers of the fundamentalists, especially the young males, but to point to the self-determination of Asian women as active agents who interpret and reinterpret, formulate and reformulate their identities and their cultural systems in a climate of continuous change.

Conclusion

Twice and thrice migrant and transnational women interpret and reinterpret their cultural systems in the changing diasporic contexts as cultural entrepreneurs. By engaging with their cultural frameworks in the context of their local and national codes and the international forces that impact on women internationally, they transform traditional cultural forms to manufacture *newer cultural forms* which derive from their ethnic traditions and which are continuously formulated in the context of their class and local cultures. Yet there is little perception of these migrant women as active agents and as negotiators of their cultural values, which are frequently presented as nonnegotiable entities enforced on them as passive victims by patriarchies and capitalist producers. The latter agencies are indeed powerful in determining cultural patterns and cultural reproduction; however, these women also have agency, which plays an important role in their choice of life-styles and their function as innovators and originators of new cultural forms and new diasporic spaces.

Not only is the role of Asian migrant women as active agents in the transnational diaspora one that is largely absent in the literature, but the cultural locations and ethnicities of these women are represented as fixed and "ethnically absolute" (Gilroy 1987: 13). The forces that are given analytic supremacy in the definition of their identities and ethnicity are those of exclusion and of external and contrived enforcement of their cultural values. In all, Asian women are portrayed as divorced from the influences of local trends and from other homogenization forces that emanate from popular culture and are internationally applicable.[6] The assumptions found in the literature are that the crucial determinants of their identities and cultural bases, especially in the context of migration and settlement, are: the nurturing forces of a homeland culture, which (at least in the early stages of migration and settlement) provides cultural reinforcement; the maintenance of ethnic boundaries through the exclusionary forces of racism; confrontations that are said to lead to identities of resistance and defiance; and the desire of diasporan Asians to emulate and aspire to particular "white" class cultures and their symbols. There is a great deal of emphasis on boundary maintenance and on the perpetuation of what are presented as clearly organized, homogeneous, and fixed cultural values. Importance is attached to the impact of rejection, with racism and discrimination as the fundamental forces in structuring their identities and cultural locations in diasporas. Ethnicity is presented as a characteristic that has fixed components and symbols and is considered to be the primary agent controlling and generating migrants' various identities and migrant cultures. Indeed, all these social mechanisms are important in structuring their lives and in determining their life chances. My concern, however, is the many other forces that are equally important in framing their experiences and for diasporic cultural reproduction.

International forces have a strong impact on migrants' engagement with global economies and on the cultural patterns negotiated in local and international economies. Thus particular ethnicities and identities are not stable, despite a common core of fundamental religious and cultural values that constitute cultural roots but shift according to the forces that operate on them. In the case of direct, twice, and thrice migrant Asian women, these identities are not just products of confrontation and rejection, and the wholesale transference of homeland culture, but emerge out of the vibrant and changing European and international cultures in which Asian women are situated and over which they have *genuine unself-conscious command*. Their cultural locations and styles are not "wholly defined by exclusion" (Hall 1989: 46) or by consciously emulating particular subcultures, but through their natural familiarity with particular economies and with their symbolic and material culture, which they appropriate from, transform, reinterpret, and reproduce in local, national, and international contexts to generate new cultural forms in continually changing transnational settings.

Notes

1. The categories of Asians and Asian women in Britain refer predominantly to South Asians, who have migrated directly from the Indian subcontinent or from the Indian diaspora. It also includes British Asians, who were born and raised in Britain. These categories are British-specific. I am not referring here to Asian Americans — the Japanese, Chinese, Koreans, Filipinos, and so on — who are categorized as Asians in the United States. It should be kept in mind that these labels constitute "contested terrain," being almost continuously negotiated. It should be equally emphasized, however, that the themes discussed in this chapter as describing British Asian women of Sikh origin are much more widely applicable to the conceptualization of the cultural locations, life-styles, and identities of Asian women in the academic and other literatures on both sides of the Atlantic.

2. She was the first woman in Britain to have been awarded a law degree by a British University (Somerville Hall, Oxford, 1889).

3. See anthropologist Micaela di Leonardo's critique of this for Italians in the United States (1984: 22). Gayatri Spivak also criticizes the desire to represent blacks positively: "But the idea of always portraying blacks or women or whatever the minority is in a new and positive light is, in the long run, deeply insulting" (1989: 86).

4. Nearly half of the ethnic minority labor force lives in London (*Employment Gazette* 1987: 18), an area (in common with southeast Britain in general) characterized by the most amount of economic activity and least amount of unemployment (*Employment Gazette* 1988: 175). There are significant differences between London and the southeast and the rest of the few, though major, urban centers in which Asians are settled.

5. "Sloane Rangerish" styles refer to those that emanate from the Sloane Ranger set, which were popularized by the "Super Sloane" Princess Diana, prior to her current queenly style. There are Asianized and Punjabized versions of Sloane Ranger fashion trends, which are particularly obvious in their interpretation of ethnic garments like the Punjabi suit (worn by a cross-section of North Indian women), put together using Sloane Ranger accessories and in accordance with the Sloane Ranger–style codes. Although the Punjabi suit has been worn by Punjabi women for centuries, over the past decade it has acquired particular significance for

younger South Asian women in diaspora communities internationally, and also on the subcontinent, as a high fashion dress form that is being creatively interpreted both by them and by leading Indian, Pakistani, and also British designers such as Zandra Rhodes. It has become very much a part of transnational South Asian culture and increasingly available through mail-order catalogues and also through fashion magazines such as *Libas, Connections,* and *Rivaz.*

6. Hebdige (1987, 1988), in developing a cartography of taste in Britain, talks about the Americanization (homogenization) of cultural styles and patterns. This powerful universalization process is currently a burning topic with retail chain store bosses and consumer markets analyzers: "There are 50 million kids in Europe, and they have *converging* lifestyles in music labels and Big Macs. The international market is a reality and consumers are becoming more similar globally" (*New Statesman and Society Magazine,* September 8, 1989; M. George 1989: 26).

References

Allen, S.
    1987   "Gender, Race and Class in the 1980's." In Charles Husband, ed., *"Race" in Britain: Continuity and Change.* London: Hutchinson.
Altorki, Soraya
    1988   "At Home in the Field." In S. Altorki and C. El Solh, eds., *Arab Women in the Field: Studying Your Own Society.* Syracuse, N.Y.: Syracuse University Press.
Andizian, S.
    1986   "Women's Roles in Organizing Symbolic Life: Algerian Female Immigrants in France." In Rita J. Simon and Caroline B. Brettell, eds., *International Migration: The Female Experience.* Totowa, N.J.: Rowman and Allanheld, pp. 245–65.
Ballhatchet, K. A.
    1980   *Race, Sex and Class under the Raj: Imperial Attitudes and Policies and Their Critics, 1793–1905.* London: Weidenfeld and Nicolson.
Bhachu, Parminder
    1985   *Twice Migrants: East African Sikh Settlers in Britain.* London and New York: Tavistock.
    1986   "Work, Marriage and Dowry among East African Sikh Women in United Kingdom." In Rita J. Simon and Caroline B. Brettell, eds., *International Migration: The Female Experience.* Totowa, N.J.: Rowman and Allanheld, pp. 229–40.
    1988   "Home and Work: Sikh Women in Britain." In Sallie Westwood and Parminder Bhachu, *Enterprising Women: Ethnicity, Economy and Gender Relations,* pp. 76–103.
    1989   "Ethnicity Constructed and Reconstructed: The Role of Sikh Women in Cultural Elaboration and Educational Processes in Britain." *Gender and Education* 3: 147–62.

1991   "Culture, Ethnicity and Class among Punjabi Sikh Women in 1990's Britain." *New Community* 17, 3: 401–12.

1992   "Identities Constructed and Reconstructed: Representations of Asian Women in Britain." In Gina Buijs, ed., *Migrant Women: Crossing Boundaries and Changing Identities*. Oxford and New York: Berg Publishers.

Brah, Avtar
1987   "Women of South Asian Origin in Britain: Issues and Concerns." *South Asia* 7, 1: 39–53.

Brown, Colin
1984   *Black and White Britain: The Third PSI Survey* London: Heinemann.

Employment Gazette
1987   *Ethnic Origin and Economic Status*, pp. 18–29. London: Her Majesty's Stationary Office.

1988   *Ethnic Origin and the Labour Market*, pp. 164–77. London: Her Majesty's Stationary Office.

Fuller, J. Overton
1952   *Madeline: The Story of Noor Inayat Khan*. London: Victor Gollancz.

George, M.
1989   *New Statesman and Society Magazine*, September 8.

Ghai, Yash
1965   *Portrait of a Minority: Asians in East Africa*, Nairobi: Oxford University Press.

1970   *Portrait of a Minority: Asians in East Africa* (revised ed.). Nairobi: Oxford University Press.

Gibson, Margaret A., and Parminder Bhachu
1988   "Ethnicity and School Performance: A Comparative Study of Sikhs in Britain and the United States." *Ethnic and Racial Studies* 11, 3: 239–62.

1991   "The Dynamics of Educational Decision Making: A Comparative Study of Sikhs in Britain and the United States." In Margaret A. Gibson and John U. Ogbu, eds., *Minority Status and Schooling*. New York: Garland Publishing Inc., pp. 63–96.

Gilroy, Paul
1987   *There Ain't No Black in the Union Jack: The Cultural Politics of Race and Nation*. London: Hutchinson.

Goody, Jack
1975   "Bridewealth and Dowry in Africa and Eurasia." In Jack Goody and Stanley Tambiah, eds., *Bridewealth and Dowry*. Cambridge: Cambridge University Press, pp. 1–58.

Hall, Stuart
1987   "Minimal Selves." *Identity Documents*. London: Institute of Contemporary Arts, pp. 44–48.

Hebdige, Dick
1987   "Towards a Cartography of Taste: 1935–1964." In Bernard Waites, Tony Bennett, and Graham Martin, eds., *Popular Culture: Past and Present*. London: Croomhelm, in association with the Open University Press.

1988 [1979]   *Subculture: The Meaning of Style*. London: Methuen.

Higham, C., and R. Moseley
     1983   *Merle: A Biography of Merle Oberon.* Kent: New England Library.
Inner London Education Authority
     1987   *Ethnic Background and Examination Results: 1985–1986.* Report B7078.
             London: Inner London Education Authority, Research and Statistics
             Office.
Leonardo, Micaela di
     1984   *Varieties of Ethnic Experience: Kinship, Class and Gender among California
             Italian Americans.* Ithaca: Cornell University Press.
Login, Dalhousie E.
     1904   *Lady Login's Recollections: Court Life and Camp Life 1820–1904.* Reprint.
             New Delhi: Rima Publishing House.
Mac an Ghaill, Mairtain
     1988   *Young, Gifted and Black.* Philadelphia: Milton Keynes, Open University
             Press.
Parmar, Pratibha
     1984   "Gender, Race and Class: Asian Women in Resistance." In Centre for
             Contemporary Cultural Studies, *The Empire Strikes Back: Race and
             Racism in 70's Britain.* London: Hutchinson, pp. 236–75.
Sahgal, Gita
     1989   "Fundamentalism on the Rise." *Spare Rib* 202: 6–7.
Spivak, Gayatri Chakravorty
     1989   "In Praise of 'Sammy and Rosie Get Laid.'" *Critical Quarterly* 31: 80–
             88.
Visram, Rozina
     1986   *Ayahs, Lascars and Princes: The Story of Indians in Britain 1700–1947.*
             London: Pluto Press.
Westwood, Sallie
     1988   "Workers and Wives: Continuities and Discontinuities in the Lives of
             Gujarati Women." In Westwood and Bhachu, *Enterprising Women:
             Ethnicity, Economy and Gender Relations,* pp. 103–31.
Westwood, Sallie, and Parminder Bhachu, eds.
     1988   *Enterprising Women: Ethnicity, Economy and Gender Relations.* London
             and New York: Routledge.

Contributors

Parminder Bhachu is the Henry R. Luce Professor of Cultural Identity and Global Processes at Clark University, Massachusetts. Previously, she was at the University of California, Los Angeles, and at London University, Institute of Education, in Britain. She is the author of *Twice Migrants: East African Sikhs in Britain* (Tavistock, 1985), co-editor, with Sallie Westwood, of *Enterprising Women: Ethnicity, Economy and Gender Relations* (Routledge, 1988), and co-editor, with Ivan Light, of *Immigration and Entrepreneurship: Culture, Capital and Ethnic Networks* (Transactions, 1993).

Verne A. Dusenbery is Assistant Professor of Anthropology and Director of International Studies at Hamline University in St. Paul, Minnesota. Trained in anthropology at Stanford University and the University of Chicago, he has written extensively on Sikhs in North America and co-edited, with N. Gerald Barrier, *The Sikh Diaspora: Migration and the Experience Beyond Punjab* (Delhi: Chanakya Publications; Columbia, Mo.: South Asia Publications, 1989). His current research is on Sikh communities in Southeast Asia.

Madhavi Kale is Helen Taft Manning Assistant Professor of History at Bryn Mawr College, where she teaches British imperial history. She is currently preparing her Ph.D. dissertation, "Casting Labor: Empire and Indentured Migration from India to the British Caribbean, 1837–1845," for publication. Her research interests include comparative slavery and emancipation, with a focus on the British Caribbean in North America and the United States, and gender and the British Empire.

John D. Kelly is Assistant Professor of Anthropology at Princeton University. He is the author of *A Politics of Virtue: Hinduism, Sexuality and Countercolonial Discourse in Fiji* (University of Chicago Press, 1991), and, together with Uttra Singh, the translator of *My Twenty-One Years in the Fiji Islands* by Totaram Sanadhya (Fiji Museum, 1991). He is currently at work on two books: *A Politics of Value: Capitalism, Colonialism and Hindu Devotionalism in Fiji*, and *Discourse, Knowledge and*

Culture: Sciences of Word and Meaning in Ancient India and Questions for an Anthropology of Knowledge.

Aisha Khan teaches in the Sociology and Anthropology Department of Swarthmore College. Her research interests include the construction of racial and ethnic identities, colonialism, postcolonial societies, social stratification, and cultural hierarchies. She has published on her fieldwork among the Garifuna (Black Carib) in Honduras and on her fieldwork among East Indians in Trinidad, addressing such issues as South Asian diasporas in the western hemisphere, the relationship between religious ideology and ethnic identity, "mixed" racial and ethnic identities, and women's labor in the informal economy. She is also co-editor of *Women Anthropologists: Biographical Sketches* (University of Illinois Press, 1989).

Madhulika S. Khandelwal is a Historian at the Asian/American Center, Queens College, New York. In 1991, she completed her doctoral dissertation, on Indian immigrants of New York City, at the Department of History at Carnegie Mellon University. She teaches courses in Asian American studies and South Asian studies, and on the South Asian diaspora. She is currently working on a book on the evolution of the Indian immigrant communities in the United States.

Susan Slyomovics is Assistant Professor in the Department of Comparative Literature at Brown University. She is the author of *The Merchant of Art: An Egyptian Hilali Epic Poet in Performance* (University of California Press, 1988) and articles on folklore, performance, and theater in the Arabo-Muslim world. She co-produced and co-directed a videotape entitled "Wedding Song: Henna Art Among Pakistani Women in New York City" (1990).

Peter van der Veer is Professor of Comparative Religion and Director of the Research Centre for the Comparative Study of Religion and Society, University of Amsterdam. He is the author of *Gods on Earth* (London; Atlantic Highlands, N.J.: Athlone, 1988) and *Religious Nationalism* (University of California Press, 1994), and co-editor (with Carol A. Breckenridge) of *Orientalism and the Postcolonial Predicament: Perspectives on South Asia* (University of Pennsylvania Press, 1993).

Steven Vertovec is Alexander von Humboldt-Stiftung Research Fellow at the Institute of Ethnology, Free University of Berlin. Previously he was Research Fellow at Oxford University School of Geography. He is author of *Hindu Trinidad: Religion, Ethnicity and Socio-Economic Change* (London: Macmillan, 1992), editor of *Aspects of the South*

Asian Diaspora (Delhi: Oxford University Press, 1991) and co-editor of *South Asians Overseas: Migration and Ethnicity* (Cambridge University Press, 1990) and *The Urban Context: Ethnicity, Social Networks and Situational Analysis* (Oxford: Berg, in press).

Sallie Westwood, Leicester University, England, has researched widely in the field of ethnic and gender studies in Ghana, India, Britain, Ecuador, and Colombia. She is the author of several books including *All Day Every Day: Factory and Family in the Making of Women's Lives* (University of Illinois Press, 1985), and co-author, with Parminder Bhachu, of *Enterprising Women* (London; New York: Routledge, 1988) and with Sarah Radcliffe, *Viva: Women and Popular Protest in Latin America* (London; New York: Routledge, 1993).

Index

Act of Abolition (1833), 6, 74
Adamson, Alan, 77
Adi Granth, 24
Africa: and African Americans, 2; and Afro-Trinidadians, 11, 96–97, 104–16; African diaspora, 1, 198; laborers from, 79, 133; Sikhs in, 9. *See also* East Africa; Slavery
Afro-Caribbeans: as laborers, 76–82; in Britain, 197–219
Afro-Trinidadians, 10–11, 85, 93–124, 150
Ahmadiyyas. *See* Islam
Akal Takhat, 24, 27
Akali Dal (Shiromani Akali Dal), 21, 27, 28, 33. *See also* Punjabis; Sikhism
Al-Azmeh, Aziz, 127 n.17
All India Sikh Student Federation, 29
Allen, Charles, 84
Allen, Sheila, 229
Altorki, Soraya, 239
Alvarez, Sonia, 199
Amritsar, 24, 37. *See also* Golden Temple
Anderson, Benedict, 3, 5, 27, 69 n.8, 96, 205
Andhra Sangam (Fiji), 49
Andizian, S., 234
Andre, J. E., 84
Andrews, C. F., 70 n.10
Anthias, Floya, 199
Anti-Slavery Society. *See* Slavery
Anwar, Naveed, 160
Appadurai, Arjun, 93, 95, 96, 97
Arunachal Ashram (New York), 187
Arya Pratinidhi Sabha (Fiji), 49
Arya Samaj, 135; in Britain, 144; in Fiji, 9, 48, 49, 63–65; in Trinidad, 135, 149–50
Asad, Talal, 8, 98, 99, 102, 147
Ashura Day Parade (New York), 161
Asia, South East, 4
Australia: and Christian missions, 48; and South Asian migration, 61–63, 190, 223–24
Ayodhya, 50, 70 n.10

Baba Balak Nath, 144
Babb, Lawrence A., 38 n.13, 46, 60, 68 n.2
Bains, Harwant, 201
Bakhash, Shaul, 127 n.14
Ballard, Roger, 22, 142
Ballhatchet, K. A., 225
Bangladeshis: in Britain, 8, 198–99, 202, 227–28; in the United States, 2, 157
Barot, R., 143
Barrier, N. Gerald, 17, 19, 26, 34
Bayly, C. A., 73
Bengal: and nationalism, 3, 5; indentured labor from, 75–80
Bengalis: in Britain, 144, 215; in New York, 188
Benyon, J., 201, 212
Bhabha, Homi, 3, 69 n.8
Bhachu, Parminder, 9, 35, 37 n.9, 223, 227, 229, 230, 231, 233, 234, 237, 239
Bhagavata Purana, 144
Bharatiya Janata Party (BJP), 70 n.10
Bhatras, in Britain, 21
Bhattias, in Britain, 144
Bhindranwale, Sant Jarnail Singh, 29, 37 n.8
Bhojpuri, in Trinidad, 134
Birbalsingh, Frank, 73, 87
Black Power movements, 87, 105, 108, 140, 197
Blackburn, Robin, 77
Bloch, Maurice, 118
Bochasanwasi Shri Akshar Purushottam Sanstha, 150
Bodnar, John, 176 n.7
Bolland, O. Nigel, 77
Borneman, John, 69 n.8
Bowen, David, 144
Bowen, John, 97, 126 n.8, 128 n.22
Brah, Avtar, 227
Brahmakumaris, 187
Brahmans, in Trinidad, 134–39, 149. *See also* Caste

Breckenridge, Carol, 3, 93, 95
Brenneis, Donald, 113
Brereton, Bridget, 99
Britain: and colonialism, 5–6, 21, 56–57, 73–75, 99, 136–39; and slavery, 75–79, 99; South Asian emigration from, 190; South Asians in, 8, 10, 12–15, 21, 23, 29–30, 34–35, 132, 141–51, 197–219, 222–41
British and Foreign Anti-Slavery Society, 75, 84. *See also* Slavery
British Caribbean, 73–88. *See also* British Guiana; Guyana; Trinidad
British Guiana, 6, 73–79, 87, 133
Brown, Colin, 229
Burghart, R., 148
Butadroka, Sakeasi, 52, 56, 69 n.9

Calcutta. *See* Bengal
Calligraphy, Islamic, 122, 169, 175
Campbell, Carl, 104
Canada: migrants in, 224; migration from, 190; multiculturalism policy, 33; Punjabis in, 6, 12, 29–34
Caribbean, South Asians in, 11, 12, 73–88, 94–125
Caribbeans, 12; in Britain, 8, 144, 197–219, 227; in New York, 181. *See also* Afro-Caribbeans
Caste: among Punjabis, 19–22, 28; in Britain, 142–50, 223–24; in British Caribbean, 73, 88; in East Africa, 233–34; in New York, 180; in Trinidad, 134–39
Census: in British Punjab, 19–20; in Fiji, 68; in Trinidad, 103; in the United States, 157, 181
Chaddah, Mehar Singh, 28–29, 37 n.7
Chamars: in Britain, 143; in British Caribbean, 79, 80
Charottar, emigration from, 143–44
Chatterjee, Partha, 69 n.8
Checkland, S. G., 74
Chen, Hsiang-shui, 184
Chinese diaspora, 1; in Britain, 197, 206; in British Caribbean, 78–80, 137; in Fiji, 54, 61; in the United States, 167, 181, 184, 192–94
Chinmoy Mission (New York), 187
Christianity: in Britain, 8; in Fiji, 9, 49–58; in Trinidad, 104, 106, 118, 122
Christian missionaries: in Fiji, 9, 43–44, 47–49; in Punjab, 19; in Trinidad, 118, 140

Christians, Indian, in New York, 186
Chuhras, 143
Cinema. *See* Mass media
Clarke, Colin, 1, 137, 194
Class: and nationalism, 7; in Britain, 14, 143, 197, 200–203, 210, 212, 214, 222–31, 234–40; in British Caribbean, 82; in Fiji, 46, 53, 59; in New York, 160, 181, 183, 185–86, 190; in Trinidad, 94, 99–101, 106–11, 137–41
Clothing: in Britain, 204, 230–35, 239; in British Caribbean, 73, 88; in Guyana, 88; in New York, 157, 167, 179, 182–83, 188, 190–91; Islamic, in Trinidad, 120–23
Clunie, Fergus, 47
Cohen, Anthony, 96
Cohen, Philip, 200, 212
Colonialism, 3–5, 87, 106. *See also* Britain
Columbia University, 182
Comins, D. W. D., 82
Commonwealth Immigrants Advisory Council, 146
Conversion: Euro-American Sikhs, 28, 35; in Fiji, 43–44, 48–49, 56–57, 62; in New York, 182, 187; in Trinidad, 105, 140
Corrigan, Philip, 69 n.8
Crapanzano, Vincent, 125 n.5
Cross, Malcolm, 138, 139
Crowley, D., 136
CSR Company (Australia), 48
Cultural Association of Bengal (New York), 180
Cumpston, I. M., 73
Czechoslovakia, 7

Daaj, 231–36. *See also* Dowry
Dance, 182; Garba, 188; Sufi, 13, 174
Dangars, in British Caribbean, 79–80
Daniels, Roger, 178, 183
Darbar Sahib. *See* Golden Temple
Datar, Rajan, 215
Davis, Susan, 159
De Verteuil, L. A. A., 77, 78, 82
Deepawali. *See* Diwali
Demerara, indentured labor in, 74–75
Democratic Labour Party (DLP). *See* Trinidad
Despres, L. A., 137
Dhanoa, S. S., 37 n.5
Dhillon, Gurdarshan Singh, 37 n.5
Dilgeer, H. S., 37 n.6

Diwali: in Britain, 145; in Fiji, 50–51, 59; in New York, 181, 191, 193
Dollimore, John, 210
Dome of the Rock (Jerusalem), representation in New York parade, 166, 171
Dorman, W. A., 176 n.6
Dowry, 14, 223, 230–37
Dress. See Clothing
Dumont, Louis, 73
Dusenbery, Verne A., 18–19, 20, 23, 26, 31, 32, 35, 36 n.1, 37 nn. 7, 11, 38 nn. 13, 15

East Africa: dowry in, 231–36; migration to Britain, 35, 142–45, 202, 223–24, 227–29; migration to the United States, 190, 223–34; Ramgharias in, 21, 35; South Asians in, 4, 144
Eickelman, Dale, 97, 102
England. See Britain
English language, 1–2, 23, 224; and Muslims in New York, 160, 169, 182; and South Asians in Britain, 143; in Fiji, 49–50, 67; in Trinidad, 134
European Community, 1–2
European diaspora, 1
European nationalism, 2–7, 174, 205–6

Fanon, Fritz, 198
Farhang, M., 176 n.6
Ferguson, James, 3, 19, 36, 94, 95
Fiji, 6, 9–10, 43–67, 82; Lautoka violence, 49–53
Fiji Labour Party, 54, 58
Fijian Christian Nationalist party, 57
Fijian People's Party, 58
Film. See Mass media
Fisher, Maxine P., 180
Flushing. See New York City, Queens
Foner, Eric, 77
Food: in Britain, 198; in British Caribbean, 73, 88; in New York, 157, 191; in New York parade, 172–74; in Swaminarayan tradition, 150; in Trinidad, 114, 120. See also Restaurants
Football. See Soccer
Forbes, R., 135
Foster, Robert, 69 n.8
Foucault, Michel, 212
Fox, Richard G., 19
France, Peter, 47
Freidenberg-Herbstein, Judith, 159

Freitag, Sandria, 11, 86, 132
Friedman, Jonathan, 119
Fryer, Peter, 206
Frykenberg, R., 132
Fuller, J. Overton, 226
Furnivall, J. S., 137

Gamble, W. H., 78, 82
Gandhi, Indira, 29
Gandhi, Mohandas, 5, 66
Gandhi, Rajiv, 29
Garba, 188
Gardner, Robert W., 180
Garrett, John, 68 n.3
Gellner, Ernest, 3
Gender: and diaspora, 218–19; and nationalism, 199–201; in Britain, 203, 206, 209–11; masculinity in Britain, 197–219; Muslim women in Trinidad, 121–22; women in Britain, 14–15, 222–41; women indentured laborers in Trinidad, 6, 74–75, 80–83, 88
Geoghegan, J., 74
George, M., 242 n.6
Ghadar Party, 31–34
Ghai, Yash, 228
Ghareeb, Edmund, 176 n.6
Gibson, Margaret A., 223, 229
Gillanders, Arbuthnot and Company, 74–77, 81
Gilroy, Paul, 201, 203, 212, 218, 240
Gladstone, John, 74–77, 79, 81
Gluckman, Max, 148
Golden Temple, 21, 24, 27, 29
Goody, Jack, 231
Gordon, Sir Arthur, 47–48
Gouldbourne, Harry, 30
Grabar, Oleg, 176 n.8
Great Britain. See Britain
Green Revolution (Punjab), 25, 29
Green, William A., 76
Gujarat, precolonial emigration, 4
Gujaratis: in Britain, 140–46, 150, 202; in Fiji, 46–47, 60, 67; in New York, 180, 187–88
Gupta, Akhil, 3, 19, 36, 94, 95
Gurdwaras: in Britain, 215; in Canada, 30, 32–33; in Fiji, 49; in New York, 180, 186; in Sikh diaspora, 22–24. See also Sikhism
Guru Granth Sahib, 12, 24–25, 37. See also Sikhism

Gurudeva, Srila Tamal Krishna Goswami,
    45, 46, 62, 63, 67, 68 n.1
Guyana, 6, 88, 104; emigration to New
    York, 157. *See also* British Caribbean; Brit-
    ish Guiana

Hall, Stuart, 201, 205, 212, 241
Handler, Richard, 19, 34, 38 n.12, 56
Hannerz, Ulf, 98
Hardy, Friedhelm, 132
Hare Krishna. *See* International Society for
    Krishna Consciousness
Health Professions Educational Assistance
    Act (1976), 179
Hebdige, Dick, 242 n.6
Hechter, M., 139
Hefner, Robert W., 38 n.14
Heineman, Joe, 163
Helweg, Arthur W., 13–14, 23, 29, 30
Helweg, Usha, 13–14
Herder, Johann Gottfried, 3, 56
Higham, C., 226
Higman, B. W., 78
Hindi language, 21, 84, 142–43, 191
Hindu Mahasabha, 132
Hinduism, Hindus, 24, 99, 132; and Sikh-
    ism, 20, 22, 25, 31; in Britain, 10, 132,
    141–51, 202; in colonial India, 8; in Fiji,
    9–10, 43–67; in Trinidad, 10, 77–78, 84–
    85, 104, 107, 110, 112, 118–22, 132–36,
    139–41, 144, 146–51, 202; in the United
    States, 10, 180, 186–87; nationalism and
    Hindutva, 2, 56, 65
Hintzen, Percy, 137, 138, 140
Hobsbawm, Eric, 3, 7, 96, 174
Hodgson, Marshall G. S., 127 n.17
Holi, 59, 191
Hosay, 11, 83–86, 104, 126
Howard, Michael, 69 n.7

Immigration and Naturalization Act (1965),
    178
Immigration and Naturalization Service, 2,
    158, 179
Indentured labor, 5–6, 9–11; in British Ca-
    ribbean, 73–88; in Fiji, 48, 50; in Trin-
    idad, 95, 97, 99, 104, 111, 117–18, 133–
    34, 149; migration to Britain, 142
India Day Parade (New York), 181
India League of America, 183
Indian National Congress, 5

Interfaith Council (Fiji), 60, 68
International Society for Krishna Conscious-
    ness (ISKCON), in Fiji, 9, 43–49, 57, 61–
    67
Iran hostage crisis, 173
Irish: in Britain, 197, 206; in the United
    States, 2, 13, 161–64, 181, 191; laborers,
    77
ISKCON. *See* International Society for
    Krishna Consciousness
Islam, Muslims: Ahmadiyya, 104–5; in Brit-
    ain, 147, 197, 202, 204, 206, 208, 227–28,
    239; in Fiji, 43–44, 48–49, 53, 57, 63; in
    India, 20, 25, 27, 31; in New York, 157–
    75, 186; in Trinidad, 10–11, 83–86, 93–
    124, 139; Muslim nationalism, 8; Shia Is-
    lam, 104, 161, 202; Sufism, 13, 162–63,
    174–75; Sunni Islam, 104, 161, 202;
    Wahabis, 107, 114
Islamic Society of Staten Island, 167
Israel. *See* Jews

Jackson Heights. *See* New York City, Queens
Jackson, P., 145
Jafria Association of North America, 161
Jagan, Cheddi, 87
Jai Narayan, Irene, 50, 59
Jainism, 187
Jalaram Bapa, 144
Jamaica, 74, 76, 84, 86, 202
James, C. L. R., 217
Jats, 20–21, 29, 35, 143, 202, 237
Jayawardena, C., 134
Jeffrey, Robin, 27
Jensen, Joan M., 178
Jews: diaspora, 1, 8–9; in Britain, 197, 206;
    in Europe, 6; in Trinidad, 137; in the
    United States, 2, 158–61, 191
Jones, T., 143
Jones, William, 3
Juergensmeyer, Mark, 26, 30, 31, 37 n.8

Kaaba, representation in New York parade,
    166, 170–71
Kabir Panth (Fiji), 49
Kaira, emigration from, 143
Kale, Madhavi, 73, 76
Kalka, I., 148
Kannada Koota (New York), 180
Kapferer, Bruce, 103, 148–49
Kaplan, Martha, 47, 55, 68 n.3, 69 n.8

Karch, Cecilia, 99
Kashmeri, Zuhair, 30
Kasinitz, Philip, 159
Kasule, Omar Hassan, 104
Kathiawar, emigration from, 143–44
Kelly, John D., 6, 50, 54, 64, 65, 82, 83
Kelton, Jane Gladden, 162
Kenya. *See* East Africa
Kerala Samajam of New York, 180
Khalistan, 12, 17–18, 22, 25, 29–30, 33–36
Khalsa. *See* Singh Sabha/Tat Khalsa Movement
Khalsa Diwan Society (British Columbia), 32
Khan, Aisha, 93, 94, 102, 106, 126 n.13, 127 n.16
Khan, Noor Inayat, 226
Khandelwal, Madhulika S., 179, 186
Khatris, 21, 143
Kirpalani, M., 135
Kirshenblatt-Gimblett, Barbara, 158, 164, 176 n.2
Kisan Sangh (Fiji), 64
Knott, K., 143, 148, 151
Kolff, D. H. A., 4
Koran, representation in New York parade, 169–70, 175
Krishna, 65, 144. *See also* International Society for Krishna Consciousness
Krishna-Kaliya Temple (Fiji), 46–47, 49
Kugelmass, Jack, 159
Kutch, emigration from, 143–44

Labour Party: Britain, 201, 203–8; Fiji, 54, 58
LaGuerre, J. G., 138
Lal, Brij V., 69 n.7, 82, 83
Lal, Victor, 69 n.7
Lamming, George, 87, 88
Language, as marker of identity, 1–2, 8–9, 19–22, 28, 35–36, 134, 137, 142–43, 149–50, 175, 182, 186, 204, 210, 224
Lansine, Kaba, 127 n.17
Lasaro, Manasa, 57
Lass, Andrew, 69 n.8
Lautoka: Mosque, 49; Sikh Gurdwara, 49. *See also* Fiji
Lawrence, Denise, 159
Leicester. *See* Britain; Red Star project
Leonard, Karen, 17, 18, 22
Leonardo, Micaela di, 241 n.3

Leva Kanbi Patels, in Britain, 144
Lewis, Bernard, 104, 127 n.14
Lewis, Gordon, 94
Ley, D., 137
Liff, Bob, 176
Light, Henry, 76
Login, Dalhousie E., 225
Lohanas, in Britain, 144
London. *See* Britain
London Missionary Society, 68
Lowenthal, David, 96, 125 n.4

Mac an Ghaill, Mairtain, 238
Madan, T. N., 27, 37 n.8
Madras, 48; indentured laborers from, 78
Maharashtra Mandal (New York), 180
Mahavira, 187
Major, Andrew J., 37 n.7
Malcolm, John, 26
Malik, Y. K., 140
Malkki, Liisa, 17, 69 n.8, 124
Mamin, Abraham, 191, 193
Mangru, Basdeo, 73
Manhattan. *See* New York City
Maraj, Bhadase Sagan, 136, 138–40
Marriage: 14, 22–23, 28, 83, 114, 144, 149, 223–24, 231–39. *See also* Dowry; Weddings
Marriott, McKim, 36 n.1
Marx, Karl, 4
Masaryk, Thomas, 7
Masjid al-Haram (Medina), representation in New York parade, 171
Mass media, 97, 222; in Britain, 14, 199, 212, 226, 238; in Fiji, 45–46, 50–54, 69 n.6; in New York, 160, 180, 182–83, 187, 191; in Trinidad, 140–41, in the United States, 173
Mauritius, Indian laborers in, 6, 74–76, 81, 133
Mazhbi Sikhs, 20–21
Mazrui, Ali, 127 n.19
Mazumdar, Sucheta, 194
McAndrew, Brian, 30
McLeod, W. H., 17–19, 22, 24, 26, 38 n.15
McNamara, Brooks, 158, 176
Melucci, Alberto, 209
Methodist Youth Fellowship (Fiji), 47, 49, 51
Michaelson, Maureen, 144
Mishra, Vijay C., 73, 87

Mitchell, Clyde, 148
Mombasa-Lake Victoria railway, 142
Moore, Brian L., 73
Morris, H. S., 137, 145
Moseley, R., 226
Muharram. *See* Hosay
Mukhi, Sunita Sunder, 181
Multiculturalism, 12, 32; in Britain, 8, 10,
    146–48, 151; in Canada, 32–33; in Fiji,
    58, 65; in the United States, 13, 194
Munim, Muhammad Abdul, 160, 173
Music: in Britain, 198–99; in Trinidad, 120;
    in the United States, 182
Muslims. *See* Islam
Muslim Center of Queens, 172
Muslim Foundation of America, 160
Muslim League, 11, 48
Muslim World Day Parade (New York), 13,
    157–76

Naipaul, Shiva, 70 n.11
Naipaul, V. S., 3, 7, 11
Namdharis, 35
Nander, Maharashtra, 24
Nandy, Ashis, 216
National Association of Canadians of
    Origins in India (NACOI), 32
National Council of Hindu Temples
    (United Kingdom), 146
National Federation Party (Fiji), 50, 54
National Front (Britain), 212
Nationalism, 2–14; and colonialism, 2–6,
    48, 137–38; and gender, 199–200; *Hin-
    dutva*, 55, 65; in Britain, 198–208, 217–
    18; Indian, 132, 182; in Fiji, 9–10, 43–44,
    52–58, 63–66; in Trinidad, 9–11, 99–104,
    113, 124, 138–41; in the United States, 2–
    3, 174; Muslim, and Pakistan, 11, 20, 27;
    Sikh, 11–13, 17–19, 23–36
Nau Durga Temple (Fiji), 53
Navratri, 145
New York City: Geeta Temple of Elmhurst,
    186–87; Hindu Temple of Flushing, 180,
    186–87; Manhattan, 157, 161–64, 178,
    180–86, 188–90; Muslim World Day Pa-
    rade, 13, 157–76; Queens, 13–14, 157,
    172, 178–94; South Asians in, 13–14
New Zealand, 224; and Christian missions,
    48; Indians in, 61–63; Punjabis in, 17
Newspapers. *See* Mass media

Norman, H. W., 83–86
Nye, M., 148

Oberoi, Harjot S., 11–12, 19, 20, 25–26, 27,
    28, 34–35, 38 n.14
Oberon, Merle, 226–27
Orhni. *See* Clothing

Pakistan: 1965 War, 29; and dowry, 235; cre-
    ation of, 11, 20, 25, 27–28; image in Trin-
    idad, 96, 112, 115; Pakistan Independence
    Day Parade (New York), 161–62, 167
Pakistanis: in Britain, 8, 14, 198–99, 202,
    227–28, 242; in the United States, 2, 13,
    157–58, 160–62, 191
Panjabi language, 18, 21, 23, 142, 191. *See
    also* Punjabis
Paranjpe, A. C., 37 n.11
Park, Robert E., 194
Parmar, Pratibha, 239
Partition of 1947, 11, 20, 25, 27–28
Patidars, in Britain, 144
Patna Sahib (Bihar), 24
Patten, John, 147
Peach, Ceri, 1, 137, 194
People's Democratic Party (PDP). *See* Trin-
    idad
People's National Movement (PNM). *See*
    Trinidad
Persian Gulf, South Asians in, 4
Pettigrew, Joyce, 37 n.8
Pitkin, H. F., 149
Pocock, David, 10, 150
Prabhupada, A. C. Bhaktivedanta Swami,
    46, 62, 65
Pratinidhi Sabha (Fiji), 49
Price, Richard, 94
Punjab, 12, 18–30, 34–36; and Partition, 11,
    25; Arya Samaj in, 135
Punjabi: diaspora, 17–36; ethnosociology,
    19–23, 26; Suba, 21, 25, 29; suits (*see*
    Clothing). *See also* Panjabi language
Punjabis, 12, 17–36; in Britain, 21, 30, 141–
    46, 202, 222, 230–39; in Canada, 6, 12, 21,
    30–34; in East Africa, 21, 142–45, 231–
    37; in New Zealand, 17; in the United
    States, 6, 12, 17–18, 21. *See also* Ghadar
    Party; Gurdwaras; Khalistan; Sikhism
Purdah, 122, 239
Puri, Harish, 31

Pushtimargis (Vallabhacharyas), in Britain, 144

Queens. *See* New York City
Queens College New Immigrants and Old Americans Project, 189

Rabuka, Sitiveni, 50, 54–57, 60
Race, racism, 1–2, 17, 32, 65; and colonialism, 8, 43, 48, 65, 73, 137–38, 211; and Sikhs, 28, 36; in Britain, 12–15, 142, 145, 147, 197–204, 208–18, 223, 240; in Fiji, 48, 54, 58, 62–63; in South Africa, 5; in Trinidad, 101, 107–8, 113–16, 122; in the United States, 160, 183, 193–94
Radhasoamis, 144
Rafeeq, Muhammed, 117
Rahman, Alaur, 199
Ramakrishna Mission, in Fiji, 48–49, 63–64, 67
Ramayana: in Britain, 144; in Fiji, 48, 50, 53; in Trinidad, 139
Ramgarhias: in Britain, 35, 202, 237; in East Africa, 21, 35
Ranger, Terence, 96, 174
Rashtriya Swayamsevak Sangh (RSS), 132
Red Star Project (Leicester), 200–219
Reddock, Rhoda, 82, 83
Reeves, Frank, 206
Restaurants: in Fiji, 45; in New York, 157, 183–84, 190–91
Rex, John, 146, 147
Richmond Hill Gurdwara, 180
Robinson, V., 145
Rosenthal, Franz, 176 n.8
Rushdie, Salman, 8, 147, 173, 197, 204
Rutz, Henry, 56
Ryan, Selwyn D., 87, 104, 107, 119, 126 n.10, 136, 138

Safran, William, 17
Saghal, Gita, 239
Sahlins, Marshall, 68 n.3
Sai Baba missions: in Britain, 144; in Fiji, 9, 43–47, 57, 60–61, 63–67
Said, Edward, 173
Saint Patrick's Day Parade (New York), 13, 161–62
Salvo, Joseph J., 158
Salwar-kameez. *See* Clothing

Samaroo, Brinsley, 104
Sanatan Dharm (Fiji), 9, 48–50, 59, 64
Sanatan Dharma Maha Sabha (Trinidad), 135–40
Sanjek, Roger, 181, 189
Sannyasi, Bhawani Dayal, 70 n.10
Santoshi Ma, 144
Saran, Paratma, 189
Saris. *See* Clothing
Satanic Verses. See Rushdie, Salman
Saurashtra, emigration from, 143
Sayer, Derek, 69 n.8
Scarano, Francisco, 77
Schimmel, Annemarie, 176 n.8
Schneider, Jo Anne, 159
Schwartz, Barton M., 73, 134, 144
Scott, David, 11, 93
Segal, Daniel, 93, 94
Sekhon, A. S., 37 n.6
Shaheen, Jack, 176 n.6
Sharma, Harish, 50
Sharma, U. M., 143
Sheperd, Verene, 82
Shia Islam. *See* Islam
Shirdi Sai Baba, 47, 144
Shiromani Akali Dal. *See* Akali Dal
Shiromani Gurdwara Parbandhak Committee, 28
Shri Shirdi Sai Baba Mandir (Fiji), 47
Sidhu, M. S., 35
Sikh: diaspora, 17–36; nationalism, 8, 11–12, 17–18, 25–29; soldiers, 5
Sikh Society of Fiji, 49
Sikhism: Adi Granth, 24; Guru Granth Sahib, 12, 24–25, 37; Guru Panth, 20, 22, 25, 35; Gurus, 23–27, 35; in India, 19–21; Takhats, 24, 27; Vaisakhi, 13, 215. *See also* Akali Dal; Ghadar Party; Gurdwaras; Khalistan; Punjab
Sikhs: and 1984 Delhi riots, 21, 29; Euro-American, 28; in Africa, 9; in Britain, 14, 23, 30, 202, 215, 217, 222, 227, 230–39; in Canada, 12, 23, 30–34; in Fiji, 49, 57; in New Zealand, 18; in the United States, 18, 23, 30–31, 159, 161, 183, 186; Jat, 20–21, 23, 35; Khatri, 20; Mazhbi, 20–21; Namdhari, 35. *See also* Punjabis
Sims, Calvin, 162, 167
Sindhi, 20, 28
Singh, Amrik, 29
Singh, Anirudh, 59, 70 n.12

Singh, Kelvin, 84
Singh, Kharak, 37 n.5
Singh, Maharaj Ranjit, 27
Singh Sabha/Tat Khalsa Movement, 20, 25, 27–28
Singh, Sirdar Jagjit, 183
Singh, Surjan, 28
Slavery, 6, 74–88, 99, 133
Slyomovics, Susan, 160
Smith, Keith, 116
Smith, M. G., 137
Smith, S. J., 145
Smith, W. C., 132
Soccer, 12–13, 200–204, 209–19
Solomos, J., 201, 212
Sorabji, Cornelia, 226
Speckmann, J. D., 73
Spivak, Gayatri C., 241 n.3
Stanley, Lord Edward, 79
Stone, Carl, 99
Stuempfle, Stephen, 127 n.15
Sufism. See Islam
Sugar industry, 47–49, 53, 64, 73–83, 138, 141
Sunni Islam. See Islam
Surat, emigration from, 143–44
Swaminarayanis: in Britain, 144, 150; in New York, 187

Tabakaucoro, Adi Finau, 51
Takbir, in New York parade, 173–75
Tambiah, Stanley, 118
Tamils: in Britain, 144; in Fiji, 49; in the United States, 180, 191
Tatla, Darshan Singh, 35
Tchen, John Kuo Wei, 184
Television. See Mass media
Thapar, Romila, 132
Tinker, Hugh, 6, 64, 73, 74, 76, 140
Tolson, Andrew, 212
Toren, Christina, 55
Trinidad: Democratic Labour Party (DLP), 136, 138–40; Federation of Unions of Sugar Workers, 138; Hindus in, 10, 132–41, 148–51; indentured labor in, 9, 11, 48, 73–88, 95, 97, 99, 104, 111, 117–18, 133–34, 149; Muslims in, 10–11, 13, 89–124; People's Democratic Party (PDP), 136, 138–39; People's National Movement

(PNM), 99–100, 106, 138–40; Sanatan Dharma Maha Sabha, 135–40. See also Afro-Trinidadians
Trouillot, Michel-Rolph, 94
Tuan, Yi-Fu, 163

United Kingdom. See Britain
United States: and colonial Trinidad, 77, 140; census in, 157; Indians in, 10, 13–14, 178–84, 188–94; Sikhs in, 23, 29–32; South Asians in, 2, 6, 17–18; 167, 222–24, 232, 235. See also Black Power movements; New York City
Urdu, 114, 142

Vaisakhi, 13, 215
Vaishnavism, 46; in Britain, 144; in Fiji, 62. See also Hinduism; International Society for Krishna Consciousness
Van den Berghe, P., 137
Vardy, Francis P., 157–58
Vasil, R. K., 139
Vasudeva Dasa, 46, 62
Veer, Peter van der, 3, 4, 99, 132, 134
Vertovec, Steven, 1, 99, 133, 134, 140, 141, 143, 145, 150, 194
Videos. See Mass media
Visa Halari Oshwalis, in Britain, 144
Vishnu Mandir (Fiji), 49
Vishva Hindu Parishad (VHP), 70 n.10, 132
Visram, Rozina, 225, 226

Wahabis. See Islam
Wallman, Sandra, 38 n.15
Warner-Lewis, Maureen, 104
Weber, Max, 46, 68 n.2
Weddings, 121, 211, 222–35. See also Dowry; Marriage
Werbner, Pnina, 14, 148
Westwood, Sallie, 200, 227
White, James T., 78–80
Williams, Brackette, 100
Williams, Eric, 87, 139
Williams, Raymond B., 10, 150
Women. See Gender
Wood, Donald, 73, 82, 99

Young, John, 43
Yuval-Davis, Nira, 199

SOUTH ASIA SEMINAR SERIES

PUBLISHED BY THE UNIVERSITY OF PENNSYLVANIA PRESS

Nation and Migration: The Politics of Space in the South Asian Diaspora, edited by Peter van der Veer. 1995.

Orientalism and the Postcolonial Predicament: Perspectives on South Asia, edited by Carol Breckenridge and Peter van der Veer. 1992.

Gender, Genre, and Power in South Asian Expressive Traditions, edited by Arjun Appadurai, Frank J. Korom, and Margaret A. Mills. 1991.

PUBLISHED BY THE SOUTH ASIA REGIONAL STUDIES DEPARTMENT, UNIVERSITY OF PENNSYLVANIA

Making Things in South Asia: The Role of the Craftsman, edited by Michael W. Meister. 1988.

The Countries of South Asia: Boundaries, Extensions, and Interrelations, edited by Peter Gaeffke and David Utz. 1988.

Science and Technology in South Asia, edited by Peter Gaeffke and David Utz. 1988.

Identity and Division in Cults and Sects in South Asia, edited by Peter Gaeffke. 1984.

This book has been set in Linotron Galliard. Galliard was designed for Mergenthaler in 1978 by Matthew Carter. Galliard retains many of the features of a sixteenth-century typeface cut by Robert Granjon but has some modifications that give it a more contemporary look.

Printed on acid-free paper.